Schuhschrift

Margit Bowler, Philip T. Duncan, Travis Major, & Harold Torrence

Schuhschrift
Papers in Honor of Russell Schuh

eScholarship Publishing, University of California

Margit Bowler, Philip T. Duncan, Travis Major, & Harold Torrence (eds.). 2019. *Schuhschrift: Papers in Honor of Russell Schuh*. eScholarship Publishing.

Copyright ©2019 the authors

This work is licensed under the Creative Commons Attribution 4.0 International License. To view a copy of this license, visit:
http://creativecommons.org/licenses/by/4.0/
or send a letter to Creative Commons, PO Box 1866, Mountain View, CA 94042, USA.

ISBN: 978-1-7338701-1-5 (Digital)
978-1-7338701-0-8 (Paperback)

Cover design: Allegra Baxter
Typesetting: Andrew McKenzie, Zhongshi Xu, Meng Yang, Z. L. Zhou, & the editors
Fonts: Gill Sans, Cardo
Typesetting software: LaTeX

Published in the United States
by eScholarship Publishing, University of California

Contents

Preface ix
Harold Torrence

1 Reason questions in Ewe 1
Leston Chandler Buell
    1.1 Introduction 1
    1.2 A morphological asymmetry 2
    1.3 Direct insertion of *núkàtà* in the left periphery 6
        1.3.1 Negation 8
        1.3.2 VP nominalization fronting 10
    1.4 Higher than focus 12
    1.5 Conclusion 13

2 A case for "slow linguistics" 15
Bernard Caron
    2.1 Introduction 15
    2.2 The case for "slow linguistics" 17
    2.3 The discovery of a "marvellous" linguist and community 19
        2.3.1 The mystery of the falling tone 21
        2.3.2 Clefts sans 'it' sans 'be', sans everything. 22
    2.4 Macrosyntax and the specificity of oral corpora 25
        2.4.1 Macrosyntax and Macrosyntactic annotation 26
        2.4.2 Dysfluencies 28
        2.4.3 Afterthoughts 31
        2.4.4 Syntactic relations over turn-taking 32

2.5 Conclusion 34

3 Ongoing changes in the linguistic landscape in the Lake Chad area 35
Norbert Cyffer
3.1 The enormous attraction of the Lake Chad area 35
    3.1.1 The languages in the area 36
3.2 The relations between Kanuri and Chadic contact languages . 38
    3.2.1 The recognition of linguistic structures 41
    3.2.2 The special relationship between Kanuri and Buduma 43
3.3 Some conclusions 47

4 Synchronic vs. diachronic naturalness: Hyman & Schuh (1974) revisited 50
Larry M. Hyman
4.1 Introduction 50
4.2 Diachronic naturalness 52
    4.2.1 Tone spreading ("horizontal assimilation") 53
    4.2.2 Register adjustments ("vertical assimilation") 54
    4.2.3 Contour simplification 55
4.3 Synchronic naturalness 57
    4.3.1 Tone shifting 58
    4.3.2 Tonal dissimilation and polarity 59
    4.3.3 Tonal downstep 60
4.4 Summary and conclusion 63

5 A first look at Krachi clausal determiners 66
Jason Kandybowicz & Harold Torrence
5.1 Introduction 66
5.2 Background on Krachi 68
5.3 Krachi determiners and clausal determiners 69
5.4 Brief comparison to Gã 74
5.5 Conclusion 76

6 Tone and length in Mende 77
William R. Leben
6.1 What this chapter owes to Russ Schuh 77
6.2 A simple, exceptionless constraint on tone 78
6.3 Polarization 79
6.4 Polar tone: Distribution 81

	6.5	Tone melodies	82
	6.6	Conclusion	87

7 Segment frequency: Within-language and cross-language similarity 88
Ian Maddieson
	7.1	Introduction	88
	7.2	Some methodological considerations	90
	7.3	Some results	93
		7.3.1 Voiced plosives	94
		7.3.2 Voiceless plosives	95
		7.3.3 Ejectives and implosives	95
	7.4	Discussion	96

8 Constructions and competitions in Dogon inflectional tonology 101
Laura McPherson
	8.1	Introduction	101
	8.2	The Dogon languages	103
	8.3	Tommo So verbal morphology	104
	8.4	Competitions between tonal overlays	107
	8.5	The morphological representation of tonal overlays	110
		8.5.1 Distributed Morphology	110
		8.5.2 Cophonology theory	113
		8.5.3 Constraint-based Construction Morphology	114
	8.6	Other languages	118
	8.7	Conclusion	120

9 Unexpected Athabaskan pronouns 122
Maura O'Leary & Blake Lehman
	9.1	Introduction	122
	9.2	Basic Hän data	123
		9.2.1 When to use objects	123
		9.2.2 Distribution of *yë-* and *wë-*	125
	9.3	Other Athabaskan Pronouns	126
		9.3.1 Focus/topicality	126
		9.3.2 Animacy	129
		9.3.3 Other Athabaskan languages	130
	9.4	Theoretical account for Hän	132
		9.4.1 When do the pronouns occur?	132
		9.4.2 Distribution of *wë-* and *yë-*	133

| | 9.5 Summary | 137 |

10 Bole suffix doubling as morphotactic extension — 139
Kevin M. Ryan
- 10.1 Introduction ... 139
- 10.2 Contexts for doubling in Bole ... 142
- 10.3 Outside-in conditioning ... 146
- 10.4 Comparative Bole-Tangale notes ... 150
- 10.5 Morphotactic analysis ... 151
- 10.6 Morphotactic extension ... 155
- 10.7 Other approaches to vacuous affix repetition ... 158

11 CiV lengthening and the weight of CV — 161
Donca Steriade
- 11.1 Two problems for CiVL ... 161
- 11.2 SWP under stress change ... 164
- 11.3 The weight of C_0V ... 168
- 11.4 No CuVL ... 172
- 11.5 The [aɪ] problem ... 172
- 11.6 Intervals and weight in hiatus ... 175

12 On morphological palatalization in Chadic — 178
H. Ekkehard Wolff
- 12.1 Introduction ... 178
- 12.2 Morphological palatalization in WC ... 181
- 12.3 Morphological palatalization in CC-A ... 182
  - 12.3.1 Y-prosody in Gǔɗe ... 183
  - 12.3.2 Y-prosody in Ga'anda ... 183
  - 12.3.3 Y-prosody in Podoko ... 185
- 12.4 Discussion ... 186
  - 12.4.1 Morphological sources of Y-prosody ... 186
  - 12.4.2 Enigmatic relationship: Final vowel i and Y-prosody ... 187
- 12.5 Summary and outlook ... 191

Preface

THE PAPERS IN THIS VOLUME honor the life and work of Russ Schuh, whose contributions to the study of African languages, Chadic languages in particular, span the course of a near 50-year career in linguistics. Russ was the fieldlinguist's fieldlinguist; smart, old-school, straightforward, down-to-earth, calm, and funny! The stacks and stacks of field notebooks in his too-small office were a testament to his extensive research and prolific publishing habits.

A prodigiously talented and dedicated fieldworker, his work set a standard for descriptive depth and detail that has rarely been equaled. In the preface to this 1998 Grammar of Miya, he wrote, "What is an optimal descriptive grammar? Ideally, it should state and illustrate every generalization and idiosyncracy of every structure that exists in the language being described." A high bar indeed! Russ admitted that he did not think that he had attained that goal in his descriptive grammar since that would be impossible, given that "language is too vast and complex and life is too short." However, he goes on to say that "'[t]his should not deter the compiler of a descriptive grammar from trying to come as close to the ideal as available data and time permit." Anyone familiar with Russ's work will know that this striving for excellence runs through all of it. He published papers in phonetics, phonology, syntax, morphology and historical/comparative linguistics. He also conducted research on such disparate topics as African poetic metrics and Korean intonation.

Although the breadth of his knowledge and interests was intimidating,

Russ was not, as his modesty was quickly revealed by his self-deprecating sense of humor. Russ's love of language extended beyond his research. For fun, he sat in on language classes in Arabic, Hebrew, Ancient Egyptian, Tigrinya, and Korean. We even studied Wolof together for a couple of years. This enthusiasm for language was also evident from the amount of time that he put into teaching and advising. Russ dedicated many hours to mentoring graduate students and served on numerous master's and doctoral committees. I was lucky enough to meet him my first year in graduate school at UCLA and his advice that I study Wolof, which I would certainly not have done otherwise, set the path for my entire career. In his teaching too, Russ set a high standard. He expended enormous energy over many years in (successful!) efforts to get undergraduates interested in linguistics and African languages. As a result, Russ consistently led the largest most popular linguistics courses that have ever been taught at UCLA. This all sounds like a LOT of work, but Russ's own view was that, "Nothing is more fun than doing my 'job', that is, research on languages and teaching linguistics. I always tell people that I get paid for doing my hobby. There is nothing that I would rather spend my time doing than discovering patterns in language data and writing them up."

With his extensive time on the ground in Africa, Russ had a keen sense for language in context, its sociolinguistic and cultural environment. Russ recognized that long-established techniques such as audio recordings and transcription alone could not capture certain aspects of living language and he integrated video as a component of his fieldwork. He remarked, "...in my field work since 2000, I have shot a lot of video and made an [sic] a lot of audio recordings. To me, at least, the multi-media materials bring the whole experience to life in a way that studying language documents written on paper cannot do." As an integral part of his research, Russ was committed to the documentation of areas of language that intersect directly with the culture of the speakers like folktales, proverbs, riddles, song, poetry, superstitions, and tongue-twisters. In addition to the video documentation of the verbal arts, Russ's work, such as the Yobe Languages Research Project resulted in the local publication (in Potiskum, Nigeria) of a number of works including *Asum Bo Ngamo* 'Wisdom in the Ngamo Language', *Terzena Gabade* 'Tales in the Bade Language', *Labar Kuzvok Də Sato Kunək Ta Vədwai* 'Stories of the Past and Now in the Duwai Language', and seven trilingual dictionaries, which will stand as lasting resources for community members and scholars. In addition to being a tireless fieldworker, Schuh also developed linguistics materials that others will be able to use in the future and which provide a permanent record of the languages that he worked on, such as his database of Chadic roots and the lexical databases that he developed for Bole, Bade, Karakare,

Ngamo, Ngizim, Duwai, and Miya.

The papers in this volume cover a wide swath of linguistic territory, just like Russ's research. This is a testament to the many ways in which Russ influenced his fellow linguists over the years as a mentor, colleague, collaborator, teacher, advisor, and friend. These papers are also reflective of the fact that he played a pivotal role in training multiple generations of fieldworkers both at UCLA, in Africa, and elsewhere. No doubt, Russ's influence will continue to be felt for years to come as his colleagues, his students and his students' students continue to go out into the world trying to describe and document the vastness and complexity of language.

Harold Torrence
University of California, Los Angeles

1

Reason questions in Ewe

Leston Chandler Buell
University of Amsterdam

1.1 Introduction

THIS PAPER DEALS WITH REASON QUESTIONS (*why* questions) in Ewe, a member of the Gbe subgroup of the Kwa language family and spoken by more than 3,000,000 people, mainly in Ghana and Togo. An Ewe reason question, illustrated in (1), has a *why* component consisting of two non-adjacent elements: sentence-initial *núkàtà* and an optional sentence-final *ɖó*.[1]

(1) Núkàtà-(é) Kòfí lè   mɔ́lì ɖù-ḿ   (ɖô)?
     why-FOC   Kofi be.at rice eat-PROG go.to
     'Why is Kofi eating rice?'

Cross-linguistically, reason questions are particularly interesting because of certain syntactic and semantic properties that distinguish them from other question types. Some such differences in Italian led Rizzi (1999) to argue for

---

[1] The following abbreviations are used in the glosses: CJ = conjoint, DJ = disjoint, FOC = focus, OM = object marker, NEG = negative, PL = plural, PROG = progressive, PROSP = prospective, PST = past, REDUP = reduplicant, REL = relative, SG = singular, SM = subject marker.

two analytical points concerning the word *perché* 'why'. First, he argued that *perché* is first introduced in the complementizer domain rather than being moved there from a lower position. Second, he argued that *perché* occupies a position higher than other focused constituents.

This paper will show that Ewe *núkàtà...ɖó* also behaves differently from other *wh* phrases in the language. Furthermore, some of these unique characteristics will be argued to show that *núkàtà...ɖó*, just like Italian *perché*, is first merged in the left periphery and occupies a higher position than other focused constituents, and further that the bipartite nature of *núkàtà...ɖó* lends support to an independent ReasonP, lower in the complementizer domain than IntP (Shlonsky & Soare, 2011).

1.2 A morphological asymmetry

IN THIS SECTION, IT WILL BE SHOWN that while the *ɖó* of the *núkàtà...ɖó* bipartite *why* component is homophonous with an element occurring in other types of adjuncts, it does not display the same morphological alternation. We begin with some basic facts about word order, questions, and adjuncts in the language.

Ewe is a language with SVOX word order, which is illustrated by the simple sentence in (2). In *wh* questions, the questioned constituent obligatorily moves to a left-peripheral position and is often also followed by the focus marker *yé/-é*, as in (3). This focus marker is optional in most contexts, a notable exception being any type of subject focus, in which case it is obligatory (Badan & Buell, 2012). Example (1) above further shows that *núkàtà* can also be followed by the focus marker.

(2) Mè-flè uǔ sià Ghǎnà sídì àkpé blâ èvè.
   1SG-buy car this Ghana cedi thousand twenty
   'I bought this car for 20,000 Ghanian cedi.'

(3) Àmékà$_i$-é Kòfí gblɔ bé yè-kpɔ́ t$_i$ lè àsìmè?
   who-FOC Kofi say that LOG-see be.at market
   'Who$_i$ did Kofi say that he saw t$_i$ at the market?'

Núkàtà 'why' is composed of three distinct morphemes. This composition and an illustration of its subparts are given in (4). Alongside *núkàtà...ɖ ó*, an alternative form *núkà ŋútí...ɖó* can also be used. Both of these forms end in a light postposition-like nominal element which can also be used as a

1.2. A morphological asymmetry

body(part) noun: *tǎ* 'head' and *ŋúti* 'body'. No differences in interpretation or syntactic behavior were found between these two forms. All examples in this article use *núkàtà...ɖó*.

(4) nú-kà? / nú-kà-tà? / àvù kà?
    thing-which / thing-which-head / dog which
    'what? / why? / which dog?'

In other contexts, both as a content noun in the literal meaning of 'head' and in its use as a light nominal element, *tǎ* usually has a rising tone, rather than the low tone found in *núkàtà*. This shows that the word *núkàtà* has been lexicalized.

Ewe questions end with a low boundary tone, which is particularly salient when the final syllable is underlyingly high. In that case the final syllable surfaces as falling. The contrast is shown with the high-toned word *kpɔ́* 'see' in (5):

(5) a. Kòfi ɖéká kò é wò-kpɔ́.
       Kofi one only-FOC 3SG-see
       'He only saw Kofi.'

   b. Àmékà-é wò-kpɔ̂?
      who-FOC 3SG-see
      'Who did he see?'

It will be noted that the reason question in (1) ends in *ɖô*, with a falling tone, while in the expository text the form *ɖó*, with a high tone, has been used as the citation form. The final fall in the example questions is due to this final low boundary tone. In non-final positions *ɖó* is pronounced with a high tone rather than a falling one.

Many adjuncts in Ewe have the form V [DP (N)], in which the V is a light verb functioning like a preposition and the N is one of a handful of light nominal elements that behave roughly as postpositions. Some examples are given in (6).

(6) a. Mè-kpɔ́ gà hŏmè áɖé [lè xɔ̀-á mè].
       1SG-see money amount some be.at room-the inside
       'I found some money in the room.'

   b. Àgbàlẽ sìà fò nŭ [tsó àvù-wó ŋú].
      book this hit mouth go.from dog-PL body
      'This book is about dogs.' (*fò nŭ* 'talk')

c. Mè-zɔ̀ [tó tsì ŋú].
  1SG-walk pass water body
  'I walked along the river.'

These adjuncts are relevant to the discussion because it will initially appear as if the sentence-final ɖó in a núkàtà question is identical to a light verb as used in other questions, while ultimately it will need to be considered a distinct lexical entry.

When the DP in such an adjunct phrase undergoes any type of A′-movement, the V is always stranded, while the light N is pied-piped (i.e., moved along with the noun), as shown in (7).[2]

(7) a. *wh* question
   [Xɔ̀ kà mè]$_i$ -é nè-kpɔ́ gà lá lè t$_i$?
   room which inside -FOC 2SG-see money the be.at
   'Which room did you find the money in?'

  b. relative clause
   Ésìà nyé tsì [sì ŋú]$_i$ mè-zɔ̀ tó t$_i$ lá.
   this be water that body 1SG-walk pass the
   'This is the river that I walked along.'

Ɖé is one of these preposition-like verbs,[3] and its use in adjuncts is illustrated in (8). Although ɖé typically designates movement ('onto', 'into', 'to', etc.), it is also used in many idiomatic contexts.

(8) a. Dàdí-á dzò gé ɖé kplɔ̃-à dzí. (movement)
   cat-the jump fall go.to table-the top
   'The cat jumped onto the table.'

  b. Kòfi kpé ɖé Ámà ŋútí ŋútɔ́. (idiomatic)
   Kofi help go.to Ama body much
   'Kofi helped Ama a lot.'

Just as ɖó and tà are used to ask a reason question in núkàtà...ɖó questions, ɖé and tǎ can be used in statements to express a reason or goal, as in (9).

---

[2] Ewe relative clauses often end in the article *lá*.

[3] *Ɖé* behaves like other preposition-like verbs except for the fact that it cannot be used as the main predicate, unlike the verbs *lè*, *tsó*, and *tó*, which appear in (6).

1.2. A morphological asymmetry

(9) Mè-yì Tógó ɖé tàkpékpé áɖé tǎ.
1SG-go Togo go.to meeting some head

'I went to Togo for a conference.'

Now we come to the connection between *ɖé* and *ɖó*. When the complement of *ɖé* is extracted, as when it is questioned, *ɖé* normally takes the form *ɖó*, although four of my six informants also accept *ɖé* in this context:

(10) a. Kplɔ̀ kà dzí-é dàdì-á dzò gé ɖô/%ɖê?
table which top-FOC cat-the jump fall go.to

'Which table did the cat jump onto?'

b. Tàkpékpé ka tǎ nè-yì Tógó ɖô/%ɖê?
meeting which head 2SG-go Togo go.to

'What kind of conference did you go to Togo for?'

What distinguishes this *ɖó* (that from which a non-reason complement has been extracted) from the *ɖó* of *núkàtà...ɖó* is that speakers who accept the form *ɖé* in the former context reject it in the latter context, as shown in (11).

(11) Núkàtà xèví-á lè dzò-dzò-ḿ ɖô/*ɖê?
why bird-the be.at REDUP-fly-PROG go.to

'Why is the bird flying?'

The simplest analysis of distribution of *ɖé* and *ɖó* is one in which there are two separate lexical entries: one for the *ɖé* that for some speakers has the *ɖé/ɖó* alternation in extraction contexts and another without the alternation for any speakers.

The behavior of *ɖé* in extraction contexts has a parallel in the Dutch preposition *naar* 'to'. This preposition has two different (sets of) forms when its complement is extracted, depending whether it indicates a motion, as in (12), or something else, as in (13).

(12) Dutch

a. De bus reed naar het vliegveld.
the bus rode to the airport

'The bus rode to the airport.'

b. Waar reed de bus naartoe/heen/*naar?
where rode the bus to

'Where did the bus ride to?'

(13) Dutch
   a. Deze zeep ruikt naar lelietjes-van-dalen.
      this soap smells to lilies-of-the-valley
      'This soap smells like lily-of-the-valley.'
   b. Waar ruikt deze zeep naar/*naartoe/*heen?
      where smell this soap to
      'What does this soap smell like?'

In this section it was shown that the *ɖó* of reason questions is not an exponent of a morphological alternation like the *ɖó* of other adjuncts.[4] In this way, reason adjuncts have been shown to differ in a certain way from other adjuncts. However, while this difference adds to the cross-linguistic evidence that reason questions are different from their non-reason counterparts, it says nothing about what position *ɖó* is merged in or occupies at the surface. We now turn to the first of these two questions.

1.3 Direct insertion of núkàtà in the left periphery

EVIDENCE IS ACCUMULATING that the merging of *why* directly in the complementizer domain is either universal or is at least a very strong cross-linguistic tendency. A particularly clear example of this evidence comes from Krachi, a Kwa language spoken in Ghana. As shown in (14), while other *wh* phrases can appear in a sentence-final position, 'why' must appear in sentence-initial position.

(14) Krachi (Kandybowicz & Torrence, 2011)
   a. Ɔtʃíw ɛ-mò bwatéo n̩fré/kɛmekɛê/nɛnɛ?
      woman AGR-kill.PST chicken where/when/how
      'Where/when/how did the woman slaughter the chicken?'
   b. *Ɔtʃíw ɛ-mò bwatéo nání?
      woman AGR-kill.PST chicken why

---

[4]While preparing the final version of this article for publication, it occurred to me that there is an additional difference between the *ɖó* of *núkàtà...ɖó* and the *ɖó* found in extracted-from adjuncts: The *ɖó* that appears with *núkàtà* is optional, while adjunct *ɖó* is obligatory. Unfortunately, I did not have easy access to data or speakers to find data on the obligatory nature of adjunct *ɖó*.

1.3. Direct insertion of núkàtà in the left periphery

  c. Nání jí ɔʧíw ɛ-mò bwatéo?
    why FOC woman AGR-kill.PST chicken
    'Why (for what reason) did the woman slaughter the chicken?'

However, at the same time, there clearly do exist types of *why* phrases that are introduced below the inflectional domain. An example of this is the clitic *i* 'what; why' in the Bantu language Sambaa.[5] As in other Bantu languages with a conjoint/disjoint alternation, the conjoint verb form in Sambaa can only appear when the element following it is inside the VP (Buell & Riedel, 2008). Therefore, the clitic *i* in (15) is VP-internal.

(15) Sambaa (Buell, 2011: p. 813)

   U-chi-ghul-iye-i?
   2SG.SM-7OM-buy-PERF.CJ-why

   'Why did you buy it?'

In such cases, including that of Sambaa, it can usually be shown that the resulting question is essentially a purpose question rather than a reason question. While purpose questions can often be used as surrogates for reason questions, the two can be distinguished by the fact that purpose questions are generally incompatible with non-volitional predicates. Using that criterion, the examples in (16) show that Ewe *núkàtà* questions are genuine reason questions.

(16) a. Núkàtà wǒ-lè dɔ̀ lé-ḿ (dó)?
     why 3SG-be.at sickness suffer-PROG go.to
    'Why is she sick?'
  b. Núkàtà gà àḍéké mé-lè é-sí (ḍó) ò?
     why money any NEG-be.at 3SG-hand go.to NEG
    'Why doesn't she have any money?'

  In the previous section, it was shown that the *núkàtà...ḍó* word order closely resembles other cases in which a [DP+light N] constituent is extracted from the position which is complement to a light V. If 'why' were introduced in the same low position as other adjuncts, we would expect the *ḍó* of *núkàtà... ḍó* to similarly be stranded in some low position below IP. Two types of evidence will now be presented to argue that, contrary to that expectation, *núkàtà...ḍó* is first merged in the left periphery.

---

[5] While the clitic *i* is also used to mean 'what', it cannot have that interpretation in (15) because the direct object is encoded with the noun class 7 object marker *chi*.

1.3.1 Negation

Buell (2011) connected Rizzi's (1999) idea that *why* first merges in the complementizer domain with negation, proposing that *why* cannot be merged under sentential negation. In English, the argument for this comes from the fact that *why* falls outside the scope of negation. One of these scopal effects is illustrated in (17), in which the sentence *But I have sung!* is felicitous as a response to a *why* question, but not to any other type of *wh* question.

(17)   a. Why haven't you sung yet? But I have sung!
       b. What kinds of performances haven't you sung in yet? #But I have sung!
       c. Who haven't you sung for/with yet? #But I have sung!

The reason question in (17a) requires the presupposition that no singing event took place. In contrast, the non-reason questions in (17b) and (17c) are incompatible with that same presupposition. Instead, they require a context in which there is a set of potential singing events, at least one of which went unrealized. This is explained if *why*, unlike the other *wh* phrases, leaves no copy or trace in a position under negation.[6]

At first glance, Ewe seems to constitute a clear counterexample to Buell's proposal, because for some speakers, *ɖó* can appear sandwiched between the two negative heads *mě* and *ò*, as in (18a), giving the impression that *ɖó* is lower than at least one of them.

(18)   a. % Núkàtà mě-gblɔ̀   ná Ámà bé   Kòfí dzó   ɖó   ò?
           why   2SG:NEG-say to Ama that Kofi leave go.to NEG
       'Why didn't you tell Ama that Kofi left?'
       b. Núkàtà mě-gblɔ̀   ná Ámà bé   Kòfí dzó   ò   ɖô?
           why   2SG:NEG-say to Ama that Kofi leave NEG go.to

However, as (18b) shows, *ɖó* can also appear to the right of the second negative head, and that is the only word order accepted by all speakers. This fact leaves open the possibility sketched in (19) that *ɖó* is not below either of the negative heads.

---

[6]Shlonsky and Soare (2011) use the pair *Why/*How didn't Geraldine fix her bike?* to make the same claim in terms of Relativized Minimality. While *why* and *how* do not have the same status in this pair, Buell (2011) shows that *how* actually can be used grammatically in such negative questions if a list of particular manners is context-salient. However, he also shows that the interpretation with respect to the scope of negation still differs between *why* and *how* in these cases.

1.3. Direct insertion of núkàtà in the left periphery

For independent reasons, Aboh (2004) has argued the very high position of the negative head ò in (19) and the movement of IP around it.[7]

(19)
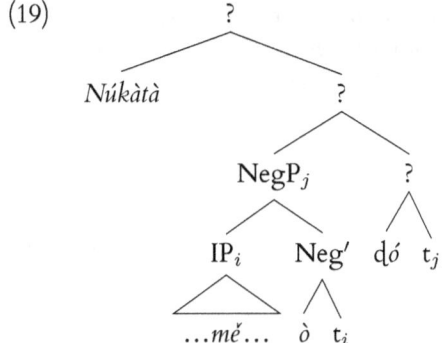

One argument that can be added for this high position is the fact that ò follows a complement clause when the matrix clause is negated, as in (20).

(20) Nyè-mé-gblɔ [CP bé Kòfi dzó] ò.
      1SG-NEG-speak   that Kofi leave NEG

'I didn't say that Kofi left.'

This fact is easily explained if ò heads a projection somewhere above IP. The sentence-final position of ò in (20) is then explained by moving the entire matrix IP to the left of ò, without prior extraposition of the complement clause.

If the analysis in (19) of sentence (18b) with ò ɖó is correct, then the problematic ɖó ò order in (18a) can be explained by assuming that a post-spell-out reordering has taken place that does not reflect the underlying syntactic hierarchy. This analysis is further supported by the fact that two of my six informants categorically reject the ɖó ò order. For those speakers, the only possible order is ò ɖó, which corresponds transparently to the syntactic structure in (19).

The structure in (19) is also comparable to Shlonsky and Soare's (2011) proposal, in which 'why' originates in a ReasonP in the complementizer region but can move to an IntP (the Interrogative Phrase first proposed by Rizzi 1999) even higher in the same region. Using data from Romanian, they argue for the following partial hierarchy of the complementizer domain.

(21) ...IntP > TopP > FocP > WhP > ReasonP...

---

[7] See also Kandybowicz (2008) for a similar particle in Nupe.

Assuming the part of their analysis that places IntP above ReasonP and that allows 'why' to move from spec-ReasonP to spec-IntP, *ɖó* could head ReasonP while *núkàtà* originates in its specifier. The NegP in (19) would then need to occupy a functional projection somewhere between IntP and ReasonP, and *núkàtà* would move from spec-ReasonP to spec-IntP. The resulting structure is depicted in (22), which omits the silent Int⁰ and F⁰ heads.

(22)

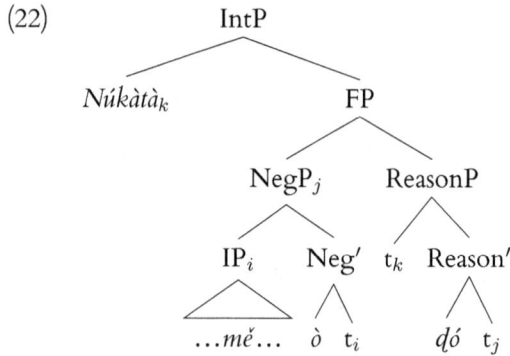

In addition to keeping 'why' entirely outside the c-command of both negation heads, this analysis, in which *ɖó* and *núkàtà* are first introduced as head and specifier of the same projection, nicely captures the fact that the two elements are related.

1.3.2 VP nominalization fronting

Although Ewe is an SVO language (23a), in progressive and prospective aspect an inversion takes place in which the object comes to precede the verb, as in (23b). The verb is followed by a nominalizing particle (*ḿ* for progressive, *gé* for prospective) which indicates which of these two aspects is intended. The object, verb, and nominalizing particle form a constituent (Buell, 2012), which for convenience we can simply call a "(VP) nominalization." As illustrated in (24), this constituent can be preposed for focus, in an operation we can call "VP nominalization fronting."[8]

---

[8] VP nominalization fronting is a type of predicate focus. For a discussion of other types of predicate focus in Ewe, see Fiedler (2012), Badan and Buell (2012), and the references therein.

1.3. Direct insertion of *núkàtà* in the left periphery

(23) a. S V O
 Ðèví lá ḍù àkɔ̀ḍú.
 child the eat banana

 'The child ate a banana.' (default aspect)

 b. S Aux [O V Nom]
 Ðèví lá lè [àkɔ̀ḍú ḍù-ḿ].
 child the be.at banana eat-PROG

 'The child is eating a banana.' (progressive aspect)

(24) a. Mè-lè [mɔ́lì ḍù gé].
 1SG-be.at rice eat PROSP

 'I'm going to eat rice.'

 b. [Mɔ́lì ḍù gé] mè-lè.
 rice eat PROSP 1SG-be.at

 'I'm going to EAT RICE.'

Instead of an object, this fronted constituent may contain a *wh* constituent (either an object or an adjunct), as in (25) and (26).[9] However, as shown in (27b), *núkàtà* 'why' is not compatible with VP nominalization fronting.

(25) [Núkà ḍù-ḿ] nè-lè?
 what eat-PROG 2SG-be.at

 'What are you eating?'

(26) [Áléké zɔ̀-ḿ] wǒ-lè?
 how walk-PROG 3SG-be.at

 'How is he walking?'

(27) a. Núkàtà nè-lè dzò-dzó-ḿ?
 why 2SG-be.at REDUP-leave-PROG

 'Why are you leaving?'

 b. *Núkàtà (dzò)-dzó-ḿ nè-lè?
 why REDUP-leave-PROG 2SG-be.at

---

[9]Some speakers do not accept *áléké* 'how' in monoclausal examples of this construction. The full range of adjunct *wh* phrases in predicate focus is better shown in multiclausal questions, which are too complex to discuss here. See Buell (2012).

Judgments on this point are so strong that when presented with them, speakers usually reject such questions after reading just the first two words, regardless of the length of the question. There is simply no way to complete a sentence starting with *núkàtà* followed by a verb stem and nominalizing particle.

The fact that a VP nominalization can contain clearly phrasal material, as in (28), in which the object is modified by a relative clause, shows that it is not formed by some extrasyntactic morphological process.

(28) Mè-lè   [[_DP_ mɔ́lì sì   Ámà ɖà   lá] ɖù ḿ   ].
      1SG-be.at   rice REL Ama cook the   eat PROG
      'I'm eating the rice that Ama made.'

Aboh (2004: ch. 6) develops an analysis in which the nominalization is formed on the main line of projection. The nominalizing particle is merged somewhere below IP and above *v*P, and the verb stem and fronted element in the nominalization (i.e., the object or *wh* phrase) subsequently move above it.[10] Let us assume that analysis. If *núkàtà* is first introduced in the complementizer domain (somewhere above IP), then it is never in a position low enough to move to this sub-IP position above the nominalizing particle, as would be necessary to form part of the nominalization constituent. Merging *núkàtà* directly in the complementizer domain thus allows us to explain the distribution of VP nominalization fronting at no extra cost.

This gives us two arguments—negation and VP nominalization fronting—that Ewe *núkàtà...ɖó*, just like Italian *perché* 'why', is first introduced in the complementizer domain. Now we turn briefly to the internal structure of that domain.

1.4 Higher than focus

BY SHOWING THAT ITALIAN *perché* 'WHY', unlike other *wh* phrases in the language, could be combined with fronted focused phrases and appear to their right, Rizzi (1999) showed that *perché* occupies a position higher than focused phrases in that language. Using the hierarchy in (21), these positions would correspond to spec-IntP and spec-FocP, respectively. The same results can be reproduced in Ewe, as shown in (29b), in which *núkàtà* is contrasted with *yèkáyì* 'when' in an embedded context, although the same pattern also holds

---

[10]Buell (2012) has argued that an alternative analysis requires an overly powerful Sidewards Movement mechanism.

1.5. Conclusion

in root questions and for other types of *wh* phrases. Of all types of *wh* phrases, only *núkàtà* can appear before a focused phrase.

(29) a. Nyè-mé-nyá núkàtà-(é) Kòfí-é wɔ̀ nú sìà ò.
 1SG-NEG-know why-FOC Kofi-FOC make thing this NEG
 'I don't know why KOFI did it.'
 b. *Nyè-mé-nyá yèkáyì-(é) Kòfí-é dzó ò.
 1SG-NEG-know when-FOC Kofi-FOC leave NEG
 'I don't know when KOFI did it.'

Thus, Ewe is similar to Italian not only in that 'why' is first merged in the complementizer domain, but also in that the position it occupies is higher than other focused elements.

Limited data also suggests that *núkàtà*, unlike other *wh* phrases, can appear to the left of a topic, as shown in (30).

(30) a. Núkàtà Kòfí yá nè-fò nǔ kplî?
 why Kofi TOP 2SG-hit mouth with:3SG
 'As for Kofi, why did you talk with him?'
 b. *yèkáyì Kòfí yá nè-fò nǔ kplî?
 when Kofi TOP 2SG-hit mouth with:3SG
 (Intended: 'As for Kofi, when did you talk with him?')

While perhaps surprising, such an ordering is predicted by the hierarchy in (21) to be possible.

1.5 Conclusion

IN THE PREVIOUS SECTIONS three analytical points were addressed. First, it was shown that *núkàtà...ɖó* is morphologically different from other adjuncts involving extraction from *ɖé*. Second, using facts from negation and VP nominalization fronting, it was argued that *núkàtà* is first merged in the complementizer domain rather than being moved there from a low position such as from within the *v*P. Finally, it was shown that the same facts used by Rizzi in Italian to argue that 'why' occupied a higher position than focused phrases could be replicated in Ewe. Furthermore, both the bipartite nature of *núkàtà... ɖó* and the combined distribution of complementizer-domain elements were shown to lend support to Shlonsky and Soare's (2011) proposed organization of the left periphery of the clause.

Ewe can thus be added to the growing number of languages that support the characterization that reason questions are universally an exclusively complementizer domain phenomenon.

Acknowledgments

I would like to thank my Ewe informants: Akuvi Adessou, Kokou Dzibril Amegan, Kate Dogbe, Jeannette Enaku, Nada Gbegble, and Elvis Yevudey. Thanks also go to Enoch Aboh, Ines Fiedler, Daan van Esch, the anonymous reviewers for this volume, and especially Jason Kandybowicz for their comments. This research was financed by Nederlandse Organisatie voor Wetenschappelijk Onderzoek (NWO) under project 360-70-300.

2

A case for "slow linguistics"

Bernard Caron
CNRS, IFRA-Nigeria, USR3336

2.1 Introduction

AS A BEGINNER HAUSAIST AND CHADICIST, I was introduced to Russell Schuh's work in the late 70's, when attending Claude Gouffé's lectures at the Ecole Pratique des Hautes Etudes. I had never met him, and I was surprised when I received a letter where he reacted to one of the very first articles I published on aspect in Hausa. My article was clumsy and fumbling, but Russell took the time to criticise it and offer suggestions to improve my approach to the topic. I was touched by his generosity and honoured that he had taken the time to share his reflections with the beginner that I was.

After defending my "Thèse d'Etat" on a Hausa dialect of the Niger Republic, as I had the opportunity to work in Nigeria for a few years, I decided to undertake the description of a lesser known Chadic language. It was only natural that in 1990, before taking up my appointment with a French research institute in Ibadan, Nigeria, I should write to him and several other renowned specialists of Chadic linguistics to ask for their advice as to which Chadic language was higher on the list of languages in need of research. I received a long, detailed letter from Russell Schuh where he made a broad description of the state of the art in the description of the whole Chadic family, branch by branch, with the location of languages and the identification of those where the information we possessed needed to be complemented, and the classification problems that were involved. As far as Nigerian Chadic languages were concerned, one language group emerged as the most worthy of interest. This was the South Bauchi language dialect cluster, with Saya as its main representative, or rather Zaar, after the autonym that I decided to use. I followed Russell Schuh's advice, and this set me on the scientific path I have been following for the past 25 years. This has literally changed my life, and I never regretted it.

Linguistics is done by people (linguists), with people (speakers, called 'informants' in our jargon), for people (other linguists, and hopefully reaching beyond the circle of linguists). It is this human aspect I would like to emphasize in my appreciation of Russell Schuh's work, and in a few examples of my own work, which I hope does not compare too badly with his.

I shared with Russell Schuh an interest in language documentation, its stress on data and the need to interpret it beyond face value. The best summary of this community of approach is found in the preface to his *Grammar of Miya* (1998), where he explains what a grammar should be:

> "What is an optimal descriptive grammar? Ideally, it should state and illustrate every generalization and idiosyncrasy of every structure that exists in the language being described. [...] The grammar should thus be organized in such a fashion and the description couched in such terminology that anyone with basic training in any tradition of linguistic theory and description could find the structures of interest and learn how they work without going beyond the description provided in the grammar itself. The grammar should be equally useful to the European structuralist working in the tradition of Andre Martinet or the American formal theorist working in the tradition of Noam Chomsky, to the semiotician concerned with the interrelations of signs or the typologist interested in cross-linguistic patterns, to the language area specialist or the general linguist. Finally, the grammar should be as comprehensible and valid in 100 years as it is today (which is not to say that the grammar might not be amended and expanded to incorporate facts unavailable to the compiler)." (Schuh, 1998: xvii)

And he has succeeded beyond expectation! His *Grammar of Miya* is my favourite grammar alongside Huddleston and Pullum (2008). This has been an inspiration and one of the reason for introducing the concept of "slow linguistics."

2.2 The case for "slow linguistics"

"SLOW LINGUISTICS" NEEDS TO BE DEFENDED in the same way as people are promoting "slow food" to fight against the infamous fast food industry. Slow linguistics takes its time to identify and prepare good quality data, carefully analysed with methods that respect its nature and structure, producing results that will endure and be appreciated for a long time.

In that respect, Russell Schuh's grammar was not a speedy exercise in adding a language name to his list of trophies. He started his fieldwork in 1982 and the book finally came out in 1996. Of course, it was slowed down by numerous teaching and administrative duties. But the grammar benefited from this slow maturation. One of the two "paramount models" to his work which he mentions in his preface, R.C. Abraham's *The Language of the Hausa People*, was published in 1959, and he mentions it as unsurpassed despite its formal quirkiness. Likewise, Russell Schuh's work stands independent from those theoretical experiments that have a life expectancy of about five years. This is fortunate, when one thinks of the African students who have to bow to the theoretical whims of their supervisor when they take their PhD in Western universities: they stay trapped in that theory imposed on them, and inflict the framework on their own students once they go back to lecture in their countries. Although Russell Schuh's wish for a grammar that "should be as comprehensible and valid in 100 years as it is today" (Schuh, 1998) may be overoptimistic, his is a much wiser option. When you have such an aim in view, you are allowed to take your time!

What makes Russell Schuh's work outstanding is that it is not merely descriptive. It is not just a list of facts randomly collected. The data is carefully analysed, from a systematic, diachronic and typological perspective, with a great amount of theoretical reflection. Let me take as an example his analysis of word order in his Miya grammar.

When studying the order of syntactic constituents in Miya, Russell Schuh does not take for granted the results of sentence elicitation. He takes into consideration not only syntactic (main vs. dependent) and morphological (TAM markers) elements but also information structure and genre (narrative vs. dialogue, reported speech, side comments, etc.). All this considered, Russell (Schuh, 1998: 281-300) argues that although Miya independent clauses typically have SXV order, VXS order is possible and is probably the most "neutral" order. In his work, he meticulously studies the relationship between Information Structure and Grammatical Relations before doing a statistical study of word order in Miya and making a generalization concerning the evolution of word order in West-Chadic languages and stressing its importance for typological studies.

In Miya, constituents of X are focused *in situ*, and the subject appears then in initial position. Subjects are focused in initial position, with restrictions on TAM markers. Outside focused sentences, nominal subjects appear sentence-finally. Topicalized subjects are of course left-dislocated, with no resumptive pronoun, and no restriction on TAM verbal markers. He suggests that in Miya, "all independent main clauses with preverbal nominal subjects may, grammatically, actually have the form TOPIC-COMMENT rather than SUBJECT-PREDICATE" (Schuh, 1998: 281). This would explain why statistically pre-verbal nominal subjects are dominant in narrations, and lead the linguist who often relies on narrations as a source of textual data to the wrong conclusions. This reconstruction of a basic constituent order against the face value of statistical evidence stresses the importance of genre and even style in the sampling of texts for linguistic studies. Of course, this takes time: the time for field work, sampling, recording, transcription and then annotation. Elicitation from a questionnaire is faster but may yield dubious results.

This type of in-depth, fine-grained analysis and annotation relies on a good understanding of the grammatical and lexical structure of the language that is documented. But as far as oral corpora are concerned, and more specifically dialogues, understanding the context, the common knowledge shared by the speakers, and even their personal history is often necessary for a proper analysis. As a consequence, much of the quality of the work we do depends on our ability to communicate with our informants.

First of all, the linguist must identify the person who possesses, beside immersion in the culture and a good competence in the language, some qualities that are not necessarily shared by everyone: communicative skills, mental agility, and an interest in abstract thinking. These qualities should hopefully match the linguist's own. When, added to this, the informant can write his own language, the linguist is blessed.

Russell Schuh, in the first chapter of his Miya grammar, gives credit to his own main informant, Vàziya Círòoma Tilde Miya, and stresses the importance of his help as regards the collection of texts.

"[…] Vaziya's ability to write Miya was invaluable. Anyone who has ever tried to transcribe recorded texts knows the tedium and frustration involved, even from languages s/he knows fairly well much less a language which s/he does not speak. But with Vaziya's written version available, it simplified the task immensely because the basic flow of the text was already there, and only specific words and constructions needed clarification." (Schuh, 1998: 9)

In the same vein, I personally would like to pay homage to the second person who has been most influential in my work on Zaar, i.e. M.S. Davan, who sadly and unexpectedly passed away at the age of 40, not long after Russell Schuh. I had been working with him for almost twenty years, and he truly deserved the first name he had chosen for himself: "Marvellous." He was a natural linguist who was not given the time to use his gifts for the development of his culture and the defence of his language.

2.3 The discovery of a "marvellous" linguist and community

AROUND 1995, I HAD BEEN WORKING for 5 years on Zaar with Sunday M. Dariya as main assistant, when I felt I needed to find somebody with whom I could communicate better on the work, and who would be more interested in the language. Sunday was a competent speaker, but had no particular interest in understanding what I was doing. And his family obligations prevented him from giving me more of his time for the large scale corpus transcription and annotation that I wanted to start at the time.

In Sunday's village where I had settled for my work, I advertised a position of assistant, offered to the many young adults who had completed their secondary school and who remained idle in the village. Very soon, five candidates volunteered. One morning, as I was teaching them the orthography I was using for transcription, I saw one young man in the audience reading over their shoulder, and pointing to them the mistakes they were making. I asked one of the applicants who was struggling with the task to leave him his seat, and it soon became obvious that that young man was by far the fastest learner. Within a couple of hours, he had mastered my orthography, which I quickly modified during the exercise, in order to make it easier for him to use. That's how I met Marvellous S. Davan, or rather Gaba as he was then called, and started working with him.

That very first day, as he found it so easy to learn, I tried my luck at teaching him how to mark the tones of the language. I gave him a list of minimal pairs in monosyllabic and disyllabic words as reference patterns, and started dictating a new word list to him. It took him 30 minutes to master the system, and return a faultless transcription. I ended the session by handing over to him a 30 minute long recording of an interview of an old man who was narrating his biography and his experience as a worker in the tin mines of the Plateau State under the British colonial occupation. Within a week, he returned a neat transcription of the cassette, marked with tones, with an interlinear translation into Hausa. A few years later, I realised that he had actually corrected what the speaker said, removing the hesitations, and changing a word here and there when he thought the man had made a mistake. I asked him to completely redo the transcription which I needed for a work on intonation, without changing anything to what the speaker had said. The passages that he had not modified ten years before came back with the same transcription, down to each single tone. He was a fast learner, a fast worker, and very precise and exact.

After working for years with Marvellous, and living within the Zaar community, a close relationship developed. I was asked to organise a cultural festival where 5 musical groups performed with their dancers. Sunday Dariya named one of his sons Bernard after me. I was turbaned "Sarkin Pada Tudun Wada Davan." I wanted to do something within the scope of my activity as a linguist that could be relevant to the community. I share with Russell Schuh the feeling that, if we need to gather data from the languages as part of our work as linguists, we need at the same time to produce "*output of interest and value to the speakers of those languages.*" (Schuh, n.d.). In a modest way that cannot compare with Russell Schuh's *Yobe Languages Research Project* on Bade, Bole, Duwai, Karekare, Maka, Ngamo and Ngizim, I have locally published a book on Zaar grammar, with a dictionary and collection of texts in Zaar, Hausa and English (Caron, 2005). I conceived the book as a linguistic help for Zaar children to have access to English starting with texts whose cultural context was familiar to them. The book was launched in Bogoro, Bauchi State, with a small price tag thanks to the financial help of the French Embassy. The Zaar community had refused to have the book distributed freely as I had planned initially. "What is free has no value" they said.

What the Zaar community was keen on getting from my work was a Zaar translation of the Bible, which I politely declined. I directed them to the SIL people in Jos, but they did not agree on the terms of their collaboration.

After a good many years of work with me, Marvellous caught the virus, and decided to start his own work. I helped him to scout the Zaar area looking for old speakers to interview about their oral traditions. He wrote and typed in Zaar a summary of his findings, which he complemented with some

2.3. The discovery of a "marvellous" linguist and community

proverbs, word lists, and a few passages from the Bible. He published the book in 2010 with the title *Bup Dzanyi Gwaay*, 'Improve yourself' (Davan, 2010). After that, Marvellous decided to teach the young children of the community to write and read in Zaar. For that, he set out to write a method, with a primer which he tested for some time in a local primary school. He registered for a BA in the Distance Learning Center that had just opened in Bogoro, Bauchi State. He also went to Jos to get some training in orthography development in a workshop organised by the SIL. But all this beautiful project was nipped in the bud by his untimely death in November 2016 in Bauchi. Let him rest in peace.

As a conclusion to this homage to Marvellous, I would like to illustrate the pivotal role he has had, as an informant, in the development of my understanding and analysis of Zaar. I will take two examples, one from phonology, and one from intonation structure.

2.3.1 The mystery of the falling tone

A phonological problem had troubled me for more than two years before I met Marvellous. It concerns tonal verb classes and more precisely, monosyllabic CV verbs with a short vowel (*du* 'to beat'; *nda* 'to enter'; *fu* 'to say'; *lə* 'to leave'; *fa* 'to drink'; *su* 'to return'; *ta* 'to climb'; *tu* 'to meet'). In the Perfective, I heard a Mid tone for all the verbs. Therefore, those verbs did not belong to the class of verbs with a lexical High tone, but rather to the lexical and morpho-phonological class of non-High verbs beginning with a voiceless obstruent.

Now, since this class of non-High verbs had a falling tone in the third person singular and plural of the Narrative, I was expecting the short list of CV verbs to behave in the same way, but it was difficult for me to check whether this was correct. The shortness of the vowel made the perception of the tone dicey, even after making my informants whistle as slowly as possible. Most of the time, however, I heard not a Mid tone but a High, sometimes with a rippling that I was tempted to interpret as a Falling tone. So, High or Falling tone? This was a pertinent question because it was possible that the falling modulation on a light syllable is systematically realized as high, in which case certain high tones could, in certain contexts, be hidden falling tones.

Could I find assistance from parallels in other parts of the language? No noun in Zaar has this syllabic structure. The only grammatical morpheme bearing the same uncertainty as to whether it is a high tone or a falling tone was the Remote Past morpheme (*ta*). Its tonal behaviour is identical with that of the Recent Past (naː), which in certain contexts takes the form nâː with a clearly perceptible falling tone because it is carried by a long vowel. The parallel between the two past tense morphemes strongly suggests the existence of such a Falling tone over the Remote Past of *ta*, that is, over a monosyllable ending in a short vowel. Is this tone "simplified" in the form of a High tone or did it keep its form, which meant that I could not hear it clearly? I could not resolve this problem just with my own ears.

A couple of years later, I devoted several days of work to the problem using CECIL, a now obsolete acoustic lab developed by SIL which could be carried to the field. But to no avail: the acoustic data was insufficient to get a pitch track that I could interpret.

And that's where Marvellous solved the problem for me in his first 30 minute long transcription. In the texts, all those monosyllabic CV verbs with a short vowel, as well as the *ta* TAM marker, were transcribed by Marvellous with a falling tone in the relevant contexts. I soon realised that Marvellous systematically transcribed the phonological value of tone, as realised after phonotactic rules had applied. I only needed to reconstruct the rules and the lexical values from his transcriptions.

I gradually came to rely totally on his intuitions. At first I doubted some transcriptions that were not consistent, thinking he had made mistakes, but soon realised that they were phenomena that had escaped my attention. Following this, my analyses became more precise, more detailed and covered more and more complex data. Marvellous's explanations of context, situations, and background knowledge of Zaar culture and village history became essential when I started doing some fine-grained corpus annotation, especially on Information Structure.

2.3.2 Clefts sans 'it' sans 'be', sans everything.

In Zaar, the possibility of dropping the copula in specifying copular clauses (Huddleston & Pullum, 2008: 1416 ff.) sometimes has the result of producing transcriptions with clefted sentences that look like left-dislocated topics. The only thing that differentiates them is intonation. Such a case is found in (1) where the speaker (Marvellous himself) talked about a game of football where he scored the sixth goal:[1]

---

[1] Zaar is transcribed using the International Phonetic Alphabet, except for /j/ which is transcribed /y/. Vocalic phonemic length is marked after the vowel by single colon (ː). Phonemic tone is marked with diacritics: á, à, â and ǎ for High, Low, Falling and Rising respectively. Mid tone is left unmarked. The following abbreviations are used in the text and in morphosyntactic transcriptions: AOR, Aorist; COND, Conditional; COP, Copula; DEF, Definite; DM, Discourse

2.3. The discovery of a "marvellous" linguist and community

(1) lim-ês máː   MYÂːN mətá   ɬya.
    six-DEF even 1SG   1SG.REM drink
    'The sixth even, it is me who scored.' (Boys-A_407) [2]

This game of football had become a bone of contention: Marvellous had been accused of not playing well. In (1) he defends himself by saying that he was the one who scored the sixth goal. *limês*, 'the sixth (goal)', is topicalised, and the subject *myâːn* is focused in the form of an independent pronoun. The corresponding "neutral" sentence (without cleft or left-dislocation), which could appear in a narration of sequential events, would read like (2):

(2) mətá   ɬya   lim-ês máː.
    1SG.REM drink six-DEF even
    'I even scored the sixth.'

A copula (either of the invariable particles *nə* 'COP1'; or *kən* 'COP2') is usually present to specify the clefted element. An equivalent of (1) would then be:

(3) lim-ês máː   nə   MYÂːN mətá   ɬya.
    six-DEF even COP1 1SG   1SG.REM drink
    'The sixth itself, it is ME who scored (it).'

In a different context, if the speaker was listing the names of the players who scored the different goals, e.g. 'Justin scored the first one, Gaba the second ...', the function of the 1SG independent pronoun would be changed to that of the topic: 'As for me, I scored the sixth one,' as in (4):

(4) myâːn, mətá   ɬya   lim-ês máː.
    1SG   1SG.REM drink six-DEF even
    'As for me, I scored the sixth itself.'

In this example, the topic is pronounced with a suspensive intonation, and followed by a pause with a pitch reset (downstep) while the main prosodic

---

Marker; fill, Pause Filler; FUT, Future; INCH, Inchoative; NEG, Negative; OBJ, Object; PL, Plural; POS, Possessive; PROX, Proximal; QUEST, Question; REM, Remote Past; RES, Resultative; SG, Singular; TAM: Tense, Aspect and Mood; VRT, Virtual. By convention, in Universal Dependencies syntax, the dependency links are tagged in lowercase, e.g. advmod, adverbial modification; conj:dicto, dysfluency; dobj, direct object; nsubj, nominal subject; obl:comp, oblique complement; punct, punctuation; svc, serial verb construction.

[2] When a reference is given for an example, it corresponds to my unpublished annotated Zaar corpus. Unreferenced examples are reconstructed for the purpose of the paper.

prominence falls on the predicate *ɬya limês*, 'score the sixth'. With no pause or stepdown, and the main prosodic prominence falling on *myâːn* 'I/me', (5a) would now become (5b) where the first element of the sentence is focused. (5b) is a prosodically marked cleft, without identifying copula, without 'it' pronoun, and without relativization:

(5) a. *myâːn* = Topic

myâːn, mətá ɬya limês máː.
1SG 1SG.REM drink six-DEF even

'(as for) me, I scored the sixth itself.'

b. MYÂːN = Focus

MYÂːN mətá ɬya limês máː.
1SG 1SG.REM drink six-DEF even

'(it is) me who (lit. I) scored the sixth itself.'

The difference between these two constructions lies in the change of place of the main prosodic prominence. It falls on *ɬya limês*, 'score the sixth' in (5a) and *myâːn* in (5b). The main prosodic prominence indicates what functions as the illocutionary nucleus and syntactic root in the utterance.[3] In a focused construction, the clefted element marked by the main prosodic prominence and/or a copula supersedes the verbal predicate as the syntactic root of the utterance. Consequently, the target of the illocutionary act moves away from the verbal predicate to specify the element of the predicative relation that is clefted. As a result, the verbal predication itself is backgrounded.

I personally relied on Marvellous's context-based explanations and paraphrases for my analyses, and looked for intonation cues to substantiate his interpretations. My own approach to the relation between the linguist and the informant may be extreme, but it is essential in the work of linguists who are not native speakers of the language they study. However, I still find it difficult to convince my colleagues of the existence of ambiguities such as the one between a topic and focus interpretation of (5a) and (5b), where the only difference is expressed by intonation.

As I became more and more involved in the study of information structure, in a bottom-up methodology based on corpus analysis, the need for an annotation system that would enable me to retrieve extensive and relevant data from large corpora became more and more urgent. That's where the

---

[3] In Dependency Grammar, the root of the utterance is the single non-governed lexical item that operates as the syntactic head of the Government Unit. (See section 4.1 for a short presentation of Dependency Relations).

concept of macrosyntax and its annotation scheme provides a powerful tool to study the interface between information structure, prosody and syntax. Once the corpus is annotated for macrosyntax, tagged and parsed, it can be queried for a study of the relative role of morphology, syntax, and prosody in establishing the relation between sound and meaning. The annotation process and its interpretation of the meaning of the data is at the foundation of corpus linguistics. This methodology has helped me to account for the specificity of oral corpora, which is at the centre of my current work in linguistics.

2.4 Macrosyntax and the specificity of oral corpora

CORPUS STUDIES IN AFRICAN LINGUISTICS must take into account an obvious fact which has methodological but also theoretical consequences: African languages (apart from Arabic and colonial languages such as English, French, etc.) have no written and grammatical tradition. They are oral languages. Oral corpora are greatly structured by the features associated with performance: dysfluencies on the one hand (hesitations, pause fillers, aborted utterances) but on the other hand, the stylistics of oral art performance, such as rhetorical repetitions, parallel constructions, etc.

Descriptive grammatical frameworks, which on the whole remain heavily indebted to prescriptive grammars of European languages, are not equipped to account for the specificities of oral data. Dysfluencies for example, which are often considered as bits of incomplete sentences, are actually the backbone of the communication process and reveal, when properly analysed, the complexity and intricate structure of this process.

This argues in favour of a new descriptive paradigm and methods specifically geared at describing oral data. Syntax most commonly takes the sentence as its defining object. However, in oral data, syntactic relations go beyond the sentence, and sometimes, beyond turn-taking. A new framework, new tools for annotation, and new tools for syntactic representation need to be devised so as to take those phenomena into account. This means taking the Illocutionary Unit as the basic unit of representation, and going beyond the limits of sentential syntax to found a new syntax called "macrosyntax."

2.4.1 Macrosyntax and Macrosyntactic annotation

In this new approach to corpus annotation, the Illocutionary Unit is taken as the basic unit of representation. The Illocutionary Unit can be compared to Cresti and Moneglia (2005)'s utterance, which they define in reference to Austin's theory of speech acts (Austin, 1962):

> "The accomplishment of an illocutionary act is the main property that a language event must have in order to be considered an utterance. [...] From an operational point of view the utterance can be defined as the minimal linguistic unit such that it allows a pragmatic interpretation in the world." (Cresti & Moneglia, 2005: 16)

The Illocutionary Unit is not necessarily congruent with intonation units, and is defined as comprising all the elements bearing a syntactic relationship with the syntactic root of the unit. This includes peripheral elements that hold a discursive relationship with the root, such as left- and right- dislocated elements, parentheses, etc. By doing so, the model lays the ground for an all-inclusive model of syntax called 'macrosyntax'. Macrosyntax subsumes 'microsyntax' which describes the relation between a head and its complements, adjuncts, determiners or modifiers.

In other words, the macrosyntactic level describes the whole set of relations holding between all the segments that make up one and only one illocutionary act (Cresti & Moneglia, 2005). A macrosyntactic punctuation marking Illocutionary Constituents and their relations has been developed in the Rhapsodie Project (RP) for French (Lacheret et al., 2014). It marks macro-syntactic boundaries (i.e. Illocutionary Units and their main components: nuclei, pre nuclei and post nuclei, including discourse markers) and limits between pile layers (disfluencies, reformulation, coordination[4]).

Illocutionary Constituents are annotated as follows: "<" follows a pre-nucleus and precedes a nucleus or another pre-nucleus; ">" precedes a post-nucleus and follows a nucleus or a previous post-nucleus; and "//" indicates the right boundary of an Illocutionary Unit.

In (6) the pre-nucleus *Ndàːdə́m máː* is a left-dislocated topic, separated from the nucleus by "<". In (7) the post-nucleus *sarkinpáːda* is a vocative separated from the nucleus by ">".

---

[4] See section 4.2. for an illustration of the use of the concept of "pile" to account for dysfluencies in oral corpora.

2.4. Macrosyntax and the specificity of oral corpora

(6) Ndàːɗəm máː < má ɫə yel=tə   áy //
    Ndadəm even < 1PL.FUT go see=3SG.OBJ eh //
    'Ndadəm < I will go and see him //' (SI_06_Girls_A_005)

(7) á   ɓân-íː   ŋǎːn   > sarkinpáːda //
    3SG.AOR finish-RES COP2.VRT.NEG2 > Sarkin_Pada //
    'Is it finished now > Sarkin Pada ?//' (SI_07_Women_A_114)'

Macrosyntactic structures can be represented using the Universal Dependencies framework[5]. See (2.1) below which represents the dependency relationships in 6:

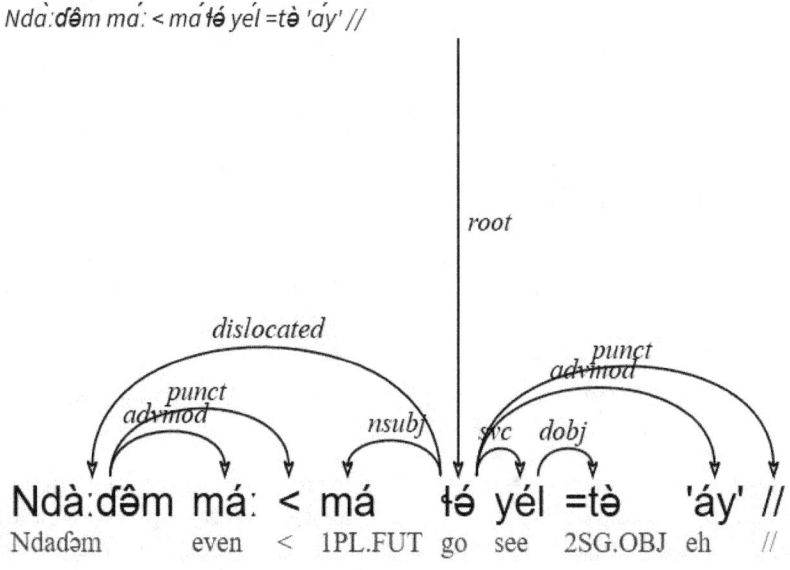

Figure 2.1: Syntactic representation of 6

Formally, a dependency is a directional relation between two words represented by an arrow: the origin of the arrow is called the governor and the target the dependent. Each dependency represents a government relation. In Fig. 2.1 an arrow tagged '*nsubj*' (nominal subject) points from *ɫə*, 'go' to *má*,

---

[5]See the Universal Dependencies website (http://universaldependencies.org/) for a detailed presentation of the theoretical framework and illustration by treebanks corpora in numerous languages.

1PL.FUT TAM and Person marker: *má* is the subject of *ɬə* and is governed by it. A government unit (GU) is a maximal unit for government. A GU has a head, which is not governed, and all the elements of the GU are dominated by this head. We call "root" the head of the Illocutionary Unit. The root of 6 is *ɬə*, 'go' in 2.1. In other words, a GU is the maximal projection of a non-governed lexeme. In our analysis, the GU is the Illocutionary Unit, i.e. the maximum macrosyntactic unit.

The following section examines three examples of the specificities of oral corpora and how they can be annotated and represented. These are: dysfluencies, afterthoughts and coordination over turn-taking. The corresponding annotation symbols will be presented and commented when they are introduced in the examples.

2.4.2 Dysfluencies

A common configuration of oral corpora that needs to be accounted for concerns dysfluencies, as in (8), an example taken from Zaar. The hesitations of the speaker result in the repetition of *kə*, separated by a pause (#), and *teː*, separated by a pause filler (yə):

(8) Tôː kə   # kə   dû teː   yə teː   gəʃi   tsən
    DM 2PL.AOR # 2PL.AOR beat around FILL around downhill like_this
    kən.
    COP2

'So, you…you would beat it towards er…towards the East like this indeed.' (Bury_Har_052)

This type of dysfluency pervades oral performances, and has to be taken into account in our description of African languages. An easy solution would be to tap into the speakers' "competence" and ask them to rephrase the sentence, removing the "mistakes" so that it can fit into our descriptive frameworks. However, these so-called mistakes are traces of cognitive processes (reformulation, etc.) that are meaningful and need to be documented.

Such a need was integrated into the work that was initiated in the 1970's in France by Claire Blanche-Benveniste and the *Groupe aixois de recherches en syntaxe* (GARS) (Blanche-Benveniste, Bilger, Rouget, van den Eynde, & Mertens, 1990). Their group was particularly innovative in their stress on documentation and oral corpora analysis. They developed a method to annotate dysfluencies of this type by turning them into a paradigm which has the same syntactic structure as coordination or apposition. They created the

2.4. Macrosyntax and the specificity of oral corpora

concept of "pile" (*empilement* in French) to describe the introduction of this paradigmatic dimension into syntax.

With coordination and apposition, elements build a paradigm in which each of them fills the same syntactic function as the first element of the paradigm. A visual representation using the GARS annotation shows clearly the paradigmatic relationship between the coordinated elements of (9):

(9) a. ka ɓəl-ni gyá: ɬərtí giní, tə ɬərtí gín, tə ɬərtí gín.
2SG.FUT dig-INCH PL root PROX and root PROX and root PROX
'You will dig these roots, and this root, and this root.'
(INT_05_Morals_SP1_117)

b. ka ɓəlni gyá: ɬərtí giní
tə ɬərtí gín
tə ɬərtí gín

'you will dig these roots
and this root
and this root.'

In macrosyntactic annotation, piles are delimited by braces: { ... }. The elements constituting the piles are separated by pipes: { __ | __ }. Various types of pipes annotate different types of piles, e.g. "|c" which annotates coordination: { __ |c __ }:

(10) ka ɓəl-ni { gyá: ɬərtí giní |c tə ɬərtí gín |c tə ɬərtí gín } //
2SG.FUT dig-INCH { PL root PROX |c and root PROX |c and root PROX } //

You will dig { these roots |c and this root |c and this root } //

The corresponding syntactic representation is shown in Figure 2.2, where the dependency tag of coordination is 'conj:coord':

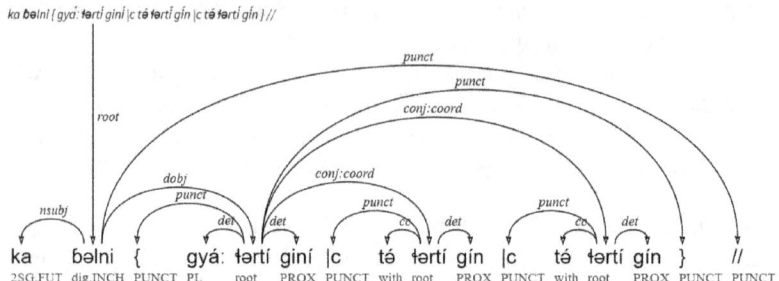

Figure 2.2: Syntactic representation of 10

The same paradigmatic relationship characterizing coordination is applied to dysfluencies, and are represented in the GARS annotation in (11):

(11) tô: kə #
    kə dû teː yə
        teː gəʃi tsən kən

'well you would...
    you would beat (it) toward er
        toward the East like this'

In macrosyntactic annotation, the piles built by dysfluencies are marked by double pipes, as in (12):[6]

(12) Tô: { kə   ‖ # kə   } dû { teː   ‖ yə teː   } gəʃi
    DM { 2PL.AOR ‖ # 2PL.AOR } beat { around ‖ fill around } East
    tsən   kən //
    like_this COP2 //

'So, { you ‖ you } would beat it { towards ‖ er... towards} the East like this indeed.' (Bury_Har_052)

The syntactic representation of dysfluencies is shown in Figure 2.3 where the dependency tag of dysfluencies is 'conj:dicto':

---

[6]In full macrosyntactic annotation, tô: and yə are called "Associated Illocutionary Units" and are surrounded by quotes.

2.4. Macrosyntax and the specificity of oral corpora

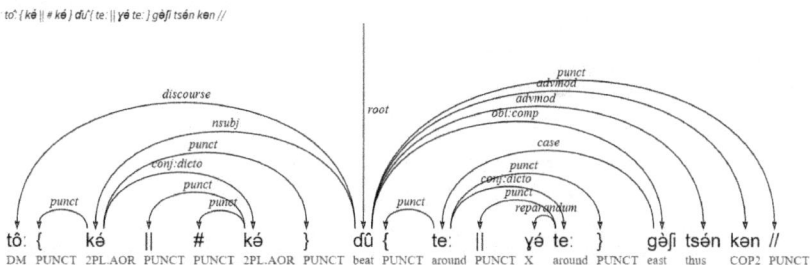

Figure 2.3: Syntactic representation of 12

This concept of 'piles' which covers coordination, apposition and dysfluencies, presents the advantage of reintegrating dysfluencies into syntax, and account for their role in discourse (reformulation, specification, elaboration of thought).

2.4.3 Afterthoughts

Afterthoughts are another example of the specificities of oral language data, as exemplified in (13):

(13) Tô: mə   ŋgyǎːr   gyaː gàːl ɓét ɗaŋ. Kóː gèri   kóː maːt.
       DM 1PL.AOR slaughter PL   cow all too   or chicken or goat

'Well we slaughtered many cows too. Or hens, or goats.' (Cal_Har_032)

In this example, the the adverbial adjunct *ɓét ɗaŋ* 'plenty too' finishes the first intonation, and the end of the unit is marked with a terminal prosodic break. Then, as an afterthought, two nouns are added, forming a discontinuous chain of three coordinated direct objects (*gyáː gàːl*, 'cows'; *gèri*, 'hens' and *maːt*, 'goat') of the verb *ŋgyáːr* 'slaughter.' The afterthought forms a second intonation unit starting with a pitch reset and finishing with its own terminal prosodic break.

The coordination operating over the final break of the first intonation unit can be represented as in (14), where the coordinated elements are in a paradigmatic relationship, and inherit their syntagmatic function from the first element of the pile:

(14) tôː mə ŋgyǎːr gyaː gàːl, ɓét ɗaŋ.
       kóː gèri
       kóː maːt.

       'well we slaughtered cows , many too.
              Or hens
              or goats.'

This poses a dilemma: if one follows the intonational clues, the constituents of the second intonation unit are syntactic orphans without governor. If one follows the syntactic structure, they are coordinated to *gàːl*, 'cow', and inherit their syntactic function from this link, but there is a discrepancy between the intonation and syntactic units.

Macrosyntax shows a way out of this dilemma by allowing syntactic relations (e.g. piling such as coordination, whether disjunctive or not) across prosodic boundaries. In (15), the coordination of the NPs in the first intonation unit (*gyàː gaːl* 'cows') and in the afterthought (*kóː gèri kóː maːt*, 'or chicken, or goat') takes place across the final prosodic boundary and over the utterance-final adverbial phrase *ɓét ɗaŋ*, 'too'. In macro-syntactic annotation, the final prosodic boundary across which the coordination operates is marked with a plus: //+. The disjunctive coordination is annotated with the symbols: { ___ lc } ... {lc___ } as in (15):[7]

(15) tôː mə   ŋgyǎːr   { gyaː gàːl lc} ɓét ɗaŋ //+ {lc kóː gèri   lc
      DM   1pl.aor slaughter { PL   cow lc} all   too //+ {lc or chicken lc
      kóː maːt } //
      or goat }//

      'well we slaughtered { many cows lc} too //+{lc or hens lc or goats} //'

(Cal_Har_ 032)

2.4.4 Syntactic relations over turn-taking

Piling through coordination can also occur across turn-taking and result in elliptic structures. Instead of considering those as either incomplete structures or structures where most of the elements have been omitted, they can be considered as a special case of coordination across turn-taking.

---

[7]See Caron (2017) for a more detailed presentation of macrosyntax and the annotation of Zaar.

2.4. Macrosyntax and the specificity of oral corpora

This is illustrated in (16) below, which is part of a passage where the first speaker [S1] is interviewed by [S2] about funeral rites. In this example, the nouns *gət* 'woman' in (16a) and (16e), and *ŋaː gət* 'girl' in (16c) are part of the same pile that spreads over several turn-takings, and share the same syntactic properties as initially stated in (16a).

The utterance in (16a) is divided in two parts: the nucleus *tá gìː tə gòs dòː?* 'where will they bury her?' and the pre-nucleus *tô ɢət kən yáː məs kúmá* 'well if it is A WOMAN that dies', a conditional dependent clause whose subject *gət*, 'woman' is clefted. The clefted element is coordinated over several turns of conversation without repeating the rest of the (16a) initial sentence.

(16) a. S1: tô **gət** kən yáː məs kúmá tá gìː
           DM woman COP.3SG.COND die too 3PL.FUT bury 3SG.OBJ
           tə gòs dòː?
           3SG.POS where
        'Well and if it is a woman that dies, they will bury her where?'

    b. S2: **gəd-àː?**
           woman-QUEST
        'A woman?'

    c. S1: **kóː ŋaː gət.**
           or young woman
        'Or a girl.'

    d. S2: **ŋaː gət** tá gìː ʃí ɓəʤəŋ > kápwâːsəŋ
           young woman 3PL.FUT bury 3PL.OBJ outside all_3PL.POS
           […]
           […]
        'Girls, they would bury them outside, all of them. […]'

    e. S1: **tə gət** ɓét kóː?
           with woman all or
        'And women too or what?'

    f. S2: m̀ː tə **gət** ɓét tá gìː ʃí dân.
           er with woman all 3PL.FUT bury 3PL.OBJ there
        'Er and women too, they would bury them there.'

                                                     (Bury_Har_20)

The elements coordinated across the turns of conversation are linked to the structure of the first question, and inherit their syntactic function from the first element of the pile: '{ gət |c kó: ŋa: gət |c tə gət ɓét } kən yá: məs […],' if it is { women |c or girls |c and women in general } that die […]').

Likewise, the noun in S2's echo-question (gaɗà:, 'women?') is part of this coordinated pile too, and inherits the same function as the coordinated elements in S1's turns. (16b) is equivalent to (17):

(17) S2: gət (kən yá: məs) a: […],
woman COP2 3SG.COND die QUEST

'(if it is) a woman (that dies) eh?'

This analysis and its accompanying annotation system elegantly underline the coherence of this large passage without postulating the existence of elements deleted through ellipsis. Each element in (16b), (16c) and (16e) is linked to the previous utterance of the speaker, and inherits its referential coordinates from this unit.

2.5 Conclusion

AS A CONCLUSION TO THIS ACCOUNT of my experience of field linguistics in all its aspects, which I started in Nigeria with Russell Schuh's initial impulse, and continued with his constant encouragement, I would like to stress that corpus linguistics has entered a new era. With the aid of computers, what I call "slow linguistics" can now be done on a large scale while gaining in quality and saving on resources, thus getting the best of both worlds. New computer programmes, using algorithms commonly referred to as "deep learning" programmes, are used to produce automatic taggers, parsers, phonetizers and sound-text aligners. Those are beginning to be developed for under-resourced languages. I am planning to experiment some of these on Zaar as a pilot language and then, why not expand these methods to the study of other languages in a future Centre for the Study of Nigerian Languages?

3

Ongoing changes in the linguistic landscape in the Lake Chad area

Norbert Cyffer
University of Vienna, Austria

3.1 The enormous attraction of the Lake Chad area

THE WIDER REGION AROUND LAKE CHAD is characterized by ongoing social, political and consequently linguistic changes. Though our knowledge about the local history is limited, there is sufficient information about the external circumstances affecting the changes of linguistic behaviour. Our increasing knowledge leads to a better understanding of the developments. In any case we have to keep in mind, that the present linguistic landscape does not correspond with that of earlier times. Over the past centuries one can observe an ongoing process of changes. Such developments have been going on until the present. These changes are ascribed to an increase and decline of political dominance, but also changes of social and religious affiliations and new developments like education, urbanisation, migration, etc.

Due to the political strength of the Kanem Empire and the spread of Islam to West Africa, which started in the 10th century, the western areas of Lake Chad became gradually populated by the Kanembu people from the east of the lake. These two factors contributed to the strength of the emerging Kanem-Borno Empire and the increasing linguistic role of Kanuri. This dominance lasted until the beginning of the 19th century. Internal conflicts and external claims to power made the empire politically faded (Hiribarren, 2017).

3.1.1 The languages in the area

The most striking linguistic upheaval in the Lake Chad area during the past millennium was the expansion of the Kanuri language to the western regions of Lake Chad. Gradually the Kanuri influence became stronger in several respects. This had several effects on the linguistic landscape.

Kanuri obtained the role of a language of wider communication

After the Kanem empire had expanded to the west of Lake Chad, the political centre was also shifted to the west and the enlarged Kanem-Borno empire emerged. This caused the Kanuri language to play a dominant role, which also expanded to areas outside the empire, e.g. in northern Cameroon, Niger and Fezzan (southern Libya).

In this context one comes across a noteworthy statement by Gerhard Rohlfs (1868). In his travel account he writes:

> "If one is to talk at all of a national language of a mixed people like Fezan, one has to mention the Kanuri or Bornu language, which is also spoken by the children. Next to it one hears Arabic, and many people also understand the Tuareg as well as the Teda and Hausa language." (Translated from German by author)

This dominance gradually faded, when Kanem-Borno got involved in power-political conflicts, which led to war activities in the first half of the 19th century (Smith, 1971).

The colonial administration of the 19th and 20th century also kept the political strength of the empire on a lower level. Kanem-Borno was spread over three colonial administrations (Nigeria, Niger, Chad). However, the recognition and respect for the religious, cultural and intellectual leadership of the Borno Emirate is unquestioned to the present day.

Kanuri influence on other languages

Kanuri exerted an important influence on the languages in the region. This refers to the lexicon as well as grammatical structures.

In his Hausa grammar Paul Newman made a very important statement about Kanuri-Hausa lexical relations (P. Newman, 2000: p. 315):

> "Kanuri loanwords date from the period of Kanuri political influence on Hausaland prior to, but continuing into, the period of Fulani domination. …The number of words borrowed from Kanuri is undoubtedly underestimated because many words of Arabic origin that are included in lists of Arabic loanwords in fact came into Hausa via Kanuri."

This fact has so far received little attention.

People gave up their own language in favour of Kanuri

This process of 'Kanurization' could be observed until the 20th century. It particularly affects speakers of Malgwa. In the course of time they gave up their language and adopted Kanuri. However, the Malgwa example is not the only case of Kanurization. For example, in the Kanuri speaking community we come across names, which also refer to designations of Chadic languages, e.g. Bade, Tera. Within the Kanuri society these are referred to as clan terms, which in this case have no direct link to immediate ethnic or linguistic relations. In the 1970s a local Kanuri leader in Damasak confirmed in his recited oral traditions the assumption that present Kanuri people had been integrated from other ethnic groups in the area. Therefore, one can conclude that many people of the area had given up their original identity in favour of Kanuri. While these developments are completed, the case of Malgwa is more recent and perhaps still going on.

The following map appeared in the travel account of Heinrich Barth (1857). It reveals interesting information about the ethnic situation of that time. The map dates back to the mid 19th century. About 20 miles north of the present Kanuri centre, Maiduguri, a place name refers to the Malgwa (= 'Ghamerghu') people: "Site of Muna the former Capital of the Ghamerghu, destroyed by the Fulbe or Fellata." It must be noted that Maiduguri has been the capital of the Borno Emirate for just over a century. Nevertheless, it is recognized to be the social, cultural and religious centre of the Kanuri people. Earlier the area was populated by speakers of Chadic languages.

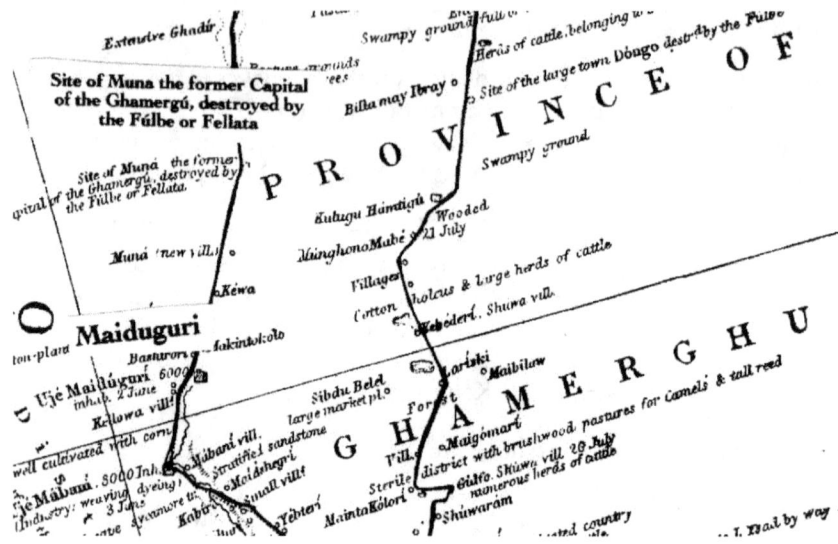

Figure 3.1: The area around Maiduguri in Heinrich Barth's map of 1857

This map helps to identify the linguistic processes. First of all it coincides with our knowledge of the recent history of the Lake Chad region. The Kanem-Borno Empire played a dominant political role in the region, which also exercised an enormous influence on the north-south and east-west trade routes. The spread of Islam is another important factor of the people of Borno's (i.e. Kanuri) identity and influence.

The map also provides useful information about the state of Kanuri penetration in the area. On the one hand it shows that the territory was closely connected with the "Ghamerghu" (Malgwa) people. On the other hand several places bear Kanuri names, e.g. Maiduguri, Maigommari (i.e. Magumeri). A larger map would also reveal, that more Kanuri place names would occur in the north. From this one can conclude that the Kanuri language was on the rise.

3.2 The relations between Kanuri and Chadic contact languages

FIGURE 3.2 BELOW PROVIDES some information about the relationships between the languages in the region. It shows that the common lexicon of

3.2. The relations between Kanuri and Chadic contact languages

contact languages is differently influenced by Kanuri and Hausa. The figures given in the table coincide largely with those given in R. Schuh's paper (Schuh, 2005b).

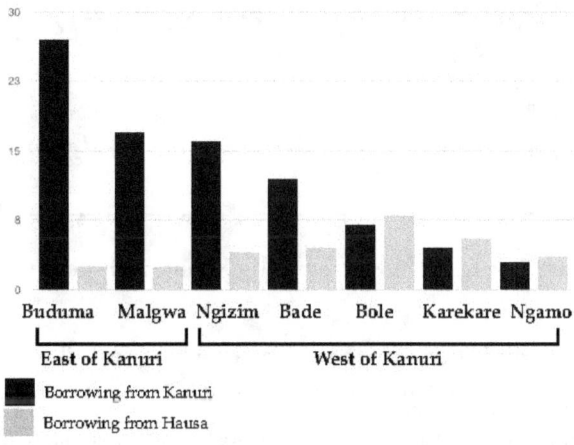

Figure 3.2: Kanuri and Hausa borrowings in Chadic contact languages (based on data from Awagana 2001, Tarbutu 2004, Dole et al. 2009, Adamu and Potiskum 2009, Gimba et al. 2009, Tikau and Yusuf 2009, and own research)

This figure helps to identify the linguistic processes. First of all it coincides with our knowledge of the recent history in the Lake Chad region. The languages Kanuri and Hausa have exercised their influence at different times. At first, it was Kanuri which was then gradually replaced by Hausa. Buduma and—to a lesser degree —Malgwa maintained close contact with Kanuri (see Figure 3.3 below).

The languages of wider communication

Kanuri had a great impact on its neighbouring languages. As outlined below, this influence was going on until the recent past. In the period of the dominant role of Kanuri, the lexicon of many contact languages shows a high rate of originally Kanuri lexemes. On the other hand, Hausa did not reach these languages to that extent. While Buduma and Malgwa in the east and southeast of the Kanuri speaking area had an intensive contact with Kanuri over time, it faded in the other languages from the first half of the 19th century.

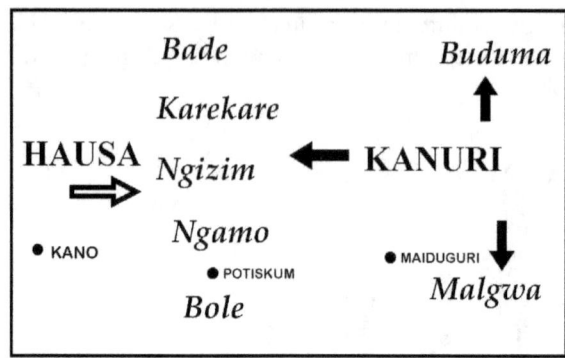

Figure 3.3: Languages affected by Kanuri and later by Hausa

What can Kanuri loans in the contact languages tell us about earlier phonological and morphological structures?

Our limited knowledge about the local history confirms that Kanuri has been a language of wider communication until the first half of the 19th century. Therefore, the lexical borrowing also reflects the phonology of that time. The causes are clearly understandable by the political and social impact of Kanuri on other peoples in the past. We have taken notice that current common processes of consonant weakening had not yet taken place at the time of borrowing.

(1)   Kanuri   Bade   Ngizim   Bole
      (Old)   (Present)
      ngálko ngálwo   ngálko   ngálko   ngálko   'better'
      káre   káre   kářai   kařê   kárai   'goods, load'
      bɔ́ci   bɔ́ji   būci   bŭshi   'mat'
      dabí   dawí   dabí   dabí   'hoe'

As earlier mentioned, a considerable number of Malgwa speakers have given up their original identity in favour of Kanuri. While this process was observed until the recent past, the same process did not apply to the Buduma people. Though relatively few in number, about 80.000 speakers or less, the people did not abandon their own social and linguistic identity. On the other hand, they maintained close contacts with the Kanuri people.

3.2.1 The recognition of linguistic structures

Earlier borrowings can also provide information about today's difficult-to-identify structures. Two examples from Bole and Buduma will illustrate this. For example, Kanuri nouns, which begin with *k*, are overrepresented. This is partly due to the fact, that the consonant *k* in many cases has a nominalizing and concretizing function.

(2) | Function | Base | Application of k |
|---|---|---|
| nominalizing prefix | suq 'market' (Arabic) | kasúwu 'market' |
| singularizing nouns | âm 'people' | kâm 'person, man' |
| general > specific | sóto 'hospitality' | kusóto 'guest' |
| verbal noun | rú 'see' verb root | kurû 'see' vn |

The basic concept of the prefix *k-* can be generalized as an original formative. The examples show, that the function can be versatile. In present Kanuri this formation pattern is no longer productive. Usually, the prefix and the noun are nowadays lexicalized and constitute a single morpheme. Of course, this does not necessarily mean that all nouns which begin with *k*, carry this feature.

Taking a look at the contact languages may help us to identify this old feature, i.e. the original morphemic status of k. An example from Buduma will show this. In Kanuri the lexeme for 'medicine' is *kurwûn*. The same lexeme, which is borrowed from Kanuri, is *rugún* in Buduma. It should be noted that the original function of *k-* was still active and productive at the time of the takeover. Therefore, in Buduma this morpheme does not appear.

(3) | | Formation | Phonological processes |
|---|---|---|
| Kanuri | k+rúgun | > kurúgun > kurúwun > kurwûn |
| Buduma | rugún | > rugún |

The Buduma loanword does not carry the nominal formative *k*. From this we may conclude that at the time of borrowing k still functioned as a separate morpheme. This historical finding cannot be applied in present Kanuri. Two forms were lexicalized to one morpheme.[1]

In the field of phonology we may also find indications, which help us to clarify unresolved questions. The following example is about the occurrence of the palatal fricative ʃ (henceforth *sh*). Most likely, this consonant did not

---

[1] J. H. Greenberg (1981) proposed that the morpheme *k* is a common Nilo-Saharan 'stage III article.' On the other hand, Margret A. Bryan (1975) suggests that it is an areal feature in northeast Africa.

have a phonemic value in old Kanuri. In present Kanuri it is an allophone of *s* when followed by the front vowels *e, i*.

(4) a. kənSê > kənshê 'coming'
 b. wúSe > wúshe 'welcome!'
 c. Sí > shí 'he, she'
 d. Síti > shíti 'side'

In borrowed words we often come across *sh* in different phonetic environments. This is due to the original sound shape in the borrowed form.

(5) a. tásha (< English) 'station'
 b. sóshi (< English) 'soldier'
 c. sháyi (< Arabic) 'tea'
 d. sharâ (< Arabic) 'law'
 e. rishô (< French) 'stove'
 f. shafô (< French) 'hat'

However, we should also note that nowadays the palatal fricative *sh* occurs also in environments other than those based on phonological rules or foreign borrowings. In order to find explanations for this, a look at the contact languages will be helpful. This can be illustrated with an example from the Bole language (Gimba et al., 2009). In present Kanuri the lexeme for sword is *kashâr*.

On the surface the sound structure seems to be untypical for Kanuri. The consonant *sh* does not occur in a place which would require the phonological process of palatalization. Also, the lexeme cannot be identified as a loanword. Therefore, either the common palatalization rule has to be modified, or another explanation must be found.

The Bole lexicon provides the comprehensible explanation. Here we obtain the entry *kasíkar* 'sword'. Outgoing from this basic form, the present Kanuri form can be deduced.

(6) | **Base** | **Palatization** | **Consonant weakening** | **Assimilation** |
kasíkar > kashíkar > kashíyar > kashâr

During the past 200 years Kanuri has undergone considerable developments of allophonic alternations. Therefore, one can conclude that these loanwords entered into the respective languages rather early and that the present phonemic rules did not exist at the time of borrowing.

3.2.2 The special relationship between Kanuri and Buduma

The linguistic relations between Kanuri and Buduma show that there have been close contacts between the speakers of the two languages. Though relatively small in number, the people, who call themselves Yedina, have retained their ethnic and linguistic identity. As they are largely surrounded by Kanuri (–Kanembu) speakers, the language shows considerable influence by the Kanuri language. As already shown, there is a high proportion of lexical borrowings. Moreover, there are also morphological and syntactic structures, which are copied from Kanuri. The other contact languages are not affected by this to such an extent. A few examples are given below.

Derivation by the noun agent morpheme -ma

Several nominal extensions were taken over from Kanuri, for example the formative of the agent noun -*ma*.

(7) **Kanuri**
cída 'work'   cidamá 'worker'
letə́ 'going' letə́ma 'traveller'
fáto 'house' fatomá 'landlord'

(8) **Buduma**
há 'cow'   hámá 'cattle breeder'
tugún 'medicine'   tugunmá 'doctor'
bandá 'fish'   bandamá 'fisherman'

This example shows that Buduma goes beyond just borrowing a lexeme. Here, the noun agent derivative acts somewhat independently and can be suffixed to original Buduma lexemes. This process is still productive.

The agent noun extension belongs to one of the more productive formations in Kanuri. Therefore, it is not surprising that it was also taken over from Kanuri. It should also be noted that the plural equivalent in Kanuri (-*wu*) was not taken over. Instead, in Buduma regular plural formations are applied (Awagana, 2001: p. 51), e.g.:

(9) **Common noun**

	Sg.	Pl.	
Kanuri	fáto	fatowá	'house'
	bə́ji	bəjiwá	'mat'
Buduma	Há	háy	'cow'
	bukwár	bukwáráy	'horse'

(10) **Extended noun**

	Sg.	Pl.	
Kanuri	fatomá	fatowú	'landlord'
	baremá	barewú	'farmer'
Buduma	baremá	baremáy	'farmer'
	kidamá	kidamáy	'worker'

The postpositions expressing relationship (-mi, -ram)

The Kanuri extensions -*mi* and -*ram*/-*rám* denote kinship relations 'son (of)' and 'daughter (of)'. Usually they are suffixed to a proper name or title of an office holder. They often become lexicalized as a new name. Both extensions are used in Buduma with the same basic meaning as in Kanuri.

(11) Kanuri
   a. Músa 'Musa' (proper noun)
   b. Músami 'Musa's son'
   c. mâi 'king'
   d. mairám 'princess'

(12) Buduma
   a. Ari 'Ari' (proper noun)
   b. Arimi 'Ari's son'
   c. may 'king'
   d. Mayram 'princess'

In Buduma the extension -*mi* was semantically extended to other concepts which are not applicable in Kanuri. For example, in order to derive a language name from an ethnic one, Kanuri applies a specific tone pattern and optional reduplication. In contrast, the formative -*mi* is applied in Buduma.

(13) Kanuri
   a. kanúri 'Kanuri person'
   b. (kanuri)kanurí 'Kanuri language'
   c. faránsa 'French person'
   d. (faransa)faransá 'French language'
   e. árab 'Arab person'
   f. (arabi)arabí 'Arabic language'

3.2. The relations between Kanuri and Chadic contact languages

(14) Buduma
    a. yediná 'Buduma person'
    b. Yedinámi 'Buduma language'
    c. ngánay 'Kanuri person'
    d. ngánaymi 'Kanuri language'
    e. abənó 'Hausa person'
    f. Abənómi 'Hausa language'

In connection with numerals we observe that in Kanuri and Buduma the extensions are replaced by the feminine counterpart. With regard to the formation of ordinal numbers Kanuri applies the extension -*mi* (< 'son of'), while Buduma uses -*ram* (< 'daughter of').[2]

(15) Kanuri
    a. kə́nyakk-**mi** 'third'
    b. kə́n'úwu-**mi** 'fifth'
    c. kə́nfíndi-**mi** 'twentieth'

(16) Buduma
    a. gakə́nnə́-**ram** 'third'
    b. hínji-**rám** 'fifth'
    c. hágə́-**ram** 'twentieth'

The preposition expressing abstractness (nəm-)

The number of suffixed extensions in Kanuri is by far higher than that of prefixed ones. Among them is the extension denoting abstractness. Buduma also took it over in the same function.

(17) Kanuri

Basic		Extended	
sáwa	'friend'	**nəm**-sáwa	'friendship'
kəjî	'sweet'	**nəm**-kəjî	'sweetness'
kâm	'person'	**nəm**-kâm	'humanity'
sháwa	'beautiful'	**nəm**-sháwa	'beauty'

---

[2] In Kanuri another extension -*ram* or -*rám* is applied to denote fees, place, instrument. Though it cannot be ruled out that there are old connections with the extension of relationship, for several reasons it is not treated here. One should also note that the tonal behaviour distinguishes the extensions (Cyffer, 1998). Therefore this derivation is regarded as a separate one.

	Category	Kanuri	Buduma	Remarks
a)	Clitic of direction	+		
b)	Indirect object	+		
c)	Adverbialization	+	+	
d)	Comparison	+		
e)	Benefaction	+		
f)	Purpose	+		
g)	Cause and reason	+	+	often extended by nanka
h)	Replacement	+		

Table 3.1: Functions and meanings of the Kanuri clitic -*ro*

(18) Buduma

Basic		Extended	
ngəlá	'friendly'	**nə́m-**ngəlá	'friendliness'
dəmú	'big'	**nə́m-**dəmú	'power'
cáy	'bitter'	**nə́m-**cáy	'bitterness'
fəlláydə	'turn (verb)'	**nə́m-**fəlláydə	'misfortune'

The postposition of direction in Kanuri and Buduma (-ro)

The clitic -*ro* is one of the widely used postpositions in Kanuri. Its basic meaning denotes direction. From this several functions and meanings emerged (Cyffer, 2010). The following table shows this. At the same time it also illustrates that Buduma took over the clitic from Kanuri, but only some of its uses.

(19) a. Káno-**ro** lenyên
'we go to Kano'

b. shí-**ro** kákkádə yíkin
'I give him a book'

c. dôi-**ro** saasâin
'they are running fast'

d. Músa Áli-**ro** kúra wo
'Musa is taller than Ali'

e. cída awányí-**ro** dikin
'I do the work for my father'

f. cída mata-**ro** Abujaro lengîn
'I go to Abuja for job search'

g. njî fijin nanka-ro lúwukinbâ
'as it is raining, I won't go out'

Buduma also took over the formative -*ro*, but on a substantially smaller scale. The probable explanation is that the formative was taken over only in those cases where a new category emerged. This applies especially in areas in which cause and reason and the formation of adverbials is expressed.

(20) Buduma (Awagana, 2001: p. 141)
   a. nəán njugó dəbú-**ró** nɔ́ké   (adverbial)
      'he chews a lot, before he swallows'
   b. ...náhəláhí nángá-**ró**   (cause and reason)
      '...because one his beating him'

Although Buduma has long been under strong Kanuri influence, the processes of language death have not occurred. Instead of applying another means of communication, the Buduma people maintained their own language and adapted it to the changing needs by lexical and grammatical borrowing from other contact languages, especially Kanuri.

3.3 Some conclusions

A CLOSER LOOK AT THE LINGUISTIC SITUATION in the western Lake Chad region provides numerous informations about aspects of language change, maintenance and loss. Even though our knowledge of the local history is limited, we come to some findings, which are of interest not only in linguistics, but also in obtaining historical insights. The history about the political power in the area is well documented. The ruling dynasties and the arrival of Islam have been well studied. However, we should be careful and not confuse the history of the ruling classes with that of the peoples in the area.

We know that the Kanuri language started to become established in the area from the 10th century. Its dominance grew gradually. The area was originally inhabited by speakers of Chadic languages. The linguistic impact of Kanuri on these languages had different effects. First of all the lexicon was affected. Terms, which did not exist in the languages concerned, were taken over. Languages, which had long lasting contacts with Kanuri, e.g. Buduma, went far beyond lexical borrowing. Especially in the morphology of nouns a considerable number of suffixed and prefixed extensions were taken over, as well as noun phrase patterns.

One has to keep in mind that Kanuri and its contact languages differ in their genetic affiliation. This entails that syntactic and morphological structures may differ in these groups. When borrowing takes place, usually the specific structure of the source language is also taken over, for example, a prefix remains a prefix, a postposition remains a postposition.

This raises the question why in one case a language threatens to disappear, whereas in another case this danger is not present. The situation of Buduma and Malgwa illustrate this well. Most likely the causes for this are the social structures of the peoples concerned. Another reason may be their habitat. With regard to Buduma, Barbara Dehnhard and Jan Patrick Heiss (personal communication) relate this fact to a tight social structure and delimitation of the surrounding peoples.

Did Kanuri also borrow from other languages?

It is common that speakers of one language have contact with those of another language. This applies, of course, also to Kanuri. First of all, one has to mention Arabic. Like other languages south of the Sahara, which have been in close contact with Islam, these languages have a considerable share of borrowings from Arabic. Kanuri is no exception. About 10% of the Kanuri lexicon can be traced back to Arabic origin. A lot of these borrowings are exported to other languages, including Hausa. Some of the lexemes obtained grammatical formatives from Kanuri, before they were passed on to other languages. With regard to borrowings from Hausa, their amount is rather limited. This is largely due to the fact that Hausa started to become a language of wider communication in the centres of the Kanuri speaking community (e.g. Maiduguri) not earlier than in the 1960s. The influence of English is even less. On the other hand, French has a larger share in the Kanuri vocabulary in Niger. The reasons for this are the different colonial administration systems in Nigeria and Niger. While in Nigeria the British system of "indirect rule" was applied, the French administration in Niger was centralistic. This resulted in the penetration of the French language down to the lowest administrative level (Bulakarima, 2001: pp. 149–156).

What's next?

In the current discussions about endangered languages in Africa, various scenarios about the future of these languages are presented. I abstain from any speculative predictions. The case of Buduma has shown, that languages with a relatively small number of speakers can survive, while others with a much

3.3. Some conclusions

larger number of speakers are indeed threatened. Many political, economic, cultural and social factors come in to determine the future developments.

4

Synchronic vs. diachronic naturalness: Hyman & Schuh (1974) revisited

Larry M. Hyman
University of California, Berkeley

4.1 Introduction

> The GNTS [Great Ngamo Tone Shift] paper is maybe the best paper I have ever written. I felt like the data was making me into a magician.
>
> (Email from Russell G. Schuh, July 11, 2005 re: Schuh 2005a; cf. Schuh 2017: 135-142)

IN 1972 RUSSELL SCHUH AND I wrote a paper entitled "Universals of Tone Rules: Evidence from West Africa." In this study, published in *Linguistic Inquiry* in 1974, we attempted to generalize from what we knew from our field experiences, from our courses at UCLA, and from what we had read and learned from others. As part of the journal review process we first had to defend ourselves against one very critical reviewer (who typed up 11 pages

4.1. Introduction

of comments single-spaced), but Jay Keyser, the editor of *LI*, decided that in addition to whatever other virtues the paper might have, the state of our knowledge of tone systems justified its publication. In honor of Russ, my purpose here is to discuss some of the issues that we raised and see how they have fared: what we got right, what we got wrong, what is still out there to be resolved. I first have to confess that I only remember rereading our paper one other time—and less carefully—before preparing the comments that I present here. However, having reread other ancient works of mine, I had been remarking to others that there are three possible reactions to re-reading something one has written a long time ago. I label them as follows, in English and Hausa:

(i) *Ignorance, rashìn sanìi.* I can't believe how little I knew then, how wrong I was, how embarrassing to make such strong pronouncements, given my youthful ignorance.

(ii) *Pride, yàbon kâi.* Hey, this isn't bad. Maybe I wouldn't say things today the way I did then, but I did a pretty good job, considering.

(iii) *Forgetfulness, màntuwaa.* I can't believe I knew all that back then. I don't remember saying that, reading those references, knowing all that. Did I really write this paper?

Having just reread Hyman and Schuh (1974), I want to add a fourth possible reaction:

(iv) *Déjà vu, naa taɓà ganinsà.* I can't believe I (we) already had those ideas back then. I thought I had just come up with these ideas recently.

This last response is reassuring, as it seems to suggest an intellectual consistency throughout one's career; however one would hope it does not instead indicate a lack of intellectual growth. Finally, the most expected reaction would probably include a mixture of emotions.[1]

In the following sections I will recapitulate and evaluate some of the generalizations in Hyman and Schuh (1974), henceforth H & S, particularly our starting point, synchronic vs. diachronic naturalness, which led us to make certain claims that require further consideration. Some of the same ideas were repeated in our two chapters in *Tone: A linguistic survey* (Fromkin 1987),

---

[1] Although I felt mostly comfortable re-reading H & S, I found it a bit embarrassing to see more than one reference to "Hyman (in preparation)," a ms. on "Synchronic vs. diachronic naturalness" that never materialized. I think we prematurely announced intended publications more in those days than now.

where we wrote on "Tone rules" (Schuh 1978) and "Historical tonology" (Hyman 1978). While H & S drew almost exclusively from West Africa (Benue-Congo and Chadic), my later chapter focused mostly on Bantu, while Russ' drew from all parts of the world.[2]

4.2 Diachronic naturalness

AMONG THE BASIC ASSUMPTIONS Russ and I shared was the impossibility of truly understanding synchronic grammar without a diachronic perspective. This was a view we derived from the simultaneous descriptive and historical work that provided so much of the focus of our graduate studies at all levels of grammar at UCLA. We not only heard Talmy Givón's adage "…today's morphology is yesterday's syntax" (Givón 1971: 413), but also sought phonetic explanations with Peter Ladefoged for the recurrent phonological patterns in one after another language. We also were influenced by the interplay between synchrony and diachrony in Natural Generative Phonology (Hooper 1973, 1976), including rule inversion (Vennemann 1972, Schuh 1972b). Lurking behind all of this was Joseph Greenberg's state-process approach to language typology and universals (J. Greenberg 1966b). In our survey of West African tone rules we attempted to take these ideas one step further, asserting that there was a difference between what was "diachronically natural" vs. "synchronically natural." Our assumption was that any diachronic tonal process (sound change) could also be a synchronic rule, but that the reverse was not the case: There are certain tone rules that could only be the result of restructuring, typically by the telescoping of multiple diachronic processes. While we were aware of the existence of unnatural or "crazy rules" (Bach and Harms 1972), our proposal was that certain recurrent restructured states could be considered SYNCHRONICALLY natural targets.

As many before us (and since), we thus assumed that "sound changes are basically phonetic in nature" (Hyman and Schuh 1974: 94), also that "…any context-sensitive sound change is…a possible synchronic phonological rule" (Hyman and Schuh 1974: 83–84). Our goal was to establish "an inventory of 'natural' rules of tone" (Hyman and Schuh 1974: 83), starting with what we considered natural phonetic tonal processes. I sketch three of these below, with brief updates of some of the advances that have been made since H & S.

---

[2]"Universals of tone rules: thirty years later" (Hyman 2007) is even more Bantucentric.

4.2.1 Tone spreading ("horizontal assimilation")

I suspect that other tonologists would agree that the most common phonetically motivated tone process is spreading from one tone-bearing unit (TBU) to the next, as in Gwari [Nupoid; Nigeria]: /súkNù/ → *súkû* 'bone', /òkpá/ → *òkpǎ* 'length'.[3] Since our work preceded the development of autosegmental tonology (Goldsmith 1976), we expressed our rules with a feature-copying format as in (1a).

(1) H tone spreading   L tone spreading
 a. /H-L/ → H-HL   /L-H/ → L-LH
 b.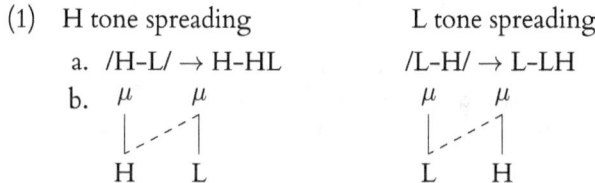

However, it is quite clear that our conception was more like (1b), where μ = TBU:

> "Spreading is an assimilatory process of the progressive or perseverative type, rather than of the regressive or anticipatory type. That is, the earlier tone appears to last too long, rather than the later tone starting too early. This in fact is the way that we would like to view this phenomenon. There is no process of tone copying or tone addition in the second syllable. Rather, the earlier tone simply enlarges its domain. What is of fundamental importance is that when the tone and the segmentals are out of phase, the tones invariably expand to the right and encompass parts of new syllables" (Hyman and Schuh 1974: 88; cf. Schuh 1978: 230).

Although we did not have an appropriate formalism, the intuition was exactly what the autosegmental framework expressed so well by dashed association lines and multiple linking. However, the bias we pointed out that tones tend to "drag on" has been confirmed in numerous subsequent phonetic studies, e.g.

> "…the F0 target for a single static tone tends to occur at the (temporal) end of the associated phonetic region…" (Akinlabi and Liberman 2000: 5)

---

[3] Tones are transcribed as follows: [á] H(igh), [ā] M(id), [à] L(ow), [â] HL falling, [ǎ] LH rising, [↓á] downstepped H.

> "Late realization of tonal targets has been demonstrated both for languages in which tones are lexical…and for those in which they are intonational…" (Kingston 2003: 86)

Such cases of tone spreading represent a natural phonologization process which occurs first where the sequenced tones are the furthest apart, e.g. creating HL and LH contours from H-L and L-H sequences, as in (1), without necessarily affecting sequences with M.[4] What is quite rare is for the reverse, anticipatory contouring to occur whereby /H-L/ and /L-H/ become HL-L and LH-H, respectively.

In H & S we were careful to state that only perseverative tone spreading can occur in "non-restrictive" tone systems which place few if any restrictions on the distribution of its /H/ and /L/ tones. Given our West African bias, we had less understanding of privative /H, Ø/ systems and of the anticipatory attraction of a tone to a prominent position. Our claim concerned the phonetic pressures on what tones (pitches) would do if left to their own devices:

> "While the exact phonetic explanation is not clear to us at this time, it appears to be the case that when there is a nonsynchrony of the tones and the segments to which the tones are assigned, the tones last too long (spreading into following syllables) rather than begin too early. Phonetically, the laryngeal adjustments required to regulate pitch changes seem to require more time than the articulatory adjustments required to produce successive segments" (Hyman and Schuh 1974: 90, note 3).

However, with the advent of autosegmental tonology, it also became possible to analyze the downstep in a derivation of /H-L-H/ to H-$^{\downarrow}$H-H as anticipatory spreading of the second H with concomitant delinking of the intervening L. See Hyman (1978, 2007) and §4.3.3 below for further discussion.

4.2.2 Register adjustments ("vertical assimilation")

In contrast with TS, which involves a "horizontal" adjustment between tone and TBU, tones may undergo a "vertical" lowering or raising in certain contexts. As schematized in (2a), natural changes include raising of a L before H or a lowering of a H after L:

---

[4]While H & S document that a language can have H tone spreading or L tone spreading without having the other, H tone spreading has since been found to be more prevalent and to occur with fewer restrictions (Hyman 2007: 7; Schuh 2018: 242).

4.2. Diachronic naturalness

(2) Vertical assimilation

    a. Natural
        L-H → M-H
        L-H → L-M

    b. Less natural
        H-L → H-M
        H-L → M-L

Thus, /nì-búː/ 'breast' is realized [nī-búː] in Mbui [Grassfields Bantu; Cameroon] (Hyman and Schuh 1974: 86), and /cèkí/ 'woman' becomes [cēkí] (→ [cēk] before pause) in Ik [Eastern Sudanic; Uganda] (Heine 1993: 17). As indicated in (2b), a H-L sequence is less likely to undergo raising of L or lowering of H. While a L to H interval is likely to undergo *compression*, as in (2a), H & S had not yet noted that a H to L interval is likely to undergo *expansion*. Thus, in Engenni [Edoid; Nigeria], a H is realized as a raised H before a L: /únwónì/ 'mouth' → [únwőnì] (Thomas 1974: 12). Such an effect has been documented phonetically in a number of languages, e.g. in Thai: "The high was significantly greater in height when followed by either the rising or low tone..." (Gandour and Potisuk 1994: 483). The double effect of lowering of H after L and raising of H before L undoubtedly feeds into the phenomenon of downdrift, the gradual lowering of an alternating sequence of Hs and Ls, the first process H & S listed as diachronically natural (Hyman and Schuh 1974: 84-85).

4.2.3 Contour simplification

H & S considered two kinds of processes converting tonal contours to level tones. First, by absorption, the endpoint of a contour is lost when followed by a tone beginning at the same level, as in (3a).

(3)   a. Natural
        LH-H → L-H
        HL-L → H-L

    b. Less natural
        L-LH → L-H
        H-HL → H-L

Thus, in Falam [Kuki-Chin; Myanmar, Bangla Desh], LH rising tones become L before both H and HL tones: /tlǎːŋ/ 'mountain' vs. *tlàːŋ lám* 'mountain road' and *tlàːŋ thlúak* 'mountain brains' (personal notes). The rising tone does not change when followed by L: *thlǎːŋ sàrìʔ* 'seven mountains.' H & S viewed absorption as a subtype of perseverative TS: if the endpoint of the contour were to spread, it would be absorbed into the following like tone. Reverse absorption, as in (3b), is less prevalent, although potentially found as a subcase of anticipatory TS (cf. note 5). P. Newman (1995: 766-767) reports optional H-HL → H-L affecting monosyllabic words in Maradi dialect of Hausa [Chadic; Niger]: *nân* 'here', *kù tsáyàa nân* 'stop here!' vs. *kù zóo nàn* 'come here!'

Other cases of contour levelling were simply identified as "contour simplification", as when Gwari ML becomes M before M or H tone. Thus, /ōzà/ 'person' first undergoes M tone spreading to *ōzû* (realized as such before L or pause), then simplifies to M-M before a non-L tone: *ōzā bmyá lō* 'the person is good.' While aware of the potential role of duration (contour tones take longer to produce than level tones) and the greater complexity of rising > falling > level tones (cf. Gordon 2001, Zhang 2001), we failed to emphasize that languages can vary in restricting contours by what precedes or follows them. Thus compare the following restrictions on LH rising tone in three closely related Kuki-Chin languages in (4).

(4)

	Hakha Lai	Falam	Kuki-Thaadow
LH-L	*	✓	*
LH-H	✓	*	*

As seen, Hakha Lai disallows LH before L, but allows it before H, while Falam does just the reverse, allowing LH before L but not before H. We can explain this difference by recognizing a conflict between articulatory vs. perceptual complexity: The LH contour in LH-L is perceptually distinct, but articulatorily complex as it involves two changes in pitch. The LH in in LH-H is less complex articulatorily with only one change in pitch, but perceptually complex, as the H part of the rise is easily masked by the following H, hence potentially subject to absorption (cf. Schuh 1978: 232-233). While Hakha Lai and Falam choose to prohibit according to articulatory vs. perceptual complexity, respectively, Kuki-Thaadow avoids both complexities in disallowing LH (and also HL) before both L and H. The effect is to limit contours to final position, a general property first noted by Clark (1983).

In addition to the above, languages may require that a contour be approached from the same pitch level (L-LH, H-HL) or by a jump up or down (L-HL, H-LH) (Hyman 2007: 12-18). A particularly striking case comes from Luba [Bantu; Democratic Republic of Congo], which is sensitive to both the preceding and following tone (Meeussen 1951, Coupez 1954: 29-33): (i) If a contour is followed by a like tone, e.g. LH-H, progressive absorption will apply: /bàdì-él-á/ → *bà-dy-èl-á* 'ils se jetaient'. (ii) If a contour is not followed, but is preceded by a like tone, e.g. L-LH, regressive absorption will apply: /bà-tù-énz-èl-è/ → *bà-tw-énz-èl-è* 'qu'ils fassent pour nous'. (iii) If a contour is neither followed nor preceded by a like tone, the full contour will be realized: /mú-tù-ám-ìl-é/ → mú-tw-ămb-ìl-é 'nous ayant dit'. This produces the following distributions (where those in parentheses are predicted, but not illustrated in Coupez's examples):

(5)
#	LH	L	→	LH-L	#	HL	L	→	H-L
#	LH	H	→	L-H	#	HL	H	→	HL-H
#	LH	#	→	—	#	HL	#	→	—
L	LH	L	→	L-H-L	L	HL	L	→	(L-H-L)
L	LH	H	→	L-L-H	L	HL	H	→	L-HL-H
L	LH	#	→	L-H	L	HL	#	→	L-H
H	LH	L	→	H-LH-L	H	HL	L	→	(H-L-L)
H	LH	H	→	H-L-H	H	HL	H	→	(H-L-H)
H	LH	#	→	H-L	H	HL	#	→	H-L

(Contour tones are also not allowed in final position.) There thus has been a lot to add to contour simplification since H & S. One final note concerns our statement: "It is not clear to us how L-F[alling] can in turn be simplified" (Hyman and Schuh 1974: 92). We now know that L-HL can simplify as L-M, L-L or L-↓L (downstepped L), among other possibilities. In Babanki [Grassfields Bantu; Cameroon] a H tone prefix + L tone stem undergoes the following derivation: /H-L/ → H-HL (by HTS) → L-HL (by prefixing lowering) → L-M (before H), L-L (before L or pause) (Hyman 1979: 167).

With these natural phonetic processes established, I now turn to consider synchronic tone rules which may not derive from a single diachronic process.

4.3 Synchronic naturalness

WHILE MOST OF WHAT WE PROPOSED concerning diachronically natural tone rules has been corroborated by subsequent work, our conclusions concerning synchronically natural tone rules beg for a reassessment. What Russ and I tried to say in H & S was that there are synchronic states that are as natural as the interacting diachronic processes that give rise to them. In the following subsections I discuss tone shifting, tonal dissimilation and polarity, and tonal downstep. In all three subsections we will see how H& S failed to consider the possibility of a /H, Ø/ privative contrast and tonal underspecification in general.

4.3.1 Tone shifting

In §4.2.1 we considered the case where a tone spreads and produces a HL or LH contour tone on the next syllable. In languages with a /H, Ø/ contrast, if the H similarly spreads in a local fashion, a H-H sequence will be produced, as in Kikerewe [Bantu; Tanzania]: /ku-bóh-el-an-a/ → *ku-bóh-él-an-a* 'to tie for each other' (Odden 1998: 177). If the H subsequently delinks from its TBU, the result is tone shifting, as in closely related Jita /ku-βón-er-an-a/ → *ku-βon-ér-an-a* 'to get for each other' (Downing 1990b: 265). Just as in the case of TS, shifting tends to be perseverative. However, anticipatory shifting also occurs, as in Totela [Bantu; Zambia] /o-ku-hóh-a/ → *o-kú-hoh-a* 'to grow' (Crane 2014: 65). Since shifting involves two sound changes (spreading and delinking), we did not consider it to be a natural diachronic process.[5] This is further supported by the fact that long-distance tone shifting occurs as a result of unbounded spreading to a designated position followed by delinking all of the Hs except the last. Thus, while Ndebele [Nguni Bantu; Zimbabwe] spreads an initial H all the way to the antepenult (Sibanda 2004: 229), closely related Zulu [South Africa] shifts the H to the antepenult (Downing 1990a: 265):

(6) a. /ú-ku-lim-is-el-a/ → ú-kú-lím-ís-e:l-a[6]
'to cause to cultivate for (s.o.)'

b. /ú-ku-hlek-is-an-a/ → u-ku-hlek-ír-a:n-a
'to amuse each other'

While it is rather common for a synchronically underlying privative H to shift to a prominent (e.g. accented) position, whether adjacent or not (cf. Hyman 1978: 263-264, Goldsmith 1987: 99), it is clear that non-local "displacement" cannot be accomplished in one diachronic step. This is particularly true in cases where the H shifts more than one word to the right, as in Giryama [Bantu; Kenya]: /á-na-mal-a ku-gul-a ŋguwo/ → *a-na-mal-a ku-gul-a ŋguúwo* 's/he wants to buy clothes' (cf. all L tone *ni-na-mal-a ku-gul-a ŋguuwo* 'I want to buy clothes,' both forms occurring with phrase-penultimate

---

[5] While *ku-βón-ér-an-a* undoubtedly represents the correct intermediate tone spreading stage leading to Jita perseverative shifting, Totela may have developed either from anticipatory tone spreading, i.e. from *o-kú-hóh-a*, or from the development and subsequent anticipation of a HL falling tone which then simplifies to L: **o-ku-hôh-a > o-ku-hóh-a > o-kú-hôh-a > o-kú-hoh-a*. Such a development has been documented in phrase-final position in the Kirundi/Kinyarwanda complex (Philippson 1991: 186) and led to the inversion of *H to a L-marked /L, Ø/ system in Ruwund (Nash 1994).

[6] A later process inserts a stem-initial L which in (6a) creates a downstep in the final output: *úkú-↓lím-ís-e:l-a* (Sibanda 2004: 229-230). See Hyman (2014) for further discussion.

4.3. Synchronic naturalness

lengthening). The reverse situation of a H shifting long-distance to a preceding prominent position is much rarer, if occurring at all. Whether shifting turns out to be local or at a distance, it is natural to avoid multiple H tones in sequence.

4.3.2 Tonal dissimilation and polarity

As in all of phonology, tonal assimilations vastly outnumber dissimilations, although the latter do occur. When these involve contours, e.g as when LH-LH becomes H-LH in Tianjin Mandarin (Chen 2000: 105) or LH-HL in Hakha Lai (Hyman and VanBik 2004: 825), it is easy to see the motivation of economizing the number of ups and downs. On the other hand, pitch changes increase when L-L changes to L-H in Munduruku [Tupi; Brazil] (Picanço 2005: 312) or H-H dissimilates to H-L or H-Ø in Bantu by Meeussen's Rule (Goldsmith 1984). Generally attributed to the Obligatory Contour Principle (Leben 1973, Goldsmith 1976), such cases of (particularly H-H) identity avoidance are rampant in the tonal literature—though underappreciated in H & S. It seems now that we can shift dissimilation into the diachronically natural category.

H & S were more convinced that tonal polarity is a synchronic epiphenomenon, distinguished from dissimilation:

> "...a synchronic state of polarized tone exists when a syllable is assigned no underlying tone, but rather takes the opposite tone of a neighboring syllable. Dissimilation differs in that a syllable is assigned an underlying tonal representation, but when it is in proximity with a syllable of identical tone, its tone changes" (Hyman and Schuh 1974: 100).

The distinction may not always be crystal clear, as authors may disagree about whether an alternating TBU has an underlying tone or not. H & S cite the opposite H vs. L tones of the Hausa particle *nee* in *yáaròo née* 'it's a boy' vs. *jàakíi nèe* 'it's a donkey.' If *nee* is underlyingly toneless, then its output tone is assigned by opposite polarity with the preceding tone. If, on the other hand, it is assumed to have an underlying /L/ tone as per Leben (1971), it instead undergoes a rule of tonal dissimilation. The synchronic situation is complex (P. Newman and Jaggar 1989) as is its history (Schuh 1989: 261). In fact, H & S assumed that all cases of polarity represent a restructuring, hence complex history. We proposed the following possible source for a polar prefix tone (Hyman and Schuh 1974: 99):

(7) a. *LH-H > L-H
    b. *LH-L > H-L

An original LH rising tone undergoes absorption before H, but "leveling" to H before L. (A different speculative account is given for Igbo *à-gá* 'going' vs. *á-zà* 'sweeping' in Hyman and Schuh 1974: 100). It is however also possible that polarity develops directly from dissimilation. In Eastern Kayah Li [Karen; Myanmar], prefixes contrast in tone when the root carries /M/ tone: *ʔì-lū* 'the Kayah New Year festival' vs. *ʔí-vī* 'to whistle.' However, they take polar tone when followed by a /H/ or /L/ root: *ʔì-khré* 'to winnow' vs. *ʔí-lò* 'to plant (seeds)' (Solnit 2003: 625). This seems to suggest that prefixes once contrasted *H and *L tones, but *H-H and *L-L dissimilated to L-H and H-L, respectively. Since polarity seems always to affect affixes or clitics, which by definition cannot stand alone, dissimilation can produce a situation where the choice of a single underlying tone becomes arbitrary (cf. Pulleyblank 1986: 204-205). One can imagine a situation, apparently unattested, where /H/ and /L/ roots are free morphemes that can occur unaffixed, but change to L and H, respectively when an affix carries the opposite tone. In this case two dissimilatory processes conspire to produce the output polar effect. Although tonal polarity tends to be restricted to specific morphemes, it is so common that it can be viewed as synchronically natural (cf. P. Newman 1995: 775-776). It is however not clear that it results from a single diachronic process acting on the absence of tone.[7] For more on tonal polarity see Cahill (2006) and references cited therein.

4.3.3 Tonal downstep

Among other tonal phenomena that were said not to be diachronically natural is phonemic downstep, the phenomenon by which a contrastive drop resets the register of the following tones. In the early 1970s it was generally believed that downstep could be contrastive only between Hs, e.g. Igbo *ísí* 'head,' *í↓sí* 'to cook,' where a succession of downsteps could also be possible, e.g. *ú↓ló ↓átó* 'the third house' (Emenanjo 1987: 13). What was not known was that some languages contrast H vs. ↓H after L, as well as L vs. ↓L, both in Bamileke-Dschang [Grassfields Bantu; Cameroon] (Hyman and Tadadjeu 1976). Both Bamileke-Dschang and Medumba (Bangangte) also have double

---

[7] With the subsequent development of extrametricality and underspecification theory, Pulleyblank (1986: 205-6) was able to account for the Margi present tense polar prefix in *á-wì yú* 'I run' vs. *à-sá yú* 'I err.' This however does not represent a natural historical source, rather another restructuring.

4.3. Synchronic naturalness

downstepped H, as in ʒú↓↓mɛn 'thing of child,' also realizable as ʒú↓ú ↓mɛn (Voorhoeve 1971: 50). A hallmark of downstep is that it is iterative, with no phonological restriction on the number of downsteps that are theoretically possible in an utterance. A number of examples have also been found for a M vs. ↓M contrast which however usually does not allow for iterative lowering. All downstep tones place a pitch ceiling on tones that follow: a H that follows a ↓H will be realized at the same level as the preceding H, not higher, and similarly for a M that follows ↓M and a L that follows ↓L.

Sticking to the case of H tone, the crucial belief of H & S was that ↓H, although widespread and hence synchronically natural, always resulted from a complex history, thus was not diachronically natural. Instead, downsteps were seen to result from an historically lost L tone wedged between Hs: "The majority of cases of DS [downstep] known to me are directly derivable from or are assumed, explicitly or implicitly, to be derived from the loss of a LO tone between two HIs…" (Schuh 1978: 239). Following Clements and Ford (1979) this came to be expressed autosegmentally as an unlinked L floating between linked Hs, as in the following Igbo derivation:

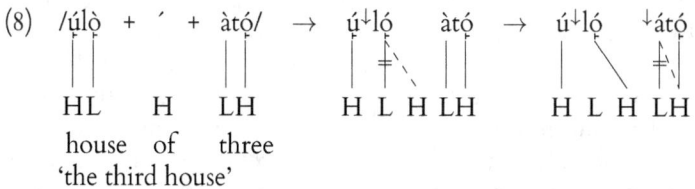

(8) /úlò + ´ + àtó/ → ú↓ló àtó → ú↓ló ↓átó

      HL H LH   H L H LH   H L H LH

      house of three
      'the third house'

As seen, there is a floating H "tonal morpheme" between the two words used also in genitive constructions, which links to the noun 'house', delinking its L tone. Similarly, the H of àtọ́ 'three' spreads leftwards, delinking its initial L. As a result, the output contains two downstepped H tones, each produced at a lower pitch than the preceding (↓)H. The result is summarized in (9a).

(9) a. H-L # H → H-↓H # H (Igbo)
    b. H # L-H → H # H-↓H (Ngizim)

This autosegmental interpretation of Igbo of course requires anticipatory spreading. Other languages such as Ngizim spread the first H perservatively, as in (9b).[8]

---

[8] Ngizim actually will not spread the H across a voiced obstruent ("depressor consonant"). Thus only the second H-L-H sequence is affected in the derivation /ná bàkó tlùwái/ → ná bàkó tlú↓wái 'I roasted the meat' (Hyman and Schuh 1974: 107).

Since we had insisted that an intervening L was required to derive a downstep, and since I had not yet gotten into Bantu (and hence did not fully appreciate /H, Ø/ privative systems), we were not prepared for Odden (1982: 179)'s demonstration that a H could automatically downstep after another H, as in Shambala [Bantu; Tanzania], where /ngótó/ → ngó⁺tó 'sheep' contrasts with H-H nyóká 'snake', derived from /nyóka/ by HTS. As Odden argues, Shambala has a /H, Ø/ system, where only /H/ is phonologically activated. Unless ⁺H always first develops from a historical lost L, certainly the majority case, we are faced with the possibility that *H-H > H-⁺H represents a natural diachronic sound change.[9] It would then fall into the category of dissimilation. In fact, there is reason to believe that Meeussen's Rule represents a telescoping of two separate changes, the first creating a downstep, the second changing the downstep to L: *H-H > H-⁺H > H-L.[10]

Before leaving this section we should, however, take note that languages may have downstep rules that are not synchronically motivated at all. Igbo is often cited as one such case, where the H tonal morpheme causes an unmotivated downstep, e.g. /ísí + ´+ éwú/ 'head of goat' → ísí é⁺wú (see Williamson 1986 and references cited therein). Of course an abstract L can be posited to account for the downstep, which has been known to be further "displaced" in other languages, e.g. Kanakuru [Chadic; Nigeria] (P. Newman 1974, cited in Schuh 1978: 233-234) and Kikuyu [Bantu; Kenya] (Clements and Ford 1979: 203-204), but these require at least a two-step diachronic derivation. Similarly, in Kalabari [Ijoid; Nigeria] one can propose a general synchronic rule of L tone insertion after a word-final L-H sequence to condition a downstep on a following H (Harry and Hyman 2014: 663-664) vs. the reverse in Aghem where a floating L is deleted after a word-final prefix+root L-H sequence so as to prevent the downstep that occurs after the same root when it has a H prefix (Hyman 1986: 212). As in the Igbo case, such specific synchronic rules are not possible sound changes, rather require a more complex diachronic scenario.

---

[9] We would in this case also have to entertain the unlikely possibility of parallel sound changes affecting other tones: *M-M > M-⁺M, usually the result of a lost L, and *L-L > L-⁺L, usually the result of a simplified contour tone, e.g. *L-HL-L > L-⁺L-L in Bamileke-Dschang (Hyman and Tadadjeu 1976: 91-92).

[10] I first presented this possibility to A.E. Meeussen himself at the workshop on l'Expansion Bantoue, April 4-16, 1977 in Viviers, France, and he approved. I mentioned this idea in Hyman (1978: 268) where, rather than appreciating the privative nature of such /H, Ø/ systems, I still considered that the H triggers were really *HL, such that *HL-H > H-⁺H > H-L.

4.4 Summary and conclusion

I BEGAN WITH THE CONVICTION that Russ Schuh and I had concerning the usefulness of distinguishing diachronic processes from the synchronic rules that result from a succession of diachronic changes. In §4.2 I presented a subset of the phonetically natural sound changes that tones often undergo, distinguishing between tone spreading, register adjustments, and contour simplifications. In §4.3 I considered recurrent synchronic phenomena which typically (always?) have a complex diachronic source: tone shifting, tonal polarity, and tonal downstep. I pointed out that some of our claims were colored by the fact that we did not fully appreciate the consequences of privative /H, Ø/ tone systems.[11] We also did not have the benefit of expressing our insights in autosegmental notation. Still, most of our claims concerning processes that can be both diachronic and synchronic seem to hold up, if only as universal tendencies: tones tend to spread perseveratively, L-H sequence intervals tend to compress (and H-L sequence intervals tend to expand), contour tones tend to be leveled out. I take these conclusions to be non-controversial.[12]

Our second position, which was that diachronic processes conspire to produce synchronically "natural" states, may seem less straightforward. Whereas our diachronic naturalness was grounded in phonetics, different principles must be involved in motivating the output synchronic states, converting tone spreading into tone shifting, tonal dissimilation into tonal polarity, and H sequences into downsteps (with or without intervening input Ls). Concerning the first it seems that as spreading takes place, the next stage is to prohibit multilinked Hs. There clearly is no advantage to an input /H/ being shifted many syllables (potentially words) to its right, which also potentially obscures the original source of the H (recall Zulu in (6b)).[13] Polarity, on the other hand, appears easier to motivate, as it is intuitively rather simple and "surely must have natural advantages in terms of production, perception, memory, and/or other psychological factors" (P. Newman 1995: 776). This leaves downstep, which can be motivated by contour simplification (HL-H, H-LH → H-$^\downarrow$H), tone spreading (H-L-H → H-H-$^\downarrow$H), or tone anticipation (H-L-H → H-$^\downarrow$H-

---

[11]I did not address the fact that there also are /L, Ø/ systems.

[12]Another generalization not addressed in above sections is that the laryngeal properties of consonants tend to affect tone, while tone much more rarely affects the laryngeal properties of consonants. While we proposed a hierarchy expressing the tendency of different consonant types to raise vs. lower tone (Hyman and Schuh 1974: 110), there has been a lot more refinement of these effects in more recent work. See, for instance, Tang (2008)'s dissertation co-directed by Russell Schuh and references cited therein.

[13]This clearly is extremely non-canonical in the sense of Corbett (2007) since an exponent of a morpheme should ideally (canonically) convene on the same morph.

H). While these all can be seen as minimizing ups and downs, the possibility of producing downstep from dissimilation (H-H → H-↓H) would require a different principle. Downstep clearly did not exist in Proto-Bantu but is so prevalent in the 500 or so daughter languages that it is hard not to see that the syntagmatic phenomenon is synchronically natural—as good or better a state than not having it at all. In short, tone shifting, tonal polarity and downstep are all good synchronic targets.

The above brief review of H & S is necessarily incomplete, as are the citations of work contemporaneous and subsequent to our efforts 45 years ago. I want to end with two final citations. The first quite surprised me as I reread it:

> "Given the alternatives of analyzing a given synchronic alternation as conditioned by some abstract phonological unit or by a grammatical category, speakers will always choose the latter course" (Hyman and Schuh 1974: 94).

I have not discussed morphological or syntactic tone, replacive tone or prosodic domains in this paper. This will have to wait for another occasion. For now I simply point out that Russ and I had the above intuition and were thus adverse to overly abstract remedies to handle synchronically odd ("crazy") tonal alternations. Which brings me to the last quote, from Russ himself:

> "…I'm busy as hell trying to tie up everything I've learned about Ngizim in the last 10 months. The tone system is very complex - I didn't know people could do such screwy things with only two tones — and it's only in the last month that I have gotten it squared away. Wallahi! Looking at these other Chadic languages really makes Hausa look different. Would you believe that Hausa does not mark aspect differences by different pronoun sets? Paul and I intend to write an article presenting evidence for this next year [the article eventually appearing as P. Newman and Schuh (1974)] …As ever, Russ."

The above appears in a letter dated August 5, 1970, mailed from Potiskum and addressed to me in Minna when we were both graduate students conducting research in Northern Nigeria. I wrote back that I was having an equally exciting (if not screwy) time with tone in Gwari, where at least we had a third, M tone (and in fact a downstepped ↓M). I only found this letter from Russ a few days ago, i.e. exactly 47 years after he wrote it. I wish I could have shared it with him. We would have had a good laugh.

4.4. Summary and conclusion

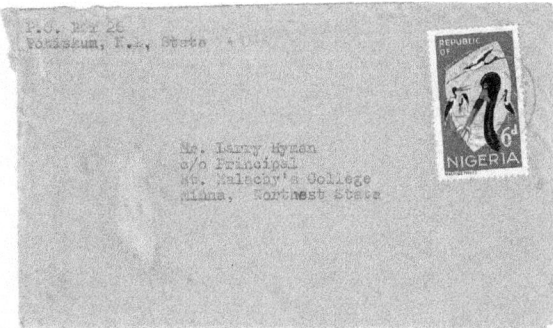

Figure 4.1: Envelope of a letter from Russell Schuh to the author in 1970

Acknowledgments

My thanks to Roxana Newman and Will Leben for their help with Hausa and to Will for other helpful input on this paper, including editorial suggestions and corrections.

5

A first look at Krachi clausal determiners

Jason Kandybowicz
The Graduate Center, CUNY

Harold Torrence
University of California, Los Angeles

5.1 Introduction

IN HIS DOCTORAL DISSERTATION, Schuh (1972a) observed that certain kinds of clauses in Ngizim, a West Chadic language of the Bade group, can occur with determiners. For example, the bracketed temporal clause in (1a) has the definite determiner *tənu* on the right edge:

(1)   a.   [Jà yka aci **tənu**], jà ndem aci   (*when* Clause)
           'When we saw him, we greeted him.'
                                     (Adapted from Schuh 1972a: 333, ex. 32)

5.1. Introduction

b. [Daa káa bii-naa gəši-k bədlamu **nən**]... (Conditional)
'If you were to get some hyena heart...'
(Adapted from Schuh 1972a: 346, ex. 74)

c. [Akuu kwá ji-n-aakun **nən**]... (*after* Clause)
'After you leave...'
(Adapted from Schuh 1972a: 356, ex. 118)

In contrast, the conditional and *after* clauses in (1)b-c have *nən* on the right edge. Schuh suggests, "...that *nən* is an indefinite determiner, which may appear at the end of adverbs by virtue of their being noun phrases" (Schuh, 1972a: 332).[1] The occurrence of a determiner-like element with a CP, a clausal determiner (CD), is not limited to Ngizim however.

In later work, Schuh shows that in Miya, a West Chadic language of the North Bauchi group, there are also clauses that occur with determiner-like elements:

(2) a. Dà fárkoo jıfana kwáa náya wún gyàɓiya **ká**...
at.first man when see girl young PRM
'To begin, when a man sees a woman...'
(Adapted from Schuh 1998: 377)

b. ...tə tán s-áa àalow-za **ká**
he if TOT-ipf love-her PRM
'...if he loves her...' (Schuh, 1998: 377)

c. Fàa kwáa zàra-tlən **ká**...
you.(m.s) when/if call-them PRM
'If you call them...' (Schuh, 1998: 372)

As the examples in (2) attest, certain temporal and conditional clauses can have the "Previous Reference Marker" (PRM) on the right periphery. Concerning (2c), Schuh remarks that, "*Kwáa* clauses always terminate with *ká*, the morpheme used in noun phrases to indicate previous reference" (Schuh, 1998: 372).

In this paper, we build on Schuh's observations in Chadic by turning to Niger-Congo and presenting a preliminary description of clausal determiners in Krachi (also spelled "Kaakye," "Kaakyi," "Kaci," "Krache," and "Krakye"), an under-documented and endangered Volta-Comoe language (J. Greenberg, 1963; Westermann & Bryan, 1952) of the North Guang branch of the

---

[1] See Schuh (1972a) for detailed discussion of the conditioning of the definite versus indefinite markers in these clauses.

Tano group of Kwa languages. Section 5.2 presents a brief introduction to the language. A description of determiners and clausal determiners in the language follows in Section 5.3. Section 5.4 briefly discusses and compares clausal determiners in the related Kwa language Gã with Krachi. Section 5.5 concludes.

5.2 Background on Krachi

KRACHI IS SPOKEN IN THE KRACHI WEST AND KRACHI EAST districts of the Volta region in central eastern Ghana. The Krachi speaking area centers around the commercial center Kete Krachi, situated on Lake Volta. Krachi is a member of the Guang subgroup of the Kwa languages. Within Guang, Snider (1998) places Krachi in the River group of the North Guang languages. Adonae (2005), however, classifies Krachi as a Central Guang language. According to Adonae, there are four dialects of Krachi: Central (spoken in Kete Krachi), West (spoken in the Kajaji, Nkomi and Odefour communities of the Sene district in the Brong Ahafo region), East (spoken in non-exclusively Krachi-speaking communities such as Dambai, Ayiremo, Kparekpare, and Tokoroano along the Oti River east of Kete Krachi), and North (spoken in the northern Volta region by a number of smaller communities along the main Krachi-Tamale road that borders the Nchumburung communities). These four Krachi varieties are mutually intelligible, but dialectal differences are easily noticed by linguistically untrained native speakers. The data from this paper are drawn exclusively from the Central Krachi dialect.[2]

Syntactically, Krachi has basic SVO word order:

(3) ɔ-kyɪ   wʊ ɛ-mɔ   bwatɛ wʊ
    CL-woman the PST-kill chicken the

  'The woman slaughtered the chicken.'

Like other Guang (especially North Guang) languages, Krachi has both noun classes[3] and a concordial agreement system. There is some disagreement as

---

[2]The Krachi data in this article are presented in the official Krachi orthography developed by the Ghana Institute for Linguistics, Literacy & Bible Translation (Dundaa, 2007). Because the orthography does not mark Krachi's two surface level tones (High and Low; cf. Adonae 2005; Snider 1990), we have omitted tone marking from our representations. The following abbreviations are used in the glosses of Krachi examples in this paper: CD – clausal determiner; CL – class marker; COMP – complementizer; FOC – focus; FUT – future; NEG – negative; POSS – possessive; PST – past; SG – singular; SPEC – specificity marker.

[3]Krachi's noun class system differentiates it from other Tano language, like Akan, which has only the remnants of a noun class system (Osam, 1994).

to the overall number of noun classes in the language. Dundaa (n.d.), for example, claims the existence of eight distinct classes, while Korboe (2002) analyzes Krachi as having eleven (see Korboe 2002 and Snider 1988 for details on the language's noun class system). As illustrated below, the noun class of a particular noun can be determined by the class prefix on the noun, which may be phonetically null in certain cases.

(4) a. ɔ-kyɪ 'woman'
    b. a-kyɪ 'women'
    c. kɪ-kpʊreki 'vulture'
    d. a-kpʊreki 'vultures'
    e. ku-gyo 'yam'
    f. i-gyo 'yams'
    g. Ø-bwatɛ 'chicken'
    h. m-bwatɛ 'chickens'

5.3 Krachi determiners and clausal determiners

THE DEFINITE ARTICLE IN KRACHI (*wʊ*) occurs postnominally following adjectives and numerals and does not inflect for noun class (i.e., number + gender). As (5) shows, the article remains the same whether it occurs with a singular or plural noun:

(5) a. kɛ-gyɪfɛ bɪbɪw ɔkʊnkʊ wʊ
       CL-cloth black one   the
       'the one black cloth'   (Adapted from Korboe (2002), ex. 32b)
    b. Anyiŋkpɪsɛ kudu wʊ bɛ-ba
       people   ten the PST-come
       'The ten people came.'   (Adapted from Korboe (2002), ex. 11c)

However, the distribution of the definite article is not the same as in English. Even common nouns without the article can be interpreted as definite, although this seems to be a property more of subjects than objects:

(6) a. Gyoro gyi mʊ-lɛ
       dog   be 3SG-POSS
       'The dog is his/hers.'   (Adapted from Korboe (2002), ex. 37f)

b. A-kyɪ   asa   bɛ fũ
CL-woman three be married

'The three women are married.'

(Adapted from Korboe (2002), ex. 16a)

Depending on its phonetic environment, the definite determiner has a number of realizations ([o, ɔ, u, wo, wu, wɔ] and possibly others). At this stage of our research, it is unclear whether the definite determiner can be dropped or is just difficult to discern at times, given that it can be very challenging to distinguish it from a preceding final vowel.

One environment in which we find clausal determiners in Krachi is the relative clause. Clausal determiners obligatorily appear at the right edges of relative clauses, which are head-initial in Krachi:

(7) a. ɔ-kyɪ   wʊ [kɛ   ɔ-dɛ]   *(wʊ)
CL-woman the COMP 3SG-sleep CD

'the woman who slept'

b. ɔ-kyɪ   kʊ [kɛ   ɔ-kya]   *(wʊ)
CL-woman SPECIF COMP PST-dance CD

'a certain woman who danced'

c. kyuŋ   wʊ kɛ   fɛ-dwɛnɛ [fɛɛ   Kwaku ɛ-ta]
guinea.fowl the COMP 2SG-think COMP Kwaku PST-pick.up
*(wʊ)
CD

'the guinea fowl that you think that Kwaku picked up'

Templatically, Krachi relative clauses take the following form.

(8) [NP DET [CP kɛ [TP S V O] CD]

That is, the clausal determiner occurs phrase-finally in relative clauses. As (7b) shows, the position of the (non-clausal) determiner is immediately following the head noun, the position where the specific indefinite determiner ($k\upsilon$), which is non-homophonous with the CD, also occurs.

A clausal determiner optionally appears at the right edge of certain matrix *wh-* questions.

(9) a. Nɛ   yɪ   fɛ   wa? (Neutral *wh-* Question)
what FOC 2SG do

'What are you doing?'

5.3. Krachi determiners and clausal determiners

    b. Nɛ yɪ fɛ wa **wʊ**!? (Emphatic *wh-* Question)
       what FOC 2SG do CD

    'What (the hell) are you doing!?'

(10) a. Nɛ yɪ fɛ kɛrɛ? (Neutral *wh-* Question)
       what FOC 2SG read

    'What are you reading?'

    b. Nɛ yɪ fɛ kɛrɛ **wʊ**!? (Emphatic *wh-* Question)
       what FOC 2SG read CD

    'What (the hell) are you reading!?'

As the translations show, the use of the clausal determiner with a *wh-* question indicates speaker disapproval or that the speaker has a negative attitude towards what is happening (consultant remark: "The speaker is angry"). This use of the clausal determiner is also found in embedded questions, which have the form of relative clauses. This is illustrated below in (11).

(11) Mɪ n-nyi yo/atɔ kɛ fɛ kɛrɛ **wʊ**!
     1SG NEG-know thing COMP 2SG read CD

    'I don't know what (the hell) you're reading!'

Although the presence of the CD does seem to add an emphatic flavor to some *wh-* questions, we have also found cases where the presence or absence of the CD in *wh-* constructions does not make an interpretive difference.

(12) a. Nsɛ yɪ ɔ-kya (**wʊ**)?
       who FOC PST-dance CD

    'Who danced?'

    b. Mɪ e-bisɛ fɛɛ nsɛ yɪ ɔ-ta kɪtɛ (**wʊ**)
       1SG PST-ask COMP who FOC PST-pick.up feather CD

    'I asked who picked up a feather.'

An interesting co-occurrence restriction on clausal determiners is found in embedded *wh-* in-situ constructions. Krachi allows for *wh*-in-situ (and partial *wh-* movement) in embedded clauses (see Torrence and Kandybowicz 2015 for a detailed description of *wh-* questions in Krachi).

(13) Mɪ e-bisɛ fɛɛ Ama ɛ-tuŋ nɛ
     1SG PST-ask COMP Ama PST-cut what

    'I asked what Ama cut.'

However, it is not possible to use the clausal determiner if the *wh*-item appears in-situ. Compare (14) below, where the clausal determiner is blocked from co-occurring with an in-situ embedded *wh*-item, with (12b), where it may optionally appear in the embedded clause accompanying a focused *wh*-element.

(14) *Mɪ e-bisɛ   fɛɛ   Ama ɛ-tuŋ   nɛ   **wʊ**
      1SG PST-ask COMP Ama PST-cut what CD

(Intended: 'I asked what Ama cut.')

Non-*wh*- focused constituents can also co-occur with an optional clausal determiner.

(15) Kweku yɪ   ɔ-kya   (**wʊ**)
     Kweku FOC PST-dance CD

'It's KWEKU who danced.'

As with the focused *wh*-questions (e.g. (12)), it is unclear what the semantic contribution of the CD is in this case.

The clausal determiner also appears in a number of embedded clausal contexts in Krachi. CDs optionally appear with sentential subjects, which are canonically factive.

(16) a. [Kɛ   Kwadu ɛ-dɛ   Kofi **wʊ**] bo ŋwaŋwa
        COMP Kwadu PST-beat Kofi CD   be surprising

   'It is surprising that Kwadu beat Kofi.'

   b. [Kɛ   Ama ɛ-watɪ   kapare wʊ brɪŋ   **wʊ**] ɛ-ha   wɛ
      COMP Ama PST-pound fufu   the quickly CD   PST-disturb 2SG

   'The fact that Ama pounded the fufu quickly disturbed you.'

The clausal determiner also appears in factive complement clauses. In contrast with their occurrence in subject clauses, the CD is obligatory in this environment, as the following data show.

(17) a. Mɪ kyɪrɪ [kɛ   mɛ dɛ   *(**wʊ**)]
        1SG hate COMP 1SG sleep CD

   'I hate (the fact that) I slept.'

   b. Yɪ bwarɛ [fɛɛ   Yaw ɛ-ta   Kofi *(**wʊ**)]
      it good   COMP Yaw PST-pick.up Kofi CD

   'It is good that Yaw picked up Kofi.'

5.3. Krachi determiners and clausal determiners

Note that determiners do not form constituents with proper names in Krachi, as demonstrated below.

(18) * Yaw ɛ-ta Kofi wʊ
Yaw PST-pick.up Kofi the
(Intended: 'Yaw picked up Kofi.')

Thus, the right edge determiner in (17b) cannot be associated with the proper name *Kofi*. It must take scope over the entire subordinate clause. The clausal determiner occurs obligatorily on the right edge of a type factive/manner clause that involves relativization of a nominalized form of the verb.

(19) Yɪ n-tɪrɪ fʊ [ke-bi wʊ [kɛ Yaw ɛ-bi Kofi kai
it NEG-bother 2SG NOM-beat the COMP Yaw PST-beat Kofi harshly
*(**wʊ**)]]
CD

'The fact that Yaw beat Kofi harshly does not bother you.'
'The way that Yaw beat Kofi harshly does not bother you.'

At least in some cases, the clausal determiner occurs in temporal clauses, although the precise conditions that license its occurrence are presently unclear.

(20) Kɛ Gyaruusi e-ŋu Yesu **wʊ**...
COMP Jairus PST-see Jesus CD
'when Jairus saw Jesus...' (Mark 5:22, GILLBT 2011)

The clausal determiner occurs on the left edge of the protasis of a simple conditional clause, as shown below.

(21) a. [Sɛ ɔ-kyɪ wʊ mɛ-mɔ bwatɛ wʊ **wʊ**] Ama ke-yo
COMP CL-woman the ?-kill chicken the CD Ama FUT-go
'If the woman kills the chicken, Ama will leave.'

b. [Sɛ Kofi mɛ-kya **wʊ**] Ama ke-yo
COMP Kofi ?-dance CD Ama FUT-go
'If Kofi dances, Ama will leave.'

We have shown that a subset of Krachi clauses are somewhat nominal in that they occur with stereotypical nominal elements like clausal determiners. Krachi clauses with the clausal determiner seem to be full CPs capable of hosting focused phrases in their left peripheries. In (22) below, the verb has been predicate clefted inside of the clause with the CD.

(22) [Kɛ [kɛ-watɪ] ji Ama ɛ-watɪ kaparɛ wʊ brɪŋ **wʊ**]
COMP NOM-pound FOC Ama PST-pound fufu the quickly CD
ɛ-ha wɛ
PST-disturb 2SG

'That Ama POUNDED the fufu quickly disturbed you.'

There is also an exclamative construction which may involve a clausal determiner, but further work is required to firmly establish this, given its complex phonological/phonetic realization. This is shown below in (23).[4]

(23) a. Ntɛ Kofi dɪɛ kya **wʊ**
PST Kofi always dance CD

'Kofi used to dance!'

b. Kɛkyɪsɛ wʊ bɔda **ŋwʊʊ**
woman the beautiful CD?

'The lady is very beautiful!'

5.4 Brief comparison to Gã

BEYOND KRACHI, CLAUSAL DETERMINERS ARE REPORTED in a number of Kwa languages (Kropp Dakubu, 1992) and New World Atlantic creoles (Lefebvre, 2015). Korsah (2017) reports on clausal determiners in Gã, a closely related Kwa language, where the definite determiner is *lɛ* (24a). Like Krachi (see (7)), headed relative clauses in the language obligatorily involve a right edge clausal determiner (24b).[5]

(24) a. tsó lɛ́
tree DEF

'the tree' (Korsah 2017: 153, ex. 4a)

b. tsó (lɛ́) ní Taki kwɔ́ *(lɛ́)
tree DEF REL Taki climb CD

'the tree that Taki climbed' (Korsah 2017: 153, ex. 4b)

In Gã matrix focus clauses, there is an optional CD.

---

[4] The kind of exclamative sentence in (23b) is pronounced at an audibly higher pitch register than ordinary declarative sentences in the language.

[5] Korsah (2017) does not have examples of relative clauses with indefinite heads (e.g., *a tree that Taki climbed*).

5.4. Brief comparison to Gã

(25) Taki ni tsɛ́ Momo (lɛ́)
      Taki FOC call Momo CD
      'Taki called Momo (as expected).' (Korsah 2017: 155, ex. 9)

In this way as well, Gã patterns like Krachi. Recall that the CD is optional in Krachi when non-*wh*-constituents are focused (15). Gã is also like Krachi in allowing in-situ *wh*- and movement when a *wh*-item originates in an embedded clause. Like Krachi too, when the in-situ option is chosen, the clausal determiner is impossible.

(26) Osa bí [akɛ Taki tsɛ namɔ (*lɛ́)]
      Osa ask COMP Taki call who CD
      'Osa asked who Taki called.' (Korsah 2017: 156, ex. 11b)

Unlike Krachi, however, when a *wh*-item from an embedded clause is extracted, the clausal determiner is obligatory.

(27) Námɔ [ni Osa le [áké Taki he] *(lɛ́)]
      what FOC Osa know COMP Taki buy CD
      'What does Osa know that Taki bought?'

      (Korsah 2017: 156, ex. 14b)

Gã clausal determiners occur with CP subjects, just as in Krachi (16). And just like Krachi, the CD is obligatory in this environment.

(28) [Ákɛ́ ámlaló lɛ́ tsé tóó nɔ́ *(lɛ́)] feé maŋ-bíí lɛ́
      COMP government DEF tear tax TOP CD do country-people DEF
      míishɛɛ
      happiness
      'That the government reduced taxes made the people happy.' (Korsah (2017: 160), ex. 23)

The clausal determiner co-occurs optionally in Gã matrix focus clauses, which may lend a flavor of expectedness. This is illustrated below. This interpretational effect is not something we have observed in Krachi.

(29) Taki ni tsɛ́ Momo (lɛ́)
      Taki FOC call Momo CD
      'TAKI called Momo (as expected).' (Korsah 2017: 155, ex. 9)

Korsah (2017) also shows that like Krachi (21) clausal determiners occur in the antecedents of conditional clauses.

(30) Kɛ́(ı) o-bá *(lɛ), m-á-yá
    COND 2SG-come CD 1SG-FUT-go
    'If you come, I will go.' (Korsah 2017: 161, ex. 24b)

The data from Gã are useful because of their similarity to the Krachi pattern. This suggests that these systems may ultimately be amenable to a unified analysis, although the data raise a number of descriptive and analytical questions.

5.5 Conclusion

IN THIS FIRST DESCRIPTION of clausal determiners in Krachi, we have shown that they occur in a number of A′ contexts, such as relativization, focus, and conditional clauses. In addition, we have briefly compared Krachi to Gã and demonstrated that there seems to be quite a lot of overlap in the distribution of CDs in the two languages. At the same time, there are a number of outstanding issues with regard to the syntax and semantics of CDs both within Krachi and in comparison to other languages. As the present work on Krachi loops back to the original observations in Schuh (1972a), we once again find ourselves in the position of learning from our beloved former teacher and mentor.

Acknowledgments

Many thanks to our native speaker consultants who provided the data for this paper: Mark Nsekou Denteh, Matthew Donkor, and Joseph Agyei Korboe. We also thank Mark Dundaa and the Ghana Institute for Linguistics, Literacy & Bible Translation (GILLBT), and Mr. Daniels Ananey Adonae for their logistical, material, and scholarly support.

6

Tone and length in Mende

William R. Leben
Stanford University

6.1 What this chapter owes to Russ Schuh

SINCE OUR FIRST MEETING in a summer French lit class at Northwestern University in 1964, I looked up to Russ for his calm vibe, his intellectual and personal honesty, and his smarts. From 1965 to 1967, we worked in the same Peace Corps project in Niger, where I cast him more consciously as a role model: mature, scholarly, imaginative, and determined to make his work count. Afterward, we kept in touch as linguistics grad students at opposite ends of the country and then as Africanist linguists in California.

Russ could sound self-deprecating. He was modest about his own achievements and had a sense of irony that made him fun to be around. As a graduate student at UCLA, in one of the departments where generative linguistics began its ascent, he once wrote that he was developing into a neo-Bloomfieldian structuralist. It sounded shocking—as intended--but it was just Russ's way of saying he was less attuned to generative linguistics than to what he soon became known for: highly reliable description and analysis based on first-hand fieldwork without a lot of theoretical baggage.

So to honor Russ, in this article I return to Mende, a Southwestern Mande language of Sierra Leone and the first language I studied as a graduate student. Mende played an important role in the approach to tone outlined in Leben (1973, 1978), but this time around, I focus on interesting distributional facts evident on the surface, with more concern for tying together what the analysis says about the language than for delving into the wealth of potential consequences Mende may still have for phonological theory.

6.2 A simple, exceptionless constraint on tone

GOOD POST-BLOOMFIELDIAN PRACTICE begins with a search for surface regularities. In Mende we are instantly rewarded with a surface generalization that seemingly has eluded researchers until now: rising tones appear only on long vowels.

Mende syllables have the form (C)V(V).[1] Several accounts of Mende posit a LH rise on short vowels underlyingly, but only surface vowels with a rise are long, as sketched in (1).

(1) NO SHORT RISE

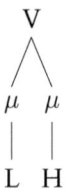

In fact, a rise is the most frequent tone found on Mende long vowels, though the glossary of about a thousand words in Spears 1967a also includes cases with H, L, HL, and LHL.[2] For the original rationale behind positing phonological LH on monomoraic syllables we turn to polarization.

---

[1] Along with short and long vowels, Spears (1967a, 1967b) also finds extra-long vowels, transcribed as V.V and often formed from two adjacent syllables by removing the intervocalic consonant, though in some cases lacking a variant with an intervening consonant, e.g. *já.á* 'touch.' Innes (1969) does not recognize V.V as a distinct category and generally transcribes these vowels as VV, and sometimes as simple V. Due to many discrepancies between these sources, I chosen to rely mainly on just one. With over 5,000 words, Innes (1969) is five times the size of Spears (1967a) but lacks the information about word structure and key tonal alternations found in Spears (1967a), a pedagogical text accompanied by a set of tapes. For this reason, Spears (1967a) is my main source of data.

[2] The surface distribution of HL is also easy to state but different from the distribution of LH. Surface HL appears on final syllables, long or short (*ngèwɔ́* 'God,' *nyàhâ* 'woman'). Word internal long syllables can also have surface HL (*póòmà* 'behind'), while on a short word-internal syllable,

6.3 Polarization

TONAL POLARITY is the taking of a tone opposite to an adjacent one, e.g. H before L and L before H. In Mende, two large classes of nouns and verbs end in a polarizing final mora, which surfaces as L before H but H before L or pause. These two Mende classes have the shapes CVV and CVCV, as shown in (a) and (b) in (2). Also, a handful of CV verbs and one noun are polarizing, and (c) in (2) includes what I believe to be a complete set from Spears (1967a).[3] High tone (H) is marked with ´ , Low tone (L) with `, and long vowels (VV) with a level tone have a tone mark on just the first V. NC sequences are single segments with the place of articulation indicated by C.

(2) Citation forms of polarizing verbs and nouns. (a) and (b) are drawn from large sets. (c) is offered as a complete list.
  a. bimoraic, 1 syllable
   pàá   'kill'   mbàá 'rice'
   hàá   'die'   hɛ̀ɛ́   'death'
   hòó   'hold'   kòó   'belly'
   sɔ̀ɔ́   'have, receive' mbɔ̀ɔ́ 'honey, dear'
  b. 2 syllables
   tàlá   'crawl'   iká   'cow'
   tɛ̀lí   'become black'   hàní   'thing'
   hìyɛ́   'get up'   kɛ̀kɛ́   'father'
   kpɔ̀wú 'shut, bury'   kòhú   'inside' (N)
  c. monomoraic, 1 syllable
   fá   'greet'   fá   'news'
   pá   'come'
   ndí   'go'
   mɛ́   'eat'

In one way or another, most analyses of Mende tone ascribe polarization to three very common factors among languages (Hyman, 2007; Hyman & Schuh, 1974).

---

phonological HL is always realized as H that triggers downstep on the following H (/taˆ tó/ = tá↓tó 'begin'). Word-final fall is common, even on a single mora. The distribution of Mende rises and falls accords well with Zhang's (2000; 2003) findings that rises are more restricted than falls and that contour tones are more likely to surface in final position than elsewhere.

[3] Two small points: The one noun in this category, *fá* 'news,' may be related to the verb *fá* 'greet.' Polar tone also applies to some pronouns like *ngi* '3sg.' and the verbal prefix *hú*-. For simplicity, I draw most examples from nouns and verbs.

(3) *Tone Absorption:* Tautosyllabic LH sequences simplify to L before H. Analogously, tautosyllabic HL sequences simplify to H before L.

```
X   X
|  =|
L   H
```

(4) *Low Tone Spreading*: The sequence L-H-H (where hyphen indicates separate syllables) becomes L-L-H.

```
X   X   X
|  ´=/
L   H
```

(5) *Contour simplification*: Before pause and before L, LH—if associated with a single TBU—is realized as H.

```
    μ
   /\
  L  H/ __ L, pause
     ↓
     Ø
```

Tone Spreading and Tone Absorption both shift the locus of a LH transition rightward. yet these changes are distinct, since in Mende Tone Absorption applies to contour tones LH and HL, while Tone Spreading applies only to L - H sequences.

With one noun from each group in (2), below are examples showing polarization at work. To the arrow's left in (6a,b,c,d,e,f) is the form after tones have been mapped by a version of the left-to-right mapping rules and Well-Formedness Condition (WFC) of Goldsmith (1976) (reformulated variously over the years in terms of rules or constraints, with differences that don't seem crucial here). The WFC requires each TBU to be linked to a tone and each tone to be linked to a TBU. To the right are the forms after Tone Absorption (6a,b,c,d) and Tone Spreading (6e,f), with dotted lines showing additions and = showing links cut. Tones left floating are removed by the Obligatory Contour Principle (OCP), proposed by Leben (1973) and named by Goldsmith

6.4. Polar tone: Distribution

(1976), which restricts melodies from having two adjacent identical tones. Exceptions to polarization in (6g,h) are discussed later.

(6)

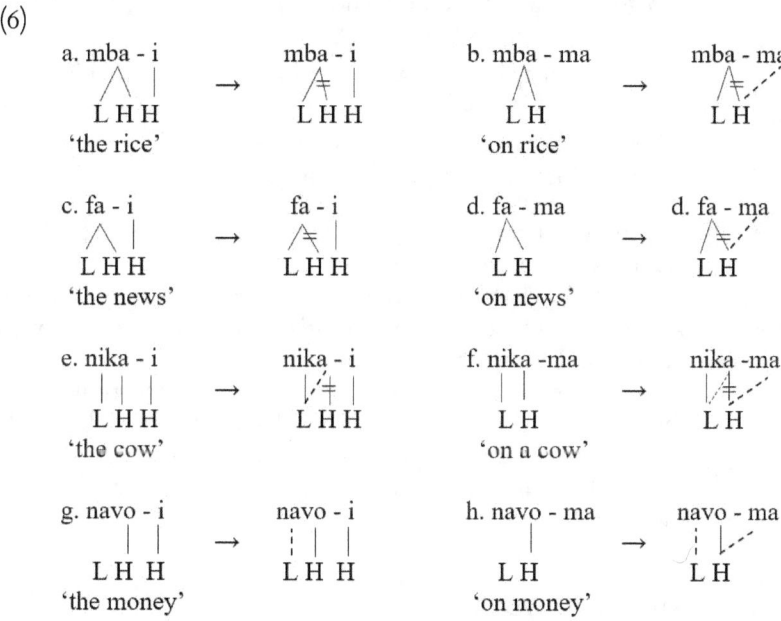

Finally, note that before pause and not sketched above, LH is realized as a surface rise on a long syllable but is simplified to H on a short syllable.

6.4 Polar tone: Distribution

IF WE EXAMINE where Mende's polar tone is and is not found, we find patterns that help us connect disparate facts about Mende tone into a unified, coherent account. Here are some key facts about the distribution of polar tone in Mende.

(7) a. Near-complementarity of polarization between words of one vs. two syllables.[4] Polarizing disyllabic words are all CVCV (where

---

[4] The near-complementarity between polarizing CVCV and CVV words makes one wonder whether at an earlier stage, polarizing Mende CVV words arose from polarizing CVCV ones. As reported by Spears (1967a, 1967b) and later sources, contemporary Mende often deletes intervocalic consonants under certain conditions, creating CVV sequences from CVCV ones.

V is short), while nearly all monosyllables with polar tone have a long vowel.[5]

b. Before polar tone, morphemes can only have L, not H (Spears 1967b, Dwyer 1978b).

c. If an earlier syllable has a rise, the final syllable cannot be polarizing.

d. Restriction to words of one and two syllables. The Spears (1967a) corpus does not give polar tone in longer words.

(7a) reflects a more general surface fact: all Mende morphemes ending in a long vowel are monosyllabic.

(7b,c) are related. The rise mentioned in (7c) is a sequence LH, and we predict that any preceding syllable in a polarizing form must be L if we rule out the melody HLH—a move that has been questioned and that gets a fresh look in the section below. (7b) rules out a form like hypothetical *bábǎ* with H before the polarizing syllable,[6] another gap that casts into doubt HLH as a licit melody. The next section shows that generalization in (7d) will follow from the melody hypothesis and from a simple analysis of exceptional non-polarizing words.

6.5 Tone melodies

TONE IN MENDE HAS A CURIOUS distribution—too many lexical tone patterns to qualify as "pitch accent" in the sense of McCawley (1978) yet too restricted for tone to be regarded as freely assigned to each tone-bearing unit (TBU) in underlying representations.

Mende's two phonological tones, H and L, are presented in Leben (1973, 1978) as forming five dominant tone melodies: H, L, HL, LH, and LHL. This is not to totally exclude Mende's other tone patterns, enumerated compellingly by Dwyer (1978b) as well as in Conteh et al. (1983), Leben (1978), Mugele and Rodewald (1991), Rodewald (1989), and Shih and Inkelas (2016). Clearly, all patterns—common, rare, and in between—need to be accounted

---

[5] This difference between words of one and two syllables—final LH vs. H before pause—plus the complementarity in the final vowels of LH words (as above, VV for monosyllables vs. V for disyllables) led Leben (1973, 1978) to wrongly assume that vowel length was not contrastive. But the distinctness of V from VV is clear from a reading of Dwyer (1978b) and Conteh, Cowper, James, Rice, and Szamosi (1983), as well as from the (c) forms in Table 2, which undergo Tone Absorption like the (a) forms yet have a short vowel like the (b) forms.

[6] One polarizing exception from Spears (1967a) and Innes (1969) is *púkpùá* 'uproot.'

6.5. Tone melodies

for. One could make this an easy task, since current rule-based and constraint-based theories are so powerful as to easily accommodate any number of purely observational accounts that generate the data. But doing justice to the data requires fitting the facts together—uncovering real patterns that may not have been obvious at first glance, making testable predictions about the language, and, ideally, developing an approach with applications across languages.

If the goal here is to fit the facts of Mende together, the five basic melodies are a good starting point for discussion, for several reasons. They form an orderly arrangement of two simple phonological tones without nearly as much overgeneration as other conceivable analyses. Dwyer (1973) was unable to reconstruct melodies other than these five for Proto-Southwestern Mande, and Dwyer's 1971 count of tone patterns in 200 words favors the notion that a handful of melodies are widely attested in core vocabulary, while others are much less frequent. Vydrin's 2004 survey of areal and genetic features of West Mande (of which Southwest Mande is a branch) observes:

> The tone-bearing unit in most of this [sic] languages of the group is not the syllable but the word: one and the same tonal pattern extends over the entire word, however long it may be, although there are some languages, such as Vai, where each syllable may carry a tone of its own.

By tone-bearing unit, Vydrin means the underlying domain of tones, not the surface unit to which in our sense a tone is assigned. Reflexes of just these five melodies are precisely what make up the tonal systems of related SWM languages Kpelle, Loko, Bandi, and Lɔma (Dwyer, 1978b; Konoshenko, 2008). Now, expanding Mende's potential melodies to include same-tone sequences HH and LL, would add considerably to the number of possible melodies. Two-tone sequences would include HH and LL, and three-tone sequences would add HHH, LLL, HHL, HLL, HHL, LHH, and LLH. Some of the added melodies could find a use, but at the cost of obscuring the ability of left-to-right tone mapping (Pulleyblank, 1986; Williams, [1971] 1976) to account for Mende's most common tone patterns.

Reducing the number of theoretically possible tone melodies was the motivation behind the OCP. But Mende has more tone patterns than can be expressed by the mechanisms presented here up to this point. For example, Mende surface forms have contrasting surface tone patterns H - L and H - HL:

(8)

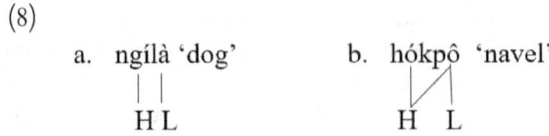

a. ngílà 'dog'
    | |
    H L

b. hókpô 'navel'
    H L

The account so far allows for (8a), using the same left-to-right mapping principle as *nìká*, but Mende has no principle to predict the link in (8b) between H and the second TBU. If a phonological characteristic is not predictable, we naturally stipulate it lexically. Thus underlying representations for (8) would look like this:

(9)

a. ngilà 'dog'

H L

b. hókpô 'navel'

H L

The prelinked tone in (9) has raised some questions, yet it is plausible that a set of irregular forms should be marked not to deviate underlyingly from their surface realization. In fact, prelinking is independently motivated in Mende. Mende's grammatical morphemes tend to be monosyllabic and, if they have a tone of their own, either L or H, and this tone is fixed: no polarization or spreading from these positions. For example, the definite marker is always -*í*, even when surrounded by material, left and right;[7] similarly for the indefinite marker, -*ngàa*. This makes sense if these morphemes are prelinked to their tones and if they are subject to a faithfulness constraint requiring no deviation from the surface tone in their underlying representations. The unpredictable tone associations in nouns and verbs behave this way as well. Prelinking of inherent tones to grammatical morphemes would also avoid the need to consider the grammatical morphemes as separate constituents, as would be the case if they were to form the domain for mapping a tone melody.

Another objection, summarized by S & I, is: "Dwyer (1978a) and Conteh et al. (1983) argued, however, that prelinking could just as well be used for all nouns in the system, obviating the autosegmental analysis." But a lexicon with all the surface links supplied would make very different predictions from one with only exceptional links. For one thing, adding links to all TBUs to all underlying forms would deprive faithfulness of a non-diacritic way to

---

[7]For examples with -*í*, see (6a,c,e,g). Note that the distinction between prelinked vs. free tones does not prevent *compacité tonale* (Green, 2013, 2017) from wiping out lexical tone in the constructions where it operates.

6.5. Tone melodies

distinguish regular cases from *nàvó*-type ones that resist polarization (compare (6e,f) to (6g,h)). For another, melodies independent of TBUs make a variety of predictions, notably (from Leben 1973) that each melody will be tend to found on Mende words no matter how many or how few syllables those words have. Third, the LH melody has special status, as polarization applies only words whose melody is LH and in fact only to a (large) subset of these. The next point will add support to the notion that words with the melody LH have a special status.

As shown in (6g,h), some exceptional LH CVCV words do not undergo polarization. Among them are *nàvó* 'money' and about two dozen others. Prelinking, the device used in (9a) to place an unpredictable link between a H and a TBU, can also capture the unpredictable behavior of the *nàvó* class with no additional stipulations. (10a,d) gives the proposed underlying forms, while (10b,e) adds a Tone Spreading context and (10c,f) shows the surface forms:

(10)

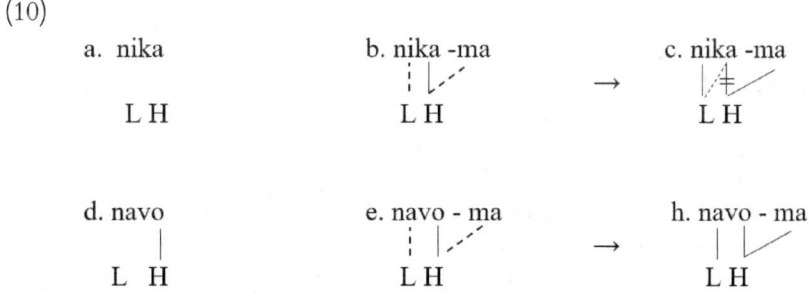

As we see, what exempts (10d) from Tone Spreading is prelinking, the only phonological feature distinguishing it from (10a). In fact, prelinking has independent merits, based on yet another class of words with a LH melody, three-syllable words. Left-to-right mapping leads us to expect a three-syllable word to have the surface pattern L-H-H, which is correct for *ndàvúlá* 'spoon,' but Mende also has L-L-H words like *làsìmó* 'amulet.' The difference is captured if we adopt the same device— prelinking vs. no prelinking—that distinguished the LH words in (10) above:

(11)

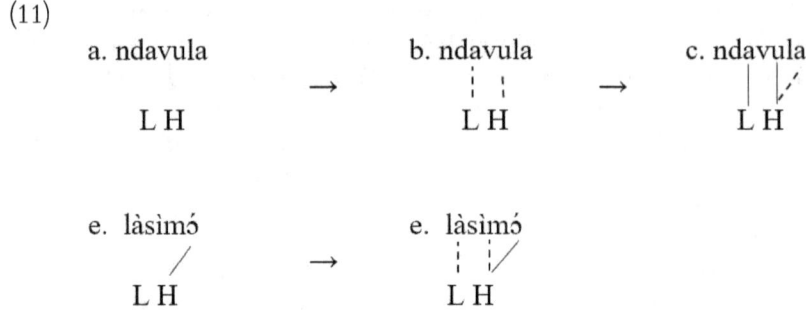

a. ndavula → b. ndavula → c. ndavula

  L H   L H   L H

e. làsìmɔ́ → e. làsìmɔ́

  L H   L H

To (11a) left-to-right mapping adds two links for (11b), and in (10c) the WFC requires a tone for the final TBU. For (11e), mapping puts L on the first TBU and the WFC requires a tone for the second TBU. That the link comes from the left is predictable from the same mapping principle that assigns tone in other cases, e.g. the second TBU of H-melody *pélé* 'house.' Note that this analysis predicts that the linked H in (11e) should be immobile, like the prelinked tone of *nàvó* in (10b). In other words, it should not undergo polarization. The prediction is correct. With polarization, we would expect the H at the end of *làsìmɔ́* to lower before the H of postposition *-ma* 'on.' But it does not. The correct form, as this analysis leads us to expect, is *làsìmɔ́-má*.[8]

To make the melody hypothesis as strong as possible, let us restrict prelinking to a single H and a single TBU of a short penult or short final syllable. Even constrained so tightly, this system of melodies and prelinks generates the nine most common noun tone patterns reported by Shih and Inkelas (2016) (S & I).

LHL	H	L H	H L	L H	H L	LHL	HL	L
μ μ μ	μ μ μ	μ μ μ	μ μ μ	μ μ μ	μ μ μ	μ μ μ	μ μ μ	μ μ μ
LHL	H	L H	H L	L H	H L	LHL	HL	L

Table 6.1: The nine most frequent tone patterns in Mende, as melodies.

The tenth most common pattern is HLH. The price for adding it would be eliminating predictions about where polarization applies.[9] An alternative is

---

[8]The class represented by (11a) is also exempt from polarization; there is no evidence that Tone Spreading applies word-internally or to doubly linked H.

[9]Dwyer (1978b): 184–185, 188–189 traces the distribution of polar tone back to proto-

to classify cases outside those handled in Table 6.1 as outliers. As pointed out earlier, limiting Mende's underlying tonal melodies to five is not the only choice, only one of conceivable starting points, but one factor that favors the five-melody model is that it makes a testable connection--between the distribution of polarizing words and their tone melodies.[10]

6.6 Conclusion

THE CENTRALITY OF MELODIES was a point of departure in my early work on Mende, and subsequent work by others, some of it cited in this article, has raised valid questions and objections, which I have tried to answer here, while correcting some previous serious oversights. But whatever the correct analysis of Mende's underlying tones, my main purpose has been to bring up some remarkable surface generalization that had escaped me until I had a look.

Acknowledgments

First, I am immensely grateful to Richard A. Spears, who first worked out Mende's tonology and impressed on me its importance for phonological theory. This paper has benefited from conversations with Mike Rodewald and from a wealth of suggestions and corrections from David Dwyer, Larry Hyman, and Keith Snider based on an earlier draft. The errors are my fault. Finally, I wish to thank Larry Hyman for uncovering Kukuya, an unrelated language that he rightly called more like Mende than Mende itself (Hyman, 1987).

Western Mande and argues that the point is not synchronically relevant. But one might ask why the pattern has remained stable for several thousand years.

[10]S & I object to "consigning the less common patterns to lexical prespecification. This approach thus tacitly bifurcated surface tone patterns into the frequent and the infrequent, choosing only to account for the former," and ending with the question, "why, if all patterns are possible, are some more common than others?" This is a reasonable question, and it may indeed point to the need for a vastly different framework, as S & I suggest, though regardless of theoretical framework, it is worth considering whether a word's frequency of use has an even greater effect on perceived regularity than its appearance in a dictionary. Contrary to the impression one gets from S & I, the autosegmental model is not inherently incompatible with expressing gradations in regularity. For example, a scale of regularity could be based on the degree of deviation from Mende's basic melodies and on what amount of lexical specification (such as prelinking) is required to generate a form.

7

Segment frequency: Within-language and cross-language similarity

Ian Maddieson
University of New Mexico

7.1 Introduction

IT HAS OFTEN BEEN REMARKED that there is a general pattern of similarity between the relative frequency of occurrence of segments within individual languages and the cross-language frequency with which segments are found in inventories (e.g. J. Greenberg 1966a). For example, of the three common voiced plosives /b, d, g/ it is often the case that /g/ is less frequently found in the words of a particular language. Cross-linguistically, among these three sounds, it is also /g/ that is most often missing from an inventory of phonemes that includes other voiced stops (Maddieson 2013). The correlation between within-language and cross-language frequency has even been invoked in discussions of phonological reconstruction in historical/comparative linguistics. In the "standard" reconstruction of Proto-Indo-European (PIE), /b/ is ex-

7.1. Introduction

tremely rare in the reconstructed lexicon, whereas in most languages with a voiced stop series /b/ is typically quite common. This observation provided one line of support for the "glottalic" reconstruction of PIE in which instead of "standard" */b, d, g/ an ejective series */p', t', k'/ is proposed for the correspondences in question (Berkes 1995). This harmonizes with the fact that in languages with ejective stops it is typically /p'/ that is rare or absent from the series.

In this paper some aspects of the overall pattern of similarity between within-language and cross-language segment frequency will be explored, using frequency data published in the literature as well as data extracted from various sources, particularly *RefLex* (Segerer and Flavier 2011-2017), a database focused on the lexicons of African languages which incorporates tools for analyzing, among other things, the number of occurrences of each segment. One notable inclusion in RefLex is the Miya dictionary compiled by Russell Schuh (ms, Schuh 2010). Individual language data will be compared with information on cross-language frequency of occurrences in inventories using *LAPSyD* (Maddieson and Flavier 2014-2017, Maddieson, Flavier, Marsico, Coupé, and Pellegrino 2013), a database on the basic phonological systems of a worldwide sample of languages.

We posit that within and cross-language frequency patterns show a correlation for two reasons. On the one hand there are processes that target specific segments for elimination or modification but which leave related segments unchanged. For example, by the Middle English period Old English (OE) /g/ is vocalized in many post-stressed positions. Thus /g/ is lost in forms such as OE '*eage*' Modern English '*eye*' (cf. German *Auge*), OE '*lagu*' Modern '*law*' (cf. Latin *lex, legis*), OE '*fugol*' Modern '*fowl*' (cf. German *Vogel*), whereas /d/ in similar positions remains, as in OE '*wudu*' Modern '*wood*', OE '*sceadu*' Modern '*shade*'. Singleton /b/ is rare in comparable positions in OE, but note forms like '*crabba*' ~ Modern '*crab*', '*ebbian*' ~ Modern '*to ebb*'. Vocalization, or weakening to a fricative or approximant (as in Dutch), affects a voiced velar plosive more frequently than voiced stops at other places since a) the articulatory gesture for /g/ is a tongue-body movement, like that required for a vowel, and b) the smaller supraglottal cavity behind a velar constriction means that pressure builds up more rapidly tending to separate the contacting surfaces.

Similarly, some segments have weaker perceptual cues to their identity than related segments. Such segments are more likely to be eliminated or perceived as something different. For example, the release burst of /p/ is weaker in amplitude than that for other voiceless stops, and it has no characteristic spectral peaks as found for stops produced by a lingual constriction (Stevens

1988: 323ff). Particularly if there is some aspiration present after the release, /p/ may be perceived as a labial or placeless fricative, i.e. as [ɸ], [f], or [h]. For example, a perceptual confusion study of American English by Weber and Smits (2003) showed that /p/ in onset or coda was heard as /h/ almost 20% of the time (even though /h/ does not occur finally in English). In modern Tokyo Japanese, all cases of Old Japanese */p/ have become either /h/ (allophonically [ɸ] before the vowel /ɯ/, [ç] before /i/) or medial /w/, except where 'reinforced' by being geminate or post-nasal (Martin 1987, Shibatani 1990), whereas most cases of */t/ and */k/ remain as such (or appear as their voiced counterparts). Because of loans and other forms, /h/ and /p/ can be contrastive but /h/ is over ten times more frequent as a simple onset consonant (Tamaoka and Makioka 2004).

On the other hand, processes that introduce new classes of segments to a language, or sounds in new positions, may also be selective and not apply across the board. Thus, for example, in the Austronesian language Bintulu of North Sarawak the implosive stops /ɓ, ɗ/ develop from earlier 'voiced aspirated' stops, which remain as such in closely related Kelabit, leading to correspondences such as Kelabit /təbʰuh/ ~ Bintulu /təɓəw/ "sugar cane", Kelabit /pədʰuh/ ~ Bintulu /lə-pədəw/ "gall". However, Kelabit /qʰ/, as in /uqʰeŋ/ "spinning (as a top)" does not seem to correspond with an implosive velar stop but with plain /q/ since no /ʛ/ occurs in Bintulu (Blust 1973, 2013; Blust and Trussel 2010-2016).

7.2 Some methodological considerations

Segment frequency in a particular language may be counted in various ways. In particular, counts may be made either based on a lexicon, or based on running text so as to reflect the relative frequency of actual usage. Lexical counts are influenced by what form is chosen for lexical entries and whether all variants of a given lemma are included, while the type of text used and the degree of standardization of the transcription employed will influence the frequencies found in a text count. However, to a large degree, the results of differently conducted counts show similarities. Figure 7.1 shows the fit between the relative frequency of French consonants in a very large lexical corpus and a large corpus of written materials, including books and the French subtitles to English-language films (New 2006).
There is high degree of coherence in the relative frequencies of segments in these two different corpora (R^2 = .86). The two segments that are markedly more frequent in text are easily accounted for in that they occur often in text

7.2. Some methodological considerations

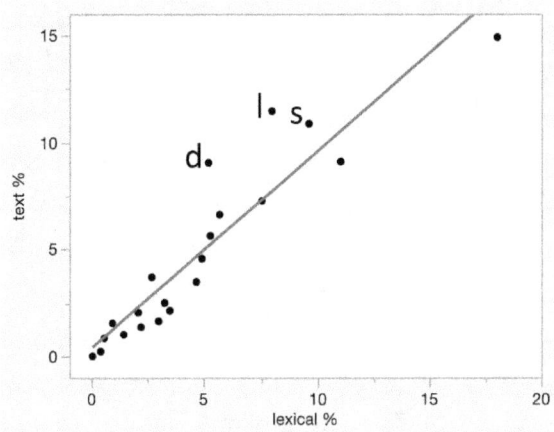

Figure 7.1: Consonant frequency (in %) in French text and lexicon

in frequently-used grammatical elements (/d/ especially in the prepositional forms *de, du, des*, and /l/ in the definite marker *le, les*). /s/ also is frequent in grammatical forms, such as 3rd person pronominals *se, son, sa, ses* and deictics like *ce, cet(te)*. Some of the low frequency consonants are less common in text since they not only occur in few words, but these words tend to be low-frequency items themselves.

A similar pattern is usually found when comparing frequencies in written and spoken texts. Figure 7.2 plots the relative frequency of consonants in written and spoken Castilian Spanish based on two large corpora, one of written news agency stories, the other of spontaneous speech. Here the frequencies are even more highly correlated ($R^2 = .95$), although /k/ and /s/ stand out as being a little more common in the spoken corpus than in the written, and /d, l, ɾ/ are a little more common in the written corpus than in the spoken. Possibly these patterns have to do with the the higher frequency of certain discourse markers, like *si* and *que*, and elision within clusters in the spoken language. However, these deviations are small.

In the discussion below we will assume that any language-specific frequency count provides useful insights into the distribution of the segments of that language, but will attempt to be sensitive to factors that may be biasing the results in one direction or another.

There are also methodological challenges in determining the frequency with which segments of particular types are found in the inventories of lan-

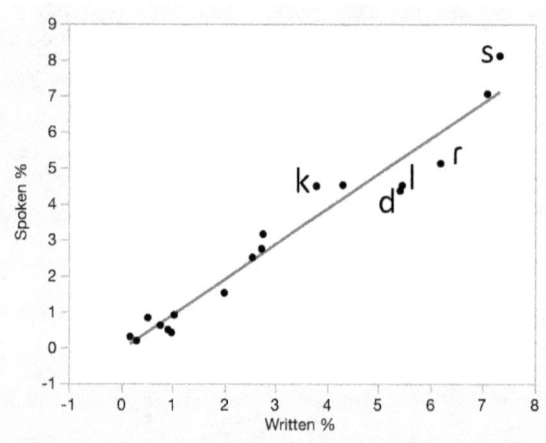

Figure 7.2: Consonant frequency in spoken and written Castilian Spanish

guages across a language sample. Although some equations of segment similarity are relatively simple, others are much more complex. For example, how many languages have a segment /t/? Conventional phonetic classification distinguishes dental [t̪] from alveolar [t]. In a small number of languages these are contrastive segments, but in many languages the same segment can be realized as either dental or alveolar even if in some, such as French and Spanish, a dental pronunciation is more common and in others, such as English and German, an alveolar pronunciation is more common. Moreover, in the available descriptions of a non-trivial number of languages, it is not specified whether a segment transcribed /t/ is normally dental or normally alveolar. Should these be considered completely distinct segments or would comparisons be more valid if the three categories (dental, alveolar, unspecified) were merged? In this and a number of similar cases the decision here is to merge. A merged category is represented with an asterisk, e.g. /*t/.

Another issue to consider is whether any sample of languages included in a survey appropriately represents languages in general. This paper uses the LAPSyD database, which is not a strictly stratified sample based on current understanding of genetic language affiliation but which does represent a very diverse range of languages with good areal balance between languages indigenous to different parts of the world. The current version includes 720 languages with some regard to the density of distinct documented languages in the six major areas recognized. In assigning languages to areas, geographical boundaries are established first, then all the languages in families predominantly based in a given area are assigned to that area. Thus, for example, Malagasy, Maori and Hawaiian are all assigned to the East and South-East Asia area together with all the other members of the Austronesian family. The current distribution of the sample languages is shown in Table 7.1.

Geographical/ genetic area	# languages
Europe, W. & S. Asia	109
E. & S. E. Asia	128
Africa	156
N. America	93
S. America	124
Oceania	109

Table 7.1: Distribution of languages in *LAPSyD* sample by geographical/genetic areas

7.3 Some results

THE RESULTS PRESENTED BELOW compare cross-language data from LAPSyD with within-language data from a selection of languages on the relative frequency of four classes of stops — voiced plosives, voiceless plosives, implosives and ejectives — occurring at three places of articulation: bilabial, the primary coronal position in the language, and velar. The within-language data are drawn from sources which vary greatly in the size of the lexicons or texts on which the counts are based. Not surprisingly, the largest sample sizes are mostly seen with major languages, as large-scale corpora are used in the speech technology industry for such languages. The nature of the sources also varies. In some cases phoneme frequency is directly taken from published counts in printed or on-line materials (e.g. French, Maltese, Bengali, Kokota). For others the frequency was calculated using tools provided with the *RefLex* database (e.g. Miya, Fulani, Basari, Ma'di). Finally, frequencies for some languages were calculated by the author from an available lexicon (e.g. Akhwakh, Kokama-Kukamiria) or taken from work on an NSF-funded research project on syllable structure carried out in the 1990's (e.g. Totonac, Wa, Thai, Igbo). This project is referenced in Maddieson and

Precoda (1992).[1]

7.3.1 Voiced plosives

As mentioned in the introduction, there is an interaction between place and voicing with respect to the frequency of plosives both within and across languages. Of the 720 languages currently in LAPSyD 432 have /b/ in their inventory of consonants, 418 have /*d/, and 377 have /ɡ/. In percentages, 60% have /b/, 58% have /*d/ and 52% have /ɡ/. If the frequency of /b/ is taken as the reference, then /*d/ has a relative frequency of 97% and /ɡ/ of 87% compared to /b/. In the Miya dictionary compiled by Russell Schuh (ms 2010) *RefLex* reports 170 occurrences of /b/, 150 of /d/ and 136 of /ɡ/ in the 1567 lexical entries imported from this dictionary. If again frequency of /b/ is taken as the reference, /d/ has 88% of /b/'s frequency and /ɡ/ has 80%. Thus, at least in this case the rank order is the same in the intra-language and cross-language data and the relative frequency differences are of a not dissimilar order of magnitude.

Counts of the within-language frequencies of /b/, /*d/ and /ɡ/ from a range of languages are shown in Table 7.2. Languages for which frequency data are available that have voiced plosives but entirely lack /ɡ/, such as Thai, Setswana, Mandinka, and Urarina are excluded. In the 33 languages in the table the frequency of /ɡ/ — expressed as a percentage of the frequency of /b/ — varies greatly (s.d. 56%), but in two-thirds of them /ɡ/ is less frequent than /b/ and the mean across the sample is 85%. A range of lower values is to be expected if there are a number of processes that affect voiced velar plosives more than those with a constriction further forward in the mouth, leading to their transformation or loss, and eventually to languages with zero /ɡ/'s.

A notably high proportion of the minority of 11 languages with more frequent /ɡ/'s than /b/'s are from Africa, six in all. However, the Austronesian language Kokota is an especially striking outlier with over 3 times more /ɡ/'s than /b/'s although this may be a case where a small sample produces

---

[1] Individual language frequency data were obtained in the following ways: calculated from data in RefLex for Miya, Basari, Fulani (Adamawa), Ma'di, Hausa (Ader dialect, Niger), Seko, Mamvu and Dan; taken from published frequency counts for Kokota, Komi, Kazakh, Hindi, Ma Manda, Woisika, Indonesian, Hebrew, Bengali, Persian, Dutch, Bardi, Mandarin, Tiriyo, Cantonese, Amharic, Kafa and Finnish and from on-line sources giving frequency counts for Italian, French, English, Catalan, Spanish, Maltese and Czech; obtained from the data compiled in the 'syllables' project for Ngizim, Wa, Igbo, Kadazan, Darai, Comanche, Totonac, Thai, Yupik and Kwakw'ala, and from personal counts by the author from published or online texts or wordlists for Amele, Akhwakh, Tapiete, Kokama, Shipibo, Qawasqar, So, Sindhi, Tera, Sawu and Maa.

unreliable results, since the counts are based on a short wordlist of just 335 items.

7.3.2 Voiceless plosives

AMONG VOICELESS PLOSIVES the counterpart of a "missing /q/" in the consonant inventory is a "missing /p/" (Maddieson 2013). In the LAPSyD language sample 688 (96%) have a plain /k/, 700 (97%) have a plain alveolar or dental stop (or both) and 631 (88%) have a plain /p/. Expressed as a percentage, the bilabial occurs with 92% of the frequency of the velar in these consonant inventories. Although there are about the same number of "missing /p/" and "missing /q/" languages, because more languages have voiceless plosives in total the overall percentage concerned is smaller in the "missing /p/" case.

Table 7.3 shows within-language frequency of /p/, /*t/ and /k/ in a sample of 43 languages. Languages for which frequency data is available but which have no /p/ in their voiceless plosive set, such as Hausa, Urarina, Kanuri and Kafa, are not included in the table. The range of variation in the /p/ as percent of /k/ measure is considerable (s.d. = 28%), but there are are no languages with an egregiously high value and many in which the frequency of /p/ is less than half that of /k/. The mean across the languages is 55%. Again, the language with the highest score is one for which the count is based on a short wordlist, in this case a list of just 382 bisyllabic words of the Tupian language Tapiete.

7.3.3 Ejectives and implosives

The patterns seen with voiced and voiceless plosives — where voicing is disfavored at the velar place and voicelessness is disfavored at the bilabial place — seem to be exaggerated when ejective and implosive stops are considered. These classes of consonants can be considered as representing hyperarticulations of voicelessness and voicedness. Ejectives guarantee the absence of voicing because of full closure of the vocal folds. Implosives usually have much higher amplitude of voicing than voiced plosives, as the lowering larynx creates lower pressure in the supralaryngeal cavity.

In the LAPSyD sample 92 languages have /ɓ/, 77 languages have /*ɗ/ and just 13 languages have /ɠ/. That is, the ratio of velar to bilabial implosives in inventories is just 14%. Correspondingly, most individual languages with implosives have very few or no words with velar examples. Some within-language data is presented in Table 7.4. Some languages with implosives at other places of articulation but no velar ones are included in the table, with absence of /ɠ/ shown by a dash in the relevant columns. They are included to demonstrate that implosives are not that infrequent overall: for example, there are more items with /ɓ/ than with /b/ in Ferry's dictionary of Basari (Ferry 1991). Among additional languages with /ɓ, *ɗ/ but no /ʄ/ are Kwaza, Hainanese, Ese Ejjia, Noon, Tsou, Movima, Goemai, Bintulu and several varieties of Karen.

The exceptionally high ratio of velar implosives in So is based on a small sample, obtained by counting all implosives in the syntactic examples and texts cited in Carlin's short grammar (Carlin 1993), and it may well be distorted by repeated occurrences of a few specific words, such as /ʄa/ "beer". Note in So, although /ʄ/ is more frequent in this data than /ɓ/, /*ɗ/ is nonetheless the most frequent implosive. The same is true for Sindhi but this source is perhaps the least trustworthy as it is based on a romanized transcription and seems not to distinguish between dental and retroflex implosives.

As for ejectives, in the LAPSyD sample 58 languages have the ejective /p'/ in their inventory, 81 have an ejective /*t'/ and 79 have the ejective /k'/. Thus the bilabial to velar ratio is 73%. Within-language frequency of occurrence data are only available for a rather small number of languages. Some data is presented in Table 7.5. Note that the back ejective of Qawasqar varies between velar and uvular and is probably more often uvular. For most of these languages /p'/ is quite rare. In the Ader dialect of Hausa, as in other Hausa varieties, it is altogether absent. In this language 64 cases of the affricate /ts'/ and 309 cases of /k'/ are reported in Caron (2014).

Considering both ejectives and implosives it is clear that the place-dependent frequency patterns within languages are more extreme than those seen with plosives. Bilabial ejectives and velar implosives are rare or absent in many of the languages that have representatives of these classes of segments at other places of articulation.

7.4 Discussion

TABLES 7.2-7.5 INDICATE that across a sample of languages it is most often the case that both bilabial voiceless plosives and ejectives are less frequent than the corresponding velar ones in lexical or text frequency. Conversely, bilabial voiced plosives and implosives are usually more frequent than velar ones. This data suggests that processes which result in the loss or replacement of /p/ or /p'/, or which prevent these segments being introduced in a language, are more commonly operative than similar processes affecting /k/ or k'/. Similarly, processes leading to loss or replacement of /ɠ/ and /ʄ/ or blocking their creation are more commonly operative than processes affect-

7.4. Discussion

ing /b/ and /ɓ/. As these processes run to term, languages which lack any words with /p/ or /q/, or with /p'/ or /ɠ/ arise even when other members of plosive, ejective and implosive series remain or are created.

The reasons for these patterns probably involve both considerations relating to production and perception, as noted in the Introduction. Ohala and Riordan (1979) have given a persuasive account of why voiced velar plosives are problematic to maintain due to the limited surface area of the supralaryngeal cavity in velars which reduces the possibility of cavity expansion, and this account also applies to velar implosives. It is less clear that a similar explanation for the rarity of /p/ and /p'/ can be found in the mechanics of production. It seems more likely that an auditory-acoustic account is required. The bilabial members of voiceless plosive and ejective series have the weakest overall amplitude of their release burst and a broad distribution of energy across the spectrum, rather than a characteristic peak in a given frequency range. In this way, they are the least easily identified members of these series.

Reasons of this kind suggest that the somewhat similar frequency patterns in cross-language and within-language frequencies of particular segments are natural outcomes of the interplay between constraints on production and perception and the cross-generational transmission of linguistic forms.

Acknowledgments

This paper is dedicated to the memory of Russ Schuh, as are all the other contributions to this volume. For me, Russ was a friend, fellow linguist, fellow field worker, fellow Africophile, and above all my running companion for innumerable miles. I am grateful to Guillaume Segerer for introducing me to the *RefLex* database used in this study, and I acknowledge the invaluable assistance of Kristin Precoda in writing the software used in the 'Syllables' project many years ago, and to Sébastien Flavier for the creation and maintenance of the *LAPSyD* environment as well as that of *RefLex*.

Language	/b/	/*d/	/g/	/g/%	Source
Kokota	30	21	92	307%	Palmer (1999)
Ngizim	253	299	414	164%	Schuh (1981)
Basari	129	170	201	156%	Ferry (1991)
Fulani	819	847	1157	141%	Tourneux and Daïrou (1998)
Ma'di	648	641	816	126%	Blackings (2000)
Komi	212	232	252	119%	Veenker (1982)
Kazakh	3636	5735	4225	116%	Kirchner (1989)
Hindi	5168	9534	5962	115%	Ghatage (1964)
Ma Manda	286	284	327	114%	Pennington (2014)
Hamer	205	153	232	113%	Petrollino (2016)
Wa	189	135	209	111%	Yan et al. (1981)
Ader Hausa	572	419	623	109%	Caron (2014)
Igbo	161	160	153	95%	Williamson (1972)
Kadazan	312	372	282	90%	Faust (1973)
Sheko	178	122	158	89%	Hellenthal (2010)
Amele	154	175	128	83%	Roberts (1987)
Miya	170	150	136	80%	Schuh (2010)
Italian	165864	594549	121624	73%	Goslin et al. (2012)
Finnish	659	9055	455	69%	Vainio (1996)
Darai	300	181	207	69%	Kotapish and Kotapish (1975)
French	17032	25431	10855	64%	New (2006)
English	10420	19125	6079	58%	Higgins (1993)
Woisika	231	147	130	56%	Stokhof (1979)
Akhwakh	542	616	263	49%	Creissels (2008)
Kafa	371	147	167	45%	Theil (2007)
Indonesian	6712	3388	2902	43%	Altmann (2005)
Catalan	149003	236919	58949	40%	Esquerra et al. (1998)
Hebrew	52258	44269	19421	37%	Silber-Varod et al. (2017)
Bengali	18728	13022	6969	37%	Mallik et al. (1998)
Spanish	31126	54284	11359	36%	Sandoval et al. (2008)
Maltese	2512670	4148424	821119	33%	Borg et al. (2011)
Czech	33348	48453	10267	31%	Bičan (n.d.)
Dutch	22932	80134	4881	21%	Zuidema (2009)

Table 7.2: Frequency of voiced plosives at major places of articulation in 33 languages. /g/ frequency is expressed as a percentage of /b/ frequency.

Language	/p/	/*t/	/k/	/p/ as %	Source
Tapiete	98	96	72	136%	González (2005)
Comanche	2454	4865	2253	109%	Wistrand-Robinson et al. (1990)
Amele	254	282	276	92%	Roberts (1987)
Bardi	996	422	1115	89%	Bowern (2012)
Mandarin	18483	45215	21727	85%	Tsoi (2005)
Czech	82945	95157	97745	85%	Bičan (n.d.)
Italian	485715	1151491	637440	79%	Goslin et al. (2012)
Kokota	29	74	37	78%	Palmer (1999)
French	27840	54049	36887	75%	New (2006)
Indonesian	6995	8364	9304	75%	Altmann (2005)
Maltese	3242782	12253833	4470418	73%	Borg et al. (2011)
English	14569	29441	20308	72%	Higgins (1993)
Kokama	725	954	1015	71%	Vallejos and Amías (2015)
Setswana	1190	2574	1697	70%	Creissels and Chebanne (2000)
Catalan	166204	283283	244778	68%	Esquerra et al. (1998)
Kadazan	429	692	642	67%	Faust (1973)
Basari	404	683	616	66%	Ferry (1991)
Totonac	996	2138	1529	65%	Aschmann (1973)
Tiriyo	166	124	223	64%	Meira (1999)
Spanish	34135	56287	55863	61%	Sandoval et al. (2008)
Wa	378	437	697	54%	Yan et al. (1981)
Shipibo	959	3014	1820	53%	Loriot et al. (1993)
Thai	422	792	814	52%	Haas (1964)
Bengali	13230	23220	26073	51%	Mallik et al. (1998)
Komi	46	75	90	51%	Veenker (1982)
Hamer	120	276	243	49%	Petrollino (2016)
Ma Manda	120	297	252	48%	Pennington (2014)
Dutch	21527	114069	47854	45%	Zuidema (2009)
Hindi	14167	21226	36131	39%	Ghatage (1964)
Fulani	521	1119	1467	36%	Tourneux and Daïrou (1998)
Kazakh	2179	5554	6368	34%	Kirchner (1989)
Yupik	302	1343	986	31%	Jacobson (1984)
Finnish	36150	184729	123070	29%	Vainio (1996)
Hebrew	18512	113334	63891	29%	Silber-Varod et al. (2017)
Ma'di	485	1031	1770	27%	Blackings (2000)
Persian	168	1459	648	26%	Nejad and Qaracholloo (2013)
Miya	74	205	309	24%	Schuh (2010)
Darai	258	320	1061	24%	Kotapish and Kotapish (1975)
Ngizim	140	377	604	23%	Schuh (1981)
Igbo	45	160	229	20%	Williamson (1972)
Woisika	104	541	587	18%	Stokhof (1979)
Cantonese	4130	16998	25671	16%	Tsoi (2005)
Akhwakh	36	255	241	15%	Creissels (2008)
Mandinka	266	1570	2059	13%	Creissels (2011)

Table 7.3: Frequency of voiceless plosives at major places of articulation in 43 languages. /p/ frequency expressed as a percentage of /k/ frequency.

Language	/ɓ/	/*ɗ/	/ʄ/	/ʄ/ as %	Source
So	4	18	10	250%	Carlin (1993)
Sindhi	65	135	105	162%	Luhana (n.d.)
Maa	289	323	178	62%	Payne and Ole-Kotikash (2008)
Tera	74	62	29	39%	P. Newman (1964)
Mamvu	340	0	115	34%	Vorbichler (1971)
Ma'di	431	339	56	13%	Blackings (2000)
Hamer	67	165	4	1%	Petrollino (2016)
Sawu	19	4	0	0%	Blust and Trussel (2010-2016)
Ngizim	69	202	—	—	Schuh (1981)
Fulani	632	812	—	—	Tourneux and Daïrou (1998)
Basari	600	355	—	—	Ferry (1991)
Ader Hausa	143	220	—	—	Caron (2014)
Dan	990	582	—	—	Vydrin (2008)

Table 7.4: Frequency of implosive stops at major places of articulation in 13 languages. /ʄ/ frequency is expressed as a percentage of /ɓ/ frequency.

Language	/p'/	/*t'/	/k'/	/p'/ as %	Source
Kwakw'ala	127	138	166	77%	Grubb (1977)
Sheko	33	48	110	33%	Hellenthal (2010)
Qawasqar	3	22	17	18%	Clairis (1985)
Kafa	5	61	114	4%	Theil (2007)
Amharic	3	166	194	2%	Bender (1974)
Akhwakh	1	139	168	0%	Creissels (2008)

Table 7.5: Frequency of ejective stops at major places of articulation in 7 languages. Frequency of /p'/ is expressed as percentage of the frequency of /k'/.

8

Constructions and competitions in Dogon inflectional tonology

Laura McPherson
Dartmouth College

8.1 Introduction

THE RELATIONSHIP BETWEEN TONE AND INFLECTION has come back into the spotlight, thanks in large part to the recent volume edited by Palancar and Léonard (2017). Though specialists in families where inflectional tone is prevalent, such as Oto-Manguean and Bantu, have long been describing these complex systems, broader theoretical interest in questions of representation and analysis have lagged behind. It would appear that for many African and Meso-American languages, the existence of inflectional tone is taken almost as a given; it is described in (hopefully) great detail, but otherwise unquestioned.

I admit this to be the case for my work on Tommo So and the Dogon language family. The Dogon languages have become known in the literature for their complex phrase-level replacive tone in the DP, with certain syntactic categories triggering tonal overlays on c-commanded words (Heath,

2016; Heath & McPherson, 2013; McPherson, 2014; McPherson & Heath, 2016). But just as this more unusual DP "tonosyntax" is common to the language family, so too are replacive overlays in verbal inflection. Consider, for example, a partial paradigm of the Tommo So verb *jɔ́bɔ́* 'run', shown in 1:[1]

(1) jɔ́bɔ̀-dɛ   IPFV Aff   'runs/will run'
    jɔ̀b-ɛ́   PFV Aff   'ran'
    jɔ́bɔ́   IMP   'run!'

In these forms, we see the tone on the verb stem change from base tone /LH/[2] to {HL} (imperfective), {L} (perfective), and {H} (imperative). These so-called "tonal overlays", which completely replace a stem's base tone, do not on their own encode ANM (aspect-negation-mood) features, but rather they co-occur with portmanteau suffixes carrying the morphosyntactic information.

Despite the prevalence of this system of replacive tone in the Dogon languages, it has received relatively little attention in the literature compared to its phrase-level counterpart. Further, it is unclear how to represent tonal overlays like these in the verbal morphology: Do they themselves expone a morphosyntactic feature or feature bundle? Is it simply stem allomorphy in particular morphosyntactic contexts? Or are tonal overlays the result of morpheme-specific phonological grammars, as in Cophonology theory (Anttila, 2002; Inkelas & Zoll, 2005; Itô & Mester, 1995)? The goal of this paper is to entangle these analyses and develop a formal account of the role of tone in Dogon verbal inflection. Following Hyman (2017), I show that inflectional overlays can be understood as a case of morphological competition, with different morphosyntactic features demanding different tonal outputs. Even though the segmental suffixes themselves are portmanteaus, I argue that overlays can be tied to single features (e.g. imperfective or negative), which compete with one another to realize their tone. I model the system using a constraint-based approach, rooted in Construction Morphology (Booij, 2010) and using elements of Realization Optimality Theory (Xu & Aronoff, 2011) and the constraint-based approach to Dogon tonosyntax (McPherson, 2014). Briefly, the lexicon contains a network of constructions, some specific and some more general, that may be linked to one another by

---

[1] The abbreviations used in this paper are: Aff 'affirmative', IMP 'imperative', IPFV 'imperfective', NEG 'negative', PFV 'perfective', REL 'relative', MCA 'main clause affirmative', MCN 'main clause negative', RCA 'relative clause affirmative', RCN 'relative clause negative'. The transcription system is roughly IPA, but with <j> for [dz], <y> for [j], and <r> for [ɾ]. High tone is marked with acute accent, low tone with grave accent, and surface underspecified (toneless) syllables are unmarked.

[2] See below for discussion of whether to consider the base tone of verbs to be lexical or not.

common features or forms. Even though more than one conflicting construction may be linked to another construction through common features, their relative network strengths predict which constructional demands are respected. These networks are formalized as constraints, with connection strengths correlating to constraint ranking or weighting.

This paper is organized as follows: In §8.2, I provide a brief introduction to the Dogon languages. In §8.3, I describe the Tommo So verbal paradigms this paper will focus on, before discussing in §8.4 how the surface form of verbs can be understood as the outcome of competitions between tonal overlays (Hyman, 2017). I turn to formal representation and analysis in §8.5, first considering Distributed Morphology and Cophonology approaches before laying out an analysis using construction constraints. In §8.6, I briefly compare the tonal grammar of Tommo So to two other Dogon languages and suggest other languages for which such an approach might be fruitful. §8.7 concludes.

8.2 The Dogon languages

THE DOGON LANGUAGES ARE A FAMILY OF LANGUAGES spoken in east central Mali, on and around the large rocky inselberg mountain of the Bandiagara Escarpment. The genetic affiliation of the family has been the subject of dispute, but it is currently thought to form its own branch of Niger-Congo (Blench, 2005), representing an early split. The family consists of around twenty languages, with exact counts made difficult by dialect chains and other fuzzy boundaries between varieties.

Most data in this paper come from my primary field notes on Tommo So; for more in-depth description, see McPherson (2013). Comparative data from other Dogon languages are drawn from Jeffrey Heath's grammars of Jamsay (2008) and Nanga (2016).

The Dogon languages are all two-tone languages, contrasting H, L, and contour tones composed of these primitives (LH, HL, and occasionally LHL); McPherson (2011) further showed that Tommo So has surface underspecification of tone [Ø], filled in by interpolation from surrounding specified syllables or boundary tones. In Tommo So, all lexical items contain one H tone stretch; in other words, there are no /L/ lexical items, nor any /HLH/. Most native vocabulary is either /H/ or /LH/, though /HL/ is also fairly well represented, largely from Fulfulde loanwords. Examples establishing the existence of lexical tone contrasts are given below, focusing on nouns:

(2) | /H/ | | /LH/ | | /HL/ | |
|---|---|---|---|---|---|
| náá | 'mother' | nàá | 'cow' | | |
| dámmá | 'village' | dàmmá | 'hoe' | támmà | 'colonial coin' |
| ísé | 'empty' | ìsé | 'dog' | ásè | 'Saturday' |

As we will see in §8.3 below, there is little evidence for lexical tone contrast in verbs.

Morphologically, the languages are characterized by isolating nominal morphology and agglutinating verbal morphology. Nearly all nominal inflection, including definiteness, number and even case, is expressed via enclitics, as shown in (3a), while verbal morphology involves suffixation, with agglutinating derivational suffixes followed by a portmanteau ANM marker and finally subject agreement (3b):

(3) a. gámmá=gɛ=mbe=ɲ̀
    cat=DEF=PL=ACC
    'the cats (accusative)'

  b. pòò-nd-ìyè-m-éélè-y
    fat-FACT-MP-CAUS-IPFV.NEG-1PL
    'we will not make (someone) fat'

This paper will set aside derivational suffixes (which are amply exemplified in McPherson and Hayes 2016) and focus solely on the portmanteau ANM suffix and tonal overlays on the stem.

8.3 Tommo So verbal morphology

IN TOMMO SO, AS IN MOST DOGON LANGUAGES, the notion of lexical tone in verbs is tenuous. In the absence of a morphologically-controlled tonal overlay, verb stems will be either /H/ or /LH/ depending upon their initial segment: vowel- and voiceless-initial roots are uniformly H-toned, while voiced obstruent-initial roots are uniformly LH-toned. Sonorant-initial roots can fall into either category, raising the possibility of tonal minimal pairs, but only one is attested: nɔ̀ɔ́ 'drink' vs. nɔ́ɔ́ 'sew', and even here there appears to be interspeaker variation. For this reason, I will refer to the tone of a verb that has not taken an overlay as its **neutral tone** rather than its lexical tone.

The lack of lexical tone contrast in verbs is unsurprising, considering that in most inflectional categories, the surface tone is entirely determined by grammatical overlays that neutralize tone distinctions. This means that

8.3. Tommo So verbal morphology

learners would be only rarely exposed to the underlying tone. For instance, we can compare the H-toned verb *kánà* in (4) with the forms in (1); in both cases, the resulting tonal forms are the same:

(4) kánà-dɛ   IPFV Aff   'does/will do'
    kàn-ì   PFV Aff   'did'
    káná   IMP   'do!'

Again, we see {HL} in the imperfective, {L} in the perfective, and {H} in the imperative (though in the case of a H-toned verb like this, this is homophonous with its neutral tone pattern).

These tonal overlays depend primarily on aspect, mood, negation, and clause type (main vs. relative); tense, if indicated, is typically encoded by an auxiliary verb and does not influence the inflection of the main verb itself. In this paper, I will concentrate on the following morphosyntactic features and their combinations:

- Imperfective (IPFV)
- Perfective (PFV)
- Negative (NEG)
- Imperative (IMP)
- Relative (REL)

As shown in the following example, verbal inflection is marked with a combination of a tonal overlay (indicated from this point onwards with superscripted tone melody after the verb stem) and a portmanteau suffix:

(5) a. jɔ́bɔ̀^{HL}-dɛ
       run-IPFV
       'runs/will run'
    b. jɔ̀b^{L}-ɛ́ɛ́lɛ̀
       run-IPFV.NEG
       'does/will not run'

In (5a), the suffix *-dɛ* indicates imperfective, along with the overlay {HL}; in (5b), there is no trace of *-dɛ*, despite also being imperfective. Instead, the portmanteau suffix *-éélè* indicates both imperfective and negative, combined with the tonal overlay {L}.[3]

The tonal overlay, but not the suffix, also depends on whether the verb is in a main clause or a relative clause. The relative clause equivalents of (5) are given in (6):

(6) a. jɔ̀bɔ́-dɛ
   run-IPFV.REL
   'that runs/will run'

   b. jɔ̀b^L-éélè
   run-IPFV.NEG.REL
   'that does/will not run'

In the negative (6b), there is no difference in form between main and relative clauses; both employ a {L} overlay. But in the affirmative (6a), the relative clause verb is characterized by neutral tone: the LH-toned verb *jɔ̀bɔ́* 'run' surfaces as *jɔ̀bɔ́-dɛ*, while a H-toned verb like *káná* 'do' surfaces as *káná-dɛ*.

Table 8.1 summarizes the main patterns of verbal inflection in Tommo So.[4]

	MCA	MCN	RCA	RCN
IPFV	X^{HL}-dɛ	X^L-éélè	X-dɛ	X^L-éélè
PFV	X^L-ɛ̀/ì	X^L-lí	X^{HL}-ɛ̀/ì	X^{HL}-lì
IMP	$X^{(H)}$	X^L-gú	—	—

Table 8.1: Schematization of Tommo So verbal inflection

Though easy to describe, it is less easy to determine the role and representation of overlays in the inflectional system. The table demonstrates clearly that segmental portmanteau morphology remains consistent between main and relative clauses (with some elements like negative [l] also repeating across

---

[3] I treat the vowel [éé] as part of the suffix, with the stem-final vowel deleted due to vowel hiatus resolution. In Heath's descriptions of related Dogon languages, different suffixes trigger vowel changes on the stem, and hence [éé] here would be part of the stem. Under such a view, the overlay would be treated as {LH}. Since this vowel consistently appears in the negative imperfective, I find it more parsimonious to treat the vowel as part of the suffix.

[4] MCA = Main Clause Affirmative; MCN = Main Clause Negative; RCA = Relative Clause Affirmative; RCN = Relative Clause Negative.

aspects), but tonal overlays may differ. However, it is not the case that overlays themselves encode relativity, since within both main and relative clauses, different overlays are found. Nevertheless, some patterns in tonal overlays do emerge, such as the correlation between negation and a {L} overlay. These patterns will be explored further in the next section.

8.4 Competitions between tonal overlays

IF WE STRIP TABLE 8.1 DOWN to just the tonal overlays (leaving the segmental morphology out), we get Table 8.2. Here, X refers to neutral tone, while – means that the inflectional category is unattested (i.e. there is no relative imperative).

	MCA	MCN	RCA	RCN
IPFV	HL	L	X	L
PFV	L	L	HL	HL
IMP	X/H	L	–	–

Table 8.2: Tonal overlays in each inflectional cell

At first glance, no overlay can be exceptionlessly identified with a single morphosyntactic feature. Even {H}, which appears just once, cannot be identified with IMPERATIVE, since the imperative negative takes {L}. {L} cannot, however, be exceptionlessly identified with negation, since it is also found in the affirmative perfective in main clauses, and {HL} is found in the perfective negative in relative clauses. {HL} correlates with IMPERFECTIVE in main clauses, but PERFECTIVE in relative clauses, and so forth. What, then, to make of these overlays, which are an invariable part of Tommo So verbal morphology?

Following Hyman (2017), I suggest that tonal overlays may in fact be exponents of morphosyntactic features or feature bundles, but since any given paradigm cell draws on multiple such features, competitions can arise. Since verb stems can, by definition, realize only a single overlay, these competitions result in what appears to be a piecemeal verb paradigm.

Hyman represents these competitions through shading, where first an exceptionless generalization is shaded in, followed by the next most exceptionless generalization to any remaining cells, and so on and so forth until the paradigm is complete. Following this procedure gives us the following:

(7) *Identifying generalizations in the Tommo So verbal paradigm*

{HL} associated with RELATIVE PERFECTIVE

	MCA	MCN	RCA	RCN
IPFV	HL	L	X	L
PFV	L	L	HL	HL
IMP	H	L	--	--

{L} associated with NEGATIVE

	MCA	MCN	RCA	RCN
IPFV	HL	L	X	L
PFV	L	L		HL
IMP	H	L	--	--

Remaining categories represented by single paradigm cells

	MCA	MCN	RCA	RCN
IPFV	HL		X	L
PFV	L	L		HL
IMP	H		--	--

First, {HL} can be identified as an overlay for the feature bundle [PERFECTIVE, +RELATIVE], without reference to negation. This overlay takes precedence over any other applicable overlays, such as the second wave, {L} for the morphosyntactic feature [NEGATIVE]. Even though the relative negative perfective has the feature [NEGATIVE], the {L} overlay is blocked because {HL} has already applied. Once these two overlays have applied, every other feature combination picks out just a single cell: {HL} for main clause imperfective, {L} for main clause perfective (or possibly just perfective, with the more specific case of relative clause perfective having been assigned {HL}), {H} for the imperative, and any remaining cells filled in with neutral tone.

Thus, the ranking for Tommo So can be summarized as follows:

(8) [PERFECTIVE, +RELATIVE] ≫ [NEGATIVE] ≫ Other

By and large, Tommo So falls into line with one of Hyman (2017)'s observations, namely that negatives tend to have identical tonal marking.

Hyman's procedure gives the impression that the highest overlay is applied first and blocks the application of lower overlays. If instead we assume that verbs are built up from lowest to highest, then each higher overlay in the scale of (8) has the power to overwrite lower overlays. Under this procedure, we can identify the following overlays and their associated morphosyntactic feature bundles:

8.4. Competitions between tonal overlays

(9) {HL}: [IMPERFECTIVE, -RELATIVE]
{L}: [PERFECTIVE]
{H}: [IMPERATIVE]
{L}: [NEGATIVE]
{HL}: [PERFECTIVE, +RELATIVE]

There is homophony in overlays, with {HL} encoding both non-relative imperfective and relative perfective, and {L} encoding both (non-relative) perfective and negative; I take this to be accidental homophony that arises from a limited inventory of possible tonal overlays. Under this view, the first three lower-ranked overlays apply first to all applicable paradigm cells; next, negative {L} applies where applicable, overwriting these earlier overlays. Finally, the highest-ranked overlay {HL} applies, overwriting either step that preceded its application. This can be visually represented as in (10):

(10) *Overwriting process in tonal overlay application*

Low-ranked overlays apply

	MCA	MCN	RCA	RCN
IPFV	HL	HL	X	X
PFV	L	L	L	L
IMP	H	H	--	--

{L} associated with NEGATIVE

	MCA	MCN	RCA	RCN
IPFV	HL		X	
PFV	L	L	L	L
IMP	H		--	--

{HL} associated with RELATIVE PERFECTIVE

	MCA	MCN	RCA	RCN
IPFV	HL		X	L
PFV	L	L	HL	HL
IMP	H		--	--

This order of application falls more in line with the "tonal layers" approach for Dinka (Anderson 1992) or the cophonological approach to Hausa replacive overlays (Inkelas, 2011), though see §8.5.2 below for the limitations of cophonology theory.

8.5 The morphological representation of tonal overlays

WHILE THIS APPROACH ADEQUATELY DESCRIBES the facts and adduces some internal structure to the paradigm of inflectional tone in Tommo So, we are still left with questions of representation and implementation in the morphological component. As already noted, verbal tone is rather superfluous in Tommo So. All of the relevant morphosyntactic information can be retrieved from either the portmanteau suffixes (in the case of AMN) or from the larger syntactic construction (in the case of main vs. relative clauses).[5] In this way, tonal overlays can be seen as a case of extended or multiple exponence (Caballero & Harris, 2012; Harris, 2017; Matthews, 1974), as similarly argued for the imperfective H tone in Mian (Fedden, 2017).

I will consider here three different possible analyses: Distributed Morphology and two constructional approaches, the incremental Cophonology theory and a globally-evaluated Construction Morphology approach similar to Realization Optimality Theory. In considering these analyses, the big questions include: 1. Whether the tonal overlays are part of the same representation as the segmental suffixes or whether they independently encode morphosyntactic features; and 2. How tonal overlays are assigned (e.g. as floating tones independent of the stem, as allomorphs of the stem, as the result of a phonological grammar, or as a result of a constructional template). Ultimately, multiple analyses are possible, and proponents of any of these theories would likely find a way to account for the data. However, I suggest that the most parsimonious account is the Construction Morphology approach, already independently required in Dogon DP tonosyntax (McPherson, 2014; McPherson & Heath, 2016).

8.5.1 Distributed Morphology

In Distributed Morphology (Halle and Marantz 1993, Harley and Noyer 1999, Embick and Noyer 2007, among others), "vocabulary items" are inserted to match morphosyntactic feature bundles spelled out by the syntax. It is thus in essence an item-based view of morphology, though proposals have been put forth to account for process morphology in the framework, as we will see below.

---

[5]Relative clause verbs can also be differentiated from main clause verbs in that they do not carry the usual subject agreement suffixes; instead, pronominal subjects are marked by preverbal independent pronouns.

8.5. The morphological representation of tonal overlays

Given this, at least two DM analyses are possible: one in which tonal overlays are themselves vocabulary items, essentially floating tones that expone morphosyntactic features, and one in which they are more epiphenomenal, either part and parcel of the stem through allomorphy or the result of a "readjustment rule", transformational rules that apply to lexical items in particular contexts.

Sande (2017) argues succinctly against DM approaches to tonal process morphology in her account of Guébie imperfective tone raising, and those arguments apply equally well here. First, she argues against the suppletive allomorphy approach on the basis on economy: in the case of Tommo So, listing every verb stem with a L-toned, HL-toned, and H-toned allomorph needlessly inflates the lexicon while at the same time missing the crucial generalization that {L}, {HL}, and {H} are predictable tonal outputs. If every stem simply has multiple allomorphs listed for different environments, what is to stop particular stems from taking a different tonal form? The fact that the same tonal overlays are consistently found in different paradigm cells becomes a happy coincidence. She goes on to show that the readjustment rule approach has been argued against even outside of the literature on grammatical tone as being unconstrained (Bye & Svenonius, 2012; Gribanova, 2015; Siddiqi, 2009) and inconsistent with the broader architecture, which has otherwise moved away from transformational rules.

Thus, if we wish to account for Tommo So verbal overlays strictly within DM, the overlays must be considered as floating tones, either associated with the portmanteau suffixes or independently exponing morphosyntactic features. The former approach—making floating tones part of the representation of portmanteau suffixes—misses generalizations about the system. For such a system to work, Tommo So would require many duplicates. For instance, we would find duplicate vocabulary items like the following:

(11) a. ^{L}-lí ↔ [PFV, NEG, -REL]
 b. ^{HL}-lí ↔ [PFV, NEG, +REL]

The fact that -lí consistently represents the negative perfective is lost here, as is the fact that {L} recurs in most of the negative cells of the paradigm.

This leaves the option of treating overlays as vocabulary items unto themselves. The list of overlays and their associated morphosyntactic features in 9 represents the necessary vocabulary items in this approach.

This raises two possible issues for the realization of tonal overlays in DM. First is the issue of extended exponence. To take an example, the vocabulary item {L} is an exponent of [NEGATIVE], as is the portmanteau suffix -éélè, which also expones [IMPERFECTIVE]. If we assume Subset Principle, that the most specific vocabulary item will be inserted first, then -éélè takes precedence (which from a hierarchical standpoint may also be predicted, assuming ASP is closer to the verb root than negation). In many approaches to DM, the insertion of a vocabulary item replaces the morphosyntactic feature(s) that it instantiates (Halle 1990; Noyer 1992, 1997; Bobaljik 2000); if this is true, then inserting -éélè would bleed the insertion of the {L} overlay, yet both appear in Tommo So in a putative case of extended exponence. To allow for such cases, Noyer distinguishes between primary and secondary exponents, where a secondary exponent is allowed to co-exist with a primary one (i.e. a secondary exponent does not discharge the morphosyntactic feature), but Stump (2001), in addition to Xu and Aronoff (2011), show that it is not always possible to determine which features are primary and which are secondary.

The second issue that arises in DM is how to deal with competition between equally compatible vocabulary items. If one vocabulary item expones more features than another, the Subset Principle dictates that the most specific wins; in the case of Tommo So tonal overlays, this means that {HL} exponing both [PERFECTIVE] and [RELATIVE] will take precedence over the other applicable overlays (such as [NEGATIVE] or a more general [PERFECTIVE]). But otherwise, we cannot predict that {L} for [NEGATIVE] with take precedence over, say, {HL} for [IMPERFECTIVE] and [-REL] (especially if [-REL] is itself considered a secondary feature), or especially an overlay for a single feature like {H} for [IMPERATIVE]. Appealing to syntactic hierarchy (as argued for by Noyer 1997) helps us little, following standard assumptions that aspect is closest to the verb, followed by negation, followed by mood: Regardless of whether it is the innermost or outermost feature that takes precedence, we see that negative {L} trumps both aspect (imperfective {HL}) and mood (imperative {H}). High sentential negation may solve this problem, but it is not clear whether negation in Tommo So is sentential, and it would still leave us with a paradox wherein the two-feature overlay {HL} for the relative perfective takes precedence over {L} for negation, but {HL} for the imperfective non-relative does not. The only way to account for such cases would be to explicitly stipulate the order of application (see Embick and Noyer 2007 footnote 14).

In sum, treating Tommo So tonal overlays as vocabulary items in a DM architecture falls short of accounting for the data without appeal to an arbitrary hierarchy of morphosyntactic features, a move that is mostly avoided in the framework. Further, by treating overlays as floating tones, the phonology would be responsible for ensuring overwriting behavior as opposed to simple concatenation. Though in principle possible for Tommo So, which lacks any

8.5. The morphological representation of tonal overlays

concatenative floating tones, this becomes more difficult for languages like Nanga (Heath, 2016), which arguably shows both types of grammatical tone. Further theoretical machinery, such as Cophonology theory, would need to be employed to differentiate between the two.

8.5.2 Cophonology theory

Another possibility, not incompatible with the DM architecture (see e.g. Sande 2017), is that tonal overlays are the result of morphology-specific phonological grammars as in Cophonology theory (Anttila, 2002; Inkelas & Zoll, 2005; Itô & Mester, 1995). These grammars, consisting of rule orderings or constraint rankings, could be associated with specific morphemes such as -*lí*, or with morphosyntactic features directly (as in Sande 2017).

As argued for in the last subsection, the generalizations of tonal overlays are better captured by associating them directly with morphosyntactic features than with the portmanteau suffixes that they accompany. In other words, a cophonology approach would have a phonological grammar specific to [NEGATIVE] resulting in an all L stem, a grammar for the feature bundle [PERFECTIVE, +REL] resulting in a {HL} overlay on the stem (with H on only the first mora), a grammar for [IMPERATIVE] resulting in an all-H stem, etc.

The same issue of competitions remains for this approach. In Cophonology theory, structure is built incrementally, usually with the result that the highest (outermost) morphosyntactic feature sees its grammar realized (see e.g. Inkelas 2011 for Hausa replacive tone). In cases where the hierarchy of tonal overlays follows a natural morphosyntactic hierarchy, such an approach is unproblematic, but in Tommo So, we arrive at the same issue found for feature discharge in DM. The closest fit we can achieve is the following hierarchy:

(12) RELATIVE ≫ NEGATIVE ≫ MOOD ≫ ASPECT

We would need to stipulate that a cophonology that makes reference to multiple features would apply at the highest feature, so that {HL} from the perfective relative could overwrite the output of the negative cophonology. The problem is that the affirmative imperfective also differs in main and relative clauses ({HL} in main clauses and neutral-toned in relative clauses, which we can take to be the absence of an overlay). Since reference must be made to [RELATIVE] to determine the overlay, then these too would be expected to trump the negative, which they do not.

As we will see below, the situation becomes even less tenable for other Dogon languages: overlays must be assessed globally, with the hierarchy or relative strengths of different overlays determined on a language-specific basis.

8.5.3 Constraint-based Construction Morphology

Though Cophonology theory is a constructional theory of morphophonology, it is only one implementation of the broader architure. I will argue here that a version based closely on Booij (2010), combined with a Realization Optimality Theory (Xu, 2011; Xu & Aronoff, 2011) and developed further for replacive tone in McPherson (2014), is the best suited to account for Tommo So inflectional tone. Crucially, while Cophonology theory involves local evaluation, with a particular grammar applied at each step in a morphological derivation, the framework employed here is global: all applicable constructions are considered in tandem, (potentially) competing with one another for realization.

In this framework, morphology is learned and implemented through **constructional schemas**, which tie together phonological, syntactic, and semantic information; the phonological component acts as a template that outputs must adhere to, rather than a constraint ranking or rule ordering deriving such an output. This is true both of segmentable affixes as well as base modification, the latter more likely to be considered the result of a cophonological grammar. To take a simple example from Booij (2010), consider the constructional schema for the English agentive suffix -*er*:

(13)   *Constructional schema for the English agentive*

Syntactically, the agentive is a noun that consists of a verb stem and an affix; semantically, it carries the meaning of one who does a predicate (co-indexed with the verb); and phonologically, the agentive is a word with the phonological content of the verb followed by the phonological sequence [ər] of the affix.

For tonal overlays, the output shows the domain of overlay application associated with a particular tonal realization (illustrated here with autosegmental notation, though nothing hinges on this decision):

8.5. The morphological representation of tonal overlays

(14) Constructional schema for Tommo So negatives

$$\{\ \}_{stem} \leftrightarrow V_{stem} \leftrightarrow [\text{NEGATIVE}]$$
$$|$$
$$\{L\}$$

As a shorthand, I have used the label "stem" to refer to the domain of overlay application, though in morphosyntactic terms this could be represented as everything below the Asp(ect) layer of structure (including the root and any derivational suffixes). The phonological representation on the lefthand side shows a {L} overlay associated with this domain.

This constructional schema can come into conflict with others, such as the following schema for the imperative:

(15) Constructional schema for Tommo So imperatives

$$\{\ \}_{stem} \leftrightarrow V_{stem} \leftrightarrow [\text{IMPERATIVE}]$$
$$|$$
$$\{H\}$$

There is no way to satisfy both constructional schemas simultaneously: the stem can either be all {H} or all {L}.

Segmental morphology is also achieved through constructional schemas, such as the following portmanteau for [IMPERATIVE, NEGATIVE]:

(16) Constructional schema for Tommo So negative imperatives (prohibitives)

$$\omega_i \leftrightarrow V_i \leftrightarrow [\text{IMPERATIVE, NEG}]$$
$$|\qquad\qquad \diagdown$$
$$[\ ]_j [gú]_k \quad V_j\ Aff_k$$

This schema resembles Booij's agentive schema more closely, with a verb (stem) followed by an affix with the phonological realization -gú. The schema says nothing about the tonal realization of the stem, which is dealt with independently by the tonal schemas above. This allows the same schema to be used even when the tone of the stem differs, such as with the imperfective suffix -dɛ in main vs. relative clauses.

Schemas such as these are linked together in the lexicon by overlap in morphosyntactic features.[6] For example, the segmental schema for the negative imperative -gú is tied to both the imperative and negative tonal schemas.

---

[6] It remains an open question whether schemas are linked together if they share phonological

However, the network connection strength from the negative is stronger, resulting in the output form taking {L} rather than the imperative's {H}. This strength is represented by the darker line:

(17) *Network connections between constructional schema for imperative and negative*

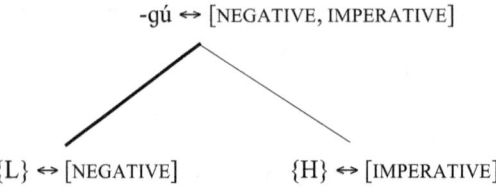

This negative tonal schema is associated with any number of other schemas in the lexicon invoking the feature [NEGATIVE], including the negative perfective *-lí* and the negative imperfective *-éélè*. These suffixal schemas may be linked to other tonal schemas as well, such as the two perfective tonal schemas {HL} for relative clauses and {L} for main clauses, and depending upon the connection strength, one or the other will prevail.[7]

Constraint-based models are, in essence, a formalization of these network connection strengths, especially the weighted constraints of Harmonic Grammar (Goldwater & Johnson, 2003; Legendre, Miyata, & Smolensky, 1990). For ease of exposition in this chapter, however, I will illustrate the data with constraint ranking, as in Optimality Theory (Prince & Smolensky, 1993).

Following McPherson (2014), I take the constructional schemas themselves as constraints ("construction constraints"), militating that outputs matching the morphosyntactic description take the proscribed morphophonological form. Note, however, that in the most common case where the morphophonological form expones a morphosyntactic feature, as in Tommo So verbal inflection, the framework is a notational variant of Realization Optimality Theory (Xu, 2011; Xu & Aronoff, 2011). The only difference is that with construction constraints, the morphophonological output may simply be an idiosyncratic phonological property of a construction rather than the

---

form; that is, it is unclear whether native speakers have connections between schemas like [NEGATIVE] and [PERFECTIVE] that both employ a {L} overlay. Here, I will assume there are no such connections.

[7] In principle, free variation could arise if two schemas were matched for strength; this would amount to two constraints that are either unranked with respect to one another or have the same weight, depending upon the mechanism of constraint evaluation.

8.5. The morphological representation of tonal overlays

instantiation of a morphosyntactic feature itself; for further discussion, see McPherson (2014).

In this approach, all applicable constructions in a spell-out domain are evaluated simultaneously, rather than structure being built incrementally from the bottom up. This crucially allows for the result of competitions to be determined on a construction-by-construction basis, rather than adhering to a fixed morphosyntactic hierarchy (with either the lowest or the highest applicable form being realized in the output).

The network connections shown in (17) are represented in the form of a tableau in (18):

(18) *Tableau for the Tommo So negative imperative*

/jɔ̀bɔ́/ [NEG, IMP]	{L} ↔ [NEGATIVE]	{H} ↔ [IMPERATIVE]	-gú ↔ [NEG, IMP]
a. jɔ̀bɔ́	*!	*	*
b. jɔ̀bɔ́-gú	*!	*	
c. jɔ́bɔ́^{H}-gú	*!		
☞ d. jɔ̀bɔ̀^{L}-gú		*	
e. jɔ̀bɔ̀^{L}		*	*!

The input consists of the root (assumed to be spelled out in vP) and the inflectional features. The applicable construction constraints in this case are the two tonal schemas for [NEGATIVE] and [IMPERATIVE] and the portmanteau suffix *-gú* for the negative imperative. The negative schema must outrank the imperative schema, since {L} surfaces in the ouput; candidates like (c) realizing the {H} overlay are not selected. It does not matter where the suffixal construction is ranked, since candidate (e), which does not realize the suffix, is harmonically bounded by candidate (d), which realizes both {L} and *-gú*. I presume a constraint against multiple exponence, such as *FEATURE SPLIT (Xu and Aronoff 2011), is low ranked in Tommo So, allowing two exponents of [NEGATIVE] to surface.

The negative tonal schema is outranked, however, by the {HL} schema for the perfective relative, as illustrated in the following tableau:

(19) *Tableau for the Tommo So negative perfective relative*

/jɔ̀bɔ́/ [NEG, PFV, +REL]	{HL} ↔ [PFV, +REL]	{L} ↔ [NEG]	-lí ↔ [NEG, PFV]
a. jɔ̀bɔ́	*!	*	*
b. jɔ̀bɔ́-lí	*!	*	
c. jɔ̀bɔ̀ᴸ-lí	*!		
☞ d. jɔ́bɔ̀ᴴᴸ-lí		*	
e. jɔ́bɔ̀ᴴᴸ		*	*!

Candidate (d) is selected as winner, which violates the tonal schema for the negative but satisfies the higher-ranked {HL} schema for the perfective relative.[8]

The crucial ranking of tonal schemas in Tommo So verbal inflection is shown in (20):

(20) {HL} ↔ [PFV, +REL] ≫ {L} ↔ [NEG] ≫ {HL} ↔ [IPFV, -REL], {L} ↔ [PFV], {H} ↔ [IMP]

To summarize, the construction constraint approach outlined here is better able to account for the data on at least two points: First, tonal overlays can themselves instantiate morphosyntactic features through the use of a constructional template, removing the need for floating tones and a separate mechanism of assigning them to the stem; they do not need to be associated solely with affixes with which they cooccur. Second, and most importantly, constructional schemas for overlays are allowed to compete with one another globally, and language-specific rankings (representing the strength of network connections in the lexicon) predict which overlay is applied. This makes the prediction that we should see both languages in which, e.g., aspect beats negation and vice versa. In the next section, I briefly provide evidence supporting this prediction.

8.6 Other languages

IF WE LOOK BEYOND TOMMO SO at other languages in the Dogon language family, we can see how each language follows its own path with regards

---

[8] The surface form is actually [jɔ́bɔ̀-lì], with L tone on the suffix, but this is accounted for by a phonological constraint *HLH (Cahill, 2007; Hyman, 2010; McPherson, 2016; Yip, 2002) which applies exceptionlessly in Tommo So. I assume this to be part of the phonological component, which applies to the output of the morphological component.

to inflectional tonal overlays (or lack thereof). In Jamsay (Heath, 2008), for example, [NEGATIVE] takes precedence over all other categories, regardless of clause type; there are no identifiable sub-patterns, since all other overlays apply to just a single cell, though we can hypothesize that an overlay like {HL} may have applied to all perfective relatives, as in Tommo So. This is demonstrated in the following table of overlays:

(21) *Paradigm of tonal overlays for Jamsay*

	MCA	MCN	RCA	RCN
IPFV	X+L		X	
PFV	L	L	HL	L
IMP	H/X		--	--

In the imperfective MCA above, "+L" indicates a floating L tone that docks to the right edge of the stem. As noted in §8.5.1 above, it is cases like these that make it difficult to treat replacive overlays as floating tones as well.

To account for the Jamsay patterns in the constraint-based framework presented here, the ranking of {HL} ↔ [PFV, +REL] and {L} ↔ [NEG] would need to be reversed with respect to Tommo So.

In Nanga (Heath, 2016), on the other hand, [NEGATIVE] plays little role. Instead, combinations of aspectual features with [±REL] apply. It is possible that {L} corresponds to [NEG, +REL], with this overlay trumped by {HL} in the perfective, but it is difficult to determine this from the data.

(22) *Paradigm of tonal overlays for Nanga*

	MCA	MCN	RCA	RCN
IPFV	X+HH		X	L
PFV	L		HL	
IMP	X+H	X	--	--

Nanga has two forms that could be fruitfully analyzed with floating tones, main clause imperfectives, whose final two moras are typically H-toned, and the imperative, with a final H tone.[9]

Comparing these three related Dogon languages, we see the reappearance of cognate tonal overlays: {HL} for [PFV, +REL], {L} for [NEG], {L} also for [PFV, -REL]. But the relative strength of each tonal schema in the network of

---

[9] There are minor complications in Nanga verbal tonology, including changes tied to subject agreement and different behavior depending upon stem length and final vowel. I have attempted to extract the main generalizations here, but any full analysis of Nanga verbal inflection will necessarily be more complicated. See Heath (2016) Chap. 10 for more in-depth discussion.

the lexicon differs, resulting in different surface patterns. The rankings for the three languages are compared in (23):

(23) a. *Tommo So:*
{HL} ↔ [PFV, +REL] ≫ {L} ↔ [NEG] ≫ {HL} ↔ [IPFV, -REL], {L} ↔ [PFV], {H} ↔ [IMP]

b. *Jamsay*
{L} ↔ [NEG] ≫ {HL} ↔ [PFV, +REL], {X+L} ↔ [IPFV, -REL], {L} ↔ [PFV], {H} ↔ [IMP]

c. *Nanga*
{X+HH} ↔ [IPFV, -REL], {L} ↔ [PFV, -REL], {HL} ↔ [PFV, +REL] ≫ {L} ↔ [NEG, +REL], {X+H} ↔ [IMP, -NEG]

This approach could hold equal promise beyond Dogon, such as in the complex verbal tonology of Bantu, where the appearance and position of a grammatical "melodic H" depends on morphosyntactic features (e.g. Odden and Bickmore 2014 and other articles in the volume) or the deeply intricate grammatical tone paradigms of Oto-Manguean (e.g. Palancar 2017).

8.7 Conclusion

I HAVE ATTEMPTED TO DIVE BELOW THE SURFACE of Tommo So verbal inflection and determine *what* its replacive tonal overlays are and *how* they are implemented in the grammar. As I have argued, tonal overlays are best considered independent exponents of morphosyntactic features that combine with portmanteau AMN suffixes in a system of multiple exponence. When multiple overlays are applicable to a single form, the overlay with greater network strength is applied, formalized as a constraint-based grammar. Crucially, these competitions are evaluated globally rather than incrementally, and network strengths (formalized as constraint ranking) are determined not by morphosyntactic hierarchies but on a language-specific basis.

Of course, it is possible to analyze the data in other ways. For instance, it is possible to view it as root allomorphy in a DM model, brushing aside the criticism of economy with the response that memory is cheap. Similarly, overlays could be viewed as cophonological grammars associated with portmanteau morphemes, even though it creates redundancies in the lexicon (e.g. by needing both ^{L}-lí and ^{HL}-lí), since language is, after all, full of redundancies. The analysis I have put forth in this paper benefits from parsimony and the fact that the same machinery is required to account for phrase-level tonal overlays, thus reconciling the two systems of replacive tone in the language.

Regardless of the ultimate analysis, the final point I wish to make here is that systems of inflectional tone offer a wealth of challenging data that push the boundaries of our morphological theories. It may be these data that are a deciding factor for one framework over another. I echo Palancar and Léonard (2017): It is time to bring inflectional tone out of the realm of the descriptive, to disentangle it, and to treat it not as an anomalous eccentricity of a small handful of languages but as a crucial element of inflectional morphology that any framework must address.

Acknowledgments

I am deeply indebted to Russ Schuh for shaping me into the linguist that I am today. He shared with me his non-wavering commitment to data, to figuring out the puzzles of language, and to think outside of the theoretical box. He was an encyclopedic resource on African languages as I worked on the grammar of Tommo So, and it is to him that I dedicate this article. I am also grateful to Bruce Hayes, for pushing me on the finer points of theory, and to Larry Hyman for many stimulating conversations about tone and competitions. Finally, thanks to Laura Kalin for her morphosyntactic insights in the preparation of this chapter. All errors and oversights are my own.

9

Unexpected Athabaskan pronouns

Maura O'Leary
University of California, Los Angeles

Blake Lehman
University of California, Los Angeles

9.1 Introduction

IN RECENT RESEARCH ON ATHABASKAN languages there has been much discussion on the distribution of Athabaskan object pronouns. Most Athabaskan languages have at least two third person singular object pronouns, and the factors which determine their distribution are widely debated. Theories include inverse voice (M. Willie, 2000), a topic/focus distinction (Hale, Jelinek, and Willie 2003; Jelinek and Willie 1996; Thompson 1989; M. Willie 1991, 2000; M. A. Willie and Jelinek 2014, a.o.), animacy (Hale, 1973; Thompson, 1996), and obviation (Aissen, 2000; Rice & Saxon, 2001; Thompson,

1989, 1996). No one theory seems to account for all Athabaskan languages, although it is generally accepted that the pronouns all stem from the same proto-Athabaskan roots.

Hän is an Athabaskan language spoken in Eagle, Alaska, US and the Dawson City area, Yukon Territory, Canada. It is extremely endangered and there are only six remaining speakers. Like other Athabaskan languages, Hän has two third person singular object pronouns occurring in complementary distribution. However, unlike with other Athabaskan languages, the distribution of Hän's pronouns can be predicted from syntax alone.

Using data collected through original field work, in this paper we provide a description and analysis of the distribution of Hän pronouns, as well as a comparison to recent accounts provided for other Athabaskan languages. We propose that there is an object position within transitive Hän verb phrases which is obligatorily filled. When this position is not filled by an overt object DP (in situ), it is filled by an object pronoun. Within this position, there are two third person object pronouns. One pronoun, *yë-*, is used when the subject is also third person. The other, *wë-*, is used when the subject is first or second person.

9.2 Basic Hän data

9.2.1 When to use objects

Hän object pronouns are used whenever an overt object is not directly adjacent to the verb. Thus, object pronouns are used when there is no overt object DP or when the object DP is in some other way non-adjacent to the verb (topicalization, adverbs intervening, etc.).

In general, the Hän word order is subject-object-verb:[1, 2]

(1) łąyy shär nähtthè'
dog bear barked.at.PFV
'The dog barked at the bear.'

When a third person subject DP is omitted, no pronoun takes its place:

(2) shär nähtthè'
bear barked.at.PFV
'It barked at the bear.'

However, when a third person object DP is omitted, a pre-verbal pronoun is used:

(3) łąyy yë-nähtthè'
dog 3O-barked.at.PFV
'The dog barked at it.'

Third person object pronouns are not only used when there is no overt object DP, as in (3). They are used whenever the object DP is not directly before the verb. For instance, (4) shows an example of topicalization in Hän, where the object, as the topic, has been moved to the beginning of the sentence. In sentences like this, where the object DP is not adjacent to the verb, an object pronoun is inserted:

---

[1] Abbreviations used in the morpheme glosses of this paper are the following: 1 = 1st person, 2 = 2nd person, 3 = 3rd person, FOC = focus marker, IMPF = imperfective, O = object, PFV = perfective, POSS = possessive, S = subject. In this paper, we use the practical orthography developed for the Eagle dialect of Hän. This orthography is largely phonemic, with most consonant symbols based on English consonants. The following is the list of Hän orthographic consonants: <b, t, d, t', k, g, k', ', tth, ddh, tth', ts, dz, ts', ch, j, ch', dhs, z, sr, zr, ł, kh, gh, h, m, w, n, r, l, y>. An apostrophe following a consonant shows that it is glottalized. For each stop/affricate, the three symbols correspond to voiceless aspirated, plain voiceless, and glottalized versions. Glottal stop is represented as <'>, and <h> is as in English. Additionally, <l> is a lateral fricative when in onset position and a sonorant as a coda. Hän has eight vowels, which, orthographically, are <i, e, a, ë, ö, u, o, ä>. The back non-low vowels <u, o> are rounded. All vowels except <ë, ö> can be written as long by doubling them. The same vowels all also have nasal counterparts, written with an ogonek accent. Low tone is represented by the grave accent over the vowel, while high tone is not written. <ë, ö> represent schwa (or a similar default vowel): <ë> in open prefix syllables, <ö> in stems. For more detail concerning Hän orthography, see Michael Krauss' introduction to Ridley (1983).

[2] It should be noted that this sentence cannot mean 'The bear barked at the dog.' Topicalization is possible in Hän, allowing a somewhat free argument order, but such topicalization is always marked by a preverbal pronoun (see O'Leary (2017) for more information on topicalization in Hän). For any sentences that could receive more than one interpretation, both interpretations are given.

9.2. Basic Hän data

(4) shär łąyy yë-nähtthè'
bear dog 3O-barked.at.PFV

'The dog barked at the bear.'
(*lit.* 'The bear, the dog barked at it.')

Note that the pronouns are used when the object DP as a whole is not adjacent to the verb. Object pronouns are never used when the object DP, no matter how large, is adjacent to the verb.

In the examples in (5), object DPs are marked with square brackets. In (5a), the object is modified by a focus marker and in (5b) the object is modified by a relative clause. However, since both DPs are immediately adjacent to the verb, any use of object pronouns is ungrammatical.

(5) a. John [sh-cär nöö] (*yë-)nè'ąyy
John my-car FOC (*3O-)3sGS.stole.PFV

'It was my car that John stole.'

b. Percy [eyy shär łąyy y-è'àww] (^yë-) jehk'ah
Percy that bear dog 3O-bit (*3O-) 3sGS.shot.PFV

'Percy shot the bear that the dog bit.'

9.2.2 Distribution of yë- and wë-

Hän has two 3rd person object pronouns: *yë-* and *wë-*. Above, we showed that *yë-* is only used when there is no overt object DP adjacent to the verb. *Wë-* follows the same distributional pattern.

These two pronouns occur in complementary distribution. *Yë-* is used when the subject is third person as well, as in (6a). *Wë-*, on the other hand, is used when the subject is first or second person, as seen in (6b).

(6) a. yë- (used when the subject is 3rd person):
yë-dädąhch'ee
3sGO-3sGS.depend.on.IMPF

'He/she depends on him/her.'

b. wë- (used when the subject is 1st or 2nd person):
wë-dädökch'ee
3sGO-1sGS.depend.on.IMPF

'I depend on him/her.'

The distribution of *yë-* and *wë-* is based purely on the person features of the subject. In the following section we describe why this is a rather surprising finding, based on the distribution of similar pronouns in other Athabaskan languages.

9.3 Other Athabaskan Pronouns

IN OTHER ATHABASKAN LANGUAGES, as in Hän, the pronouns corresponding to *yë-* and *wë-* function as third person object pronouns. These pronouns are all descended from the Proto-Athabaskan *yə- and *wə-, and are normally referred to as *yi-/bi-* pronouns, or simply y/b pronouns (Thompson, 1996).

The distribution of these pronouns varies across languages within the Athabaskan family. Broadly, there are two patterns that the y/b pronouns follow. In Apachean (Southern Athabaskan) languages, they are used obligatorily in every transitive sentence, while in Northern Athabaskan languages, they are used only when there is no overt object DP in the sentence (Rice & Saxon, 2001). Hän, as shown above, does not quite follow either of these patterns.

In both Southern and other Northern Athabaskan languages, the y/b pronouns only occur when the subject of the clause is also third person. In contrast, in Hän, *wë-* appears when the sentence subject is first or second person (see (8) above).

Additionally, the function of the y/b alternation in Hän diverges from the function of the same alternation in other Athabaskan languages. In other languages, the alternation has been argued to encode a number of distinctions, including focus or topicality (Hale et al., 2003; Platero, 1982; Rice & Saxon, 2001; Thompson, 1996; Uyechi, 1996), animacy (Hale, 1973; Thompson, 1996), obviation (Aissen, 2000; Thompson, 1989; M. Willie, 1991), and inverse voice (Thompson, 1996; M. Willie, 2000). In this section, examples of the distribution and function of y/b pronouns in several Athabaskan languages will be examined both as an overview of the role these pronouns play in the Athabaskan family and to contrast that role with our proposed analysis for Hän *yë-/wë-*, which is outlined in Section 9.4.

9.3.1 Focus/topicality

In Apachean languages, the y/b alternation has been argued to encode animacy (Hale, 1973), and more recently, topicality (Hale et al., 2003; Rice & Saxon, 2001; Thompson, 1996; Uyechi, 1996). This section gives examples

9.3. Other Athabaskan Pronouns

from two Apachean languages, Jicarilla Apache and Navajo, showing how the y/b alternation encodes topicality in these languages.

The following examples from Jicarilla Apache show how the y/b alternation in that language encodes topicality. The reflex of the 'y' pronoun, *yi-*, occurs when the subject is topical, as in (7a). Evidence for the topicality of the subject noun phrase *'ishkiyįį* 'boy' comes from the fact that (7a) is elicited as a response to the question 'What did the boy do?'. The reflex of the 'b' pronoun, *mi-* occurs when the object is topical, as in (7b). In this sentence, the object *chékéé* 'girl' is the topic, supported by the fact that this sentence is elicited by the question 'What happened to the girl?'.

(7) Jicarilla Apache
    a. 'ishkiyįį chékéé y-aa'į
        boy   girl   YI-sees

       'The boy sees the girl'   (Uyechi, 1996: 127)
       (*Answer to* 'What did the boy do?')

    b. chékéé 'ishkiyįį m-aa'į
        girl   boy   BI-sees

       'The girl is seen by the boy'   (Uyechi, 1996: 127)
       (*Answer to* 'What happened to the girl?')

The Jicarilla Apache data shows how the y/b alternation encodes topicality in cases where there are verb-external subject and object DPs. The following data, from Navajo, shows a case where this pronoun alternation also encodes topicality, but when both subject and object are pronominal.

In Navajo, as in Jicarilla Apache, the 'y' pronoun, *yi-*, is used when the subject is topical. In (8), the pronominal third person subject is topical, so the verb is marked by *yi-*. The sentence in (8) is elicited as the answer to 'What did he do?', providing evidence that the pronominal subject is indeed topical.

(8) Navajo

    yiztał
    YI-3sGO-3sGS-kick.PFV

    'He (topic) kicked him'   (Rice & Saxon, 2001: 1)
    (*Answer to* 'What did he do?')

The only way that (9) differs from (8) is that the object, rather than the subject, of the verb 'kick' is topical. In this case, the verb is marked with *bi-*. This sentence answers the question 'What happened to him?'.

(9) bistał
BI-3sGO-3sGS-kick.PFV

'He (topic) was kicked by him.'/'He kicked him (topic).'
(*Answer to* 'What happened to him?')

In addition to providing the *yi-/bi-* alternation as encoding topicality, the Navajo examples show that the alternation is not directly associated with subject/object inversion in that language, as both subject and object are pronominal in (8) and (9).

In Koyukon, a Northern Athabaskan language, Thompson (1996) argues that the pronominal distinction encodes an "inverse voice" construction, which is similar, but not identical to the topicality distinction seen in the Apachean languages. In this construction "a clause with a topical (or more important) object is marked differently than one in which the subject is the more topical argument" (Thompson, 1996: 88). Although this definition sounds similar to the straightforward topicality analysis for Jicarilla Apache and Navajo, the following examples will show that inverse voice is a slightly different construction. In Koyukon, *ye-* can mark both subject and object. When the object is less topical than the subject, *ye-* marks the object (10b). When the object is more topical than the subject, the object is represented by *be-*, with *ye-* appearing as the subject pronoun position (10a).

(10) Koyukon
   a. be–ye–neeł'aanh
      3sGO–3sGS-see

      'S/he is looking at him/her (topic).'   (Thompson, 1996: 88)
   b. ye-neeł'aanh
      3sGO–see

      'S/he (topic) is looking at him/her.'

Koyukon is one of a number of Athabaskan languages that does not allow subject/object inversion, so the alternation between *ye-* and *be-* may be related to topicality or discourse referent tracking in this language. The fact that, in certain circumstances like (10a), both *ye-* and *be-* can occur in the same clause will be relevant to the proposed analysis of the y/b alternation in Hän outlined in Section 4.

The function of the y/b alternation in Hän does not appear to be related to topicality/focus or any type of inverse construction. The following examples show cases in which a subject can be topicalized/focused without the use of either a 'y' or 'b' pronoun (11a), an object can be topicalized/focused with no object pronoun (11b), and (11c) shows that leftward movement of an object DP requires the use of a pronoun (*yë-*).

(11) a. Topical/focused subject, no pronoun
[John nöö] sh-cär (*yë-)nè'ąyy
John FOC my-car (*3O-)3sGS.steal.PFV

'It was John who stole my car.'

b. Topical/focused object, no pronoun
John [sh-cär nöö] (*yë-)nè'ąyy
John my-car FOC (*3O-)3sGS.steal.PFV

'It was my car that John stole.'

c. Leftward movement of object DP, pronoun required
[Sh-cär nöö] John *(yë-)nè'ąyy
my-car FOC John *(3O-)3sGS.steal.PFV

'It was my car that John stole.'

The above examples show that a topicality or focus analysis will not be able to account for the distribution of y/b pronouns in Hän, as well as suggesting that the alternation is more of a syntactic than pragmatic or semantic phenomenon in Hän than in any of Jicarilla Apache, Navajo, or Koyukon.

9.3.2 Animacy

In Hän's closest linguistic and geographic neighbor, Gwich'in, the y/b alternation behaves in an entirely different way from Jicarilla Apache, Navajo, and Koyukon. First, in Gwich'in these pronouns occur only as oblique objects (objects of postpositions). The alternation of the y/b pronouns (Gwich'in reflexes *ya-/va-*) in this language is determined by the animacy of the subject. In (12), the subject is 'Susan', and animate subject; the oblique pronominal object is realized as *ya-*:

(12) Gwich'in

Susan yakak nadhat
Susan y-on stand.IMPF

'Susan is standing on it/him/her.' (Thompson, 1996: 86)

In (13), the subject is *kii* 'rock', which is inanimate. In this sentence, which forms a near minimal pair with (12), the pronominal oblique object is realized as *va-*:

(13) Kii vakak nànaii
 rock b-on fall.PFV
 'A rock fell on it/him/her.'

The above examples show primarily how the y/b alternation in Gwich'in encodes animacy. Another important aspect of the function of alternation that can be taken away from these examples is that the y/b alternation, although it involves object pronouns, can be conditioned by features of the subject as well as of the object. This will be important for determining the function of the y/b alternation in Hän in the following section.

9.3.3 Other Athabaskan languages

Although the main categories of analyses proposed for the y/b alternation throughout the Athabaskan language family are topicality and animacy, as discussed above, there are other characteristics of the distribution of these pronouns in several languages in the family that appear to be relevant to the analysis of Hän *yë-/wë-*.

In Hupa, a Pacific Coast Athabaskan language spoken in Northwest California, *yi-* is a subject prefix, while *bi-/mi-* is an oblique object prefix and a possessor prefix (Thompson, 1996: 92). This lends more support to a relationship between at least the 'y' pronoun and the subject of a clause. Further support for this relationship can be seen in the fact that in other Athabaskan languages, the third person object pronoun is always null when the subject is non-third person (Young & Morgan, 1980: 64). This is similar to the Hän *yë-/wë-* alternation, with *wë-* appearing wherever an object pronoun in other languages would be expected to be null.

As discussed above for Koyukon, subject/object inversion does not appear to play a role in the distribution of y/b pronouns in other Athabaskan languages, despite initial appearances. The paradigm from San Carlos Apache shown below provides further evidence for this fact. *Yi-* and *bi-* are oblique object pronouns in this language, and the four sentences below show that both pronouns can occur regardless of the order of verb-external subject and object.

(14) San Carlos Apache
   a. O S b-V
      John gat   biká' nagu
      John cedar b-on fall.PFV

      'The cedar fell on John.' (Thompson, 1996: 84)
   b. S O b-V
      gat   John biká' nagu
      cedar John b-on fall.PFV

      'The cedar fell on John.'
   c. S O y-V
      John gat   yiká' nagu
      John cedar y-on fall.PFV

      'John fell on the cedar.'
   d. O S y-V
      gat   John yikà' nagu
      cedar John y-on fall.PFV

      'John fell on the cedar.'

In Eyak, a member of the Na-Dené family (along with Athabaskan languages and Tlingit) the general third person object pronoun is '*u*- (cognate with Hän *wë*-) (Thompson, 1996: 94). This pronoun occurs in all constructions that involve a third person pronominal object and does not alternate with the Eyak reflex of the 'y' pronoun. This will be relevant to our proposed analysis of the Hän *yë-/wë-* alternation below, as we will argue *wë-* is actually always present in third person pronominal object constructions. The fact that this type of distribution of the 'b' pronoun is attested in a related language lends support to this type of analysis.

Despite the above evidence, the pattern of distribution of y/b pronouns in the Athabaskan family as a whole is far from clear or uniform. While the pronouns are derived from the same historical source, their function in each language appears to vary greatly. The following section proposes an analysis of the alternation in Hän that is unique among previous analyses of the phenomenon in other languages in the family.

9.4 Theoretical account for Hän

HÄN'S TWO THIRD PERSON OBJECT PRONOUNS clearly behave differently than analogous pronouns in other Athabaskan languages. And it seems that the use and distribution of these pronouns can be predicted based only on syntax. More specifically, the pronouns are used when there is no overt object DP directly next to the verb, and the choice of *yë-* vs *wë-* is based on the person feature of the subject. This section proposes a theoretical account for these two observations.

9.4.1 When do the pronouns occur?

First, we must establish what triggers the use of object pronouns in Hän. They are used whenever there is no overt object DP (as in (3) repeated below as (15a), or when the object DP is not adjacent to the verb (as in (4) repeated below as (15b).

(15) a. łąyy yë-nähtthè'
   dog 3OBJ-barked.at.PFV
   'The dog barked at it.'

     b. shär łąyy yë-nähtthè'
   bear dog 3O-barked.at.PFV
   'The dog barked at the bear.'
   (*lit.* 'The bear, the dog barked at it.')

We propose that the object DP originates in an object position within transitive VPs, and that in Hän, this position must be filled for the sentence to be grammatical. Therefore, whenever the object position is not filled by the full object DP, it is filled by an object pronoun instead.

For instance, if the object DP is moved from its original position, a pronoun is inserted to fill the empty object position left behind. In (16), the full DP is topicalized to the left periphery (Manker, 2014; O'Leary, 2017; Rizzi, 1997). The object DP position cannot be left empty, and so the object pronoun *yë-* is inserted in the gap left by the topicalized object to create the grammatical sentence which was seen in (15b).

9.4. Theoretical account for Hän

(16)

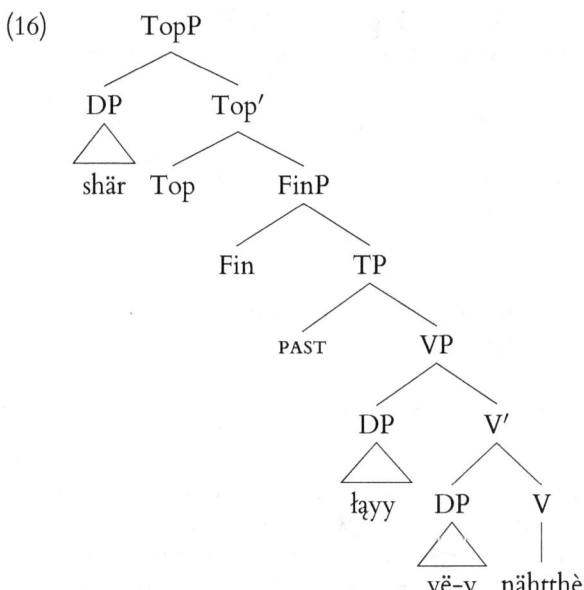

9.4.2 Distribution of wë- and yë-

The other observation that should be formally explained is the distribution of *wë-* and *yë-*. So far we have seen that *yë-* is used when the subject is third person and *wë-* is used when the subject is first or second person. We propose that *wë-* is the underlying form of both object pronouns in Hän, and that it undergoes a morphophonological change under the right conditions to become *yë-*.

A strong piece of evidence supporting this theory is that *wë-* is the prefix used for third person singular possessives:

(17) Third person singular possessive:

wë-'ìww
3SG.POSS–beads

'his/her beads'

All other object pronouns (which are realized as verbal prefixes) are identical to their possessive counterparts. As shown in Table 9.1 and Table 9.2, every object pronoun is identical to the possessive prefix of the same person and number, with the exception of the third person singular pronoun *yë-*.

	Singular	Plural
1st person	shë-	ni-
2nd person	në-	khwë-
3rd person	wë-/yë-	hu-

Table 9.1: Object pronouns/prefixes

	Singular	Plural
1st person	shë-	ni-
2nd person	në-	khwë-
3rd person	wë-	hu-

Table 9.2: Possessive prefixes

If the underlying third person singular object pronoun is, as we have proposed, always *wë-* underlyingly, then we would have the added benefit that there would be no difference between object pronoun prefixes and possessive prefixes. If the underlying third person singular object morpheme is *wë-*, then there must be some process that creates *yë-* when the subject is also third person.

In Hän morphology, null morphemes commonly effect the phonological realization of adjacent morphemes. For instance, each verb stem is associated with one of four classifier morphemes: *-d-*, *-l-*, *-ł-*, or ∅. Each of these morphemes, including the null classifier, drastically changes the phonological realization of the adjacent subject pronouns (which, like object pronouns are realized as verbal prefixes).

Another relevant feature of Hän verbal morphology, which is largely templatic, is that subject morphemes occur in several different morpheme "slots" depending on the subject's person and number features. All singular subjects as well as second person plural subjects are represented by morphemes that occur directly before the verb. These morphemes are phonologically affected by/combined with the adjacent classifier and modal morphemes; with that in mind, we have listed these morphemes together in the template in (18) below. The third person and first person plural subject agreement morphemes each have their own slot within the complex morpheme template. A template showing the order of the relevant verbal prefixes is shown in (18):

(18) Subject and object prefix template:
 3plS–O–1plS–...–Class/Subj/Aspect-Verb

9.4. Theoretical account for Hän

Based on the wide spread of subject agreement morphemes, we believe that there could easily be other templatic slots which contain morphemes that are inflected based on subject features. Therefore, we propose that there is a morpheme directly preceding the object morpheme which shows agreement with the person features of the subject. This is similar to Navajo, which also has a subject agreement position directly before the object (Speas, 1990).

To account for the Hän data, we propose that the first and second person subject agreement morpheme is ∅, shown in (19a). The third person subject agreement morpheme is *y-*, shown in (19b).[3]

(19) a. 1st/2nd person agreement morpheme ∅:
(hë)-∅-wë-(trë)-...
3PLS–OAgr–3sGO–1PLS–...–verb

b. 3rd person agreement morpheme -*y-*:
(hë)-y-wë-(trë)-...
3PLS–OAgr–3sGO–1PLS–...–verb

When the 3rd person subject agreement marker *y-* co-occurs with the third person singular object pronoun *wë-*, they merge to make *yë-*, as shown in (20). We propose that the 3rd person subject agreement marker *y-* phonologically impacts only the third person singular object pronoun and not any of the other object pronouns, as the other pronouns do not begin with glides and are unaffected by /j-/.

(20) a. Underlying:
y–wë–dädạhch'ee
3S–3sgO–3sgS.depend.on.IMPF

b. Surface:
yë–dädạhch'ee
3S+3sgO–3sgS.depend.on.IMPF

'He/she depends on him/her.'

This theory, of course, splits what used to be one alternating pronoun into two separate adjacent morphemes. Under this theory, the historical *y-* and *b-*

---

[3] The third person plural subject and first person plural subject morphemes which occur on either side of the object morphemes are both provided in the template, although they would clearly never co-occur. Additionally, *wë-* would never co-occur with the third person plural subject morpheme, and *yë-* would never co-occur with the first person plural subject morpheme. Note that other subject morphemes (besides third plural and first plural) are expressed in a single morpheme along with classifier and aspect immediately before the verb stem.

pronouns do not fill the same slot in the Hän verbal morpheme template. In fact, the theory that we suggest above assume that the Hän equivalents of *y-* and *b-* co-occur.

If this is correct, then the co-occurence of *y-* and *b-* is not unique to Hän. In Koyukon, another Athabaskan language, the two pronouns also co-occur:

(21) Koyukon

be-ye-neeł'aanh
3sGO-3sGS-see

'S/he is looking at him/her (topic).' (Thompson, 1996: 88)

9.5 Summary

WE PRESENT HERE THAT the distribution of object pronouns in Hän is drastically different that the distributions in other Athabaskan languages, despite the likelihood that they all descended from the same Proto-Athabaskan pronouns. Other Athabaskan object pronouns are distributed based on topic, voice, animacy, or other semantic factors. On the other hand, Hän third person singular object pronouns are distributed based on purely syntactic features.

Hän object pronouns occur whenever there is no overt object DP adjacent to the verb, which we posit is due to an object position within the VP that must be filled in order to create a grammatical (transitive) sentence. Within that position, one object pronoun is used when the subject is third person, and the other elsewhere. We propose that the object pronoun is always *wë-* underlyingly, and that a third person subject pronoun *y-* may precede it, leading to a surface *yë-* when the subject and object are both third person.

We hope that further research into the distribution and behavior of these pronouns will lead to a more complete understanding of the incredibly complex verbal domain found in Hän and other Athabaskan languages.

Acknowledgments

This work is based on original data collected at the 2016 Institute on Collaborative Language Research, held at the University of Alaska, Fairbanks. Many thanks to speakers Ruth Ridley, Ethel Beck, and Percy Henry, as well

9.5. Summary

as Willem De Reuse, the participants of the Hän practicum at the 2016 Institute on Collaborative Language Research, and the organizers of the same institute. This work also benefitted from comments from the participants of the 2017 Workshop on American Indigenous Languages.

10

Bole suffix doubling as morphotactic extension

Kevin M. Ryan
Harvard University

10.1 Introduction

SUFFIX DOUBLING IN BOLE is a type of multiple exponence, in the sense that it involves multiple realizations of a single morphological feature within a single prosodic/morphological word (Caballero and Harris 2012, Caballero and Inkelas 2013, Harris 2017). More specifically, it is a case of semantically vacuous affix repetition, whereby the same morpheme appears multiple times within the word without independent justification from syntax, semantics, or phonology. This type of repetition is to be distinguished from cases of multiple affixation in which each instance contributes independently to the meaning. In (1), for instance, the Tagalog causative prefix *pa* can be repeated indefinitely, but each repetition introduces another causative shell (Maclachlan 1989). Thus, there is no multiple exponence.

10.1. Introduction

(1) a. pa-kulóʔ   'to boil something'
     b. pa-pa-kulóʔ   'to make someone boil something'
     c. pa-pa-pa-kulóʔ   'to cause someone to make someone boil something'

Furthermore, multiple exponence is usually taken to exclude compound-like structures with multiple inflection that can be analyzed as agreement. For example, Vedic Sanskrit has a type of compound called a "double dual" in which each member is inflected for the dual, even though each member is semantically singular (Ryan 2006, Kiparsky 2010). In other words, the inflections reflect the total number of the compound, not the number of each member. *Mātárāpitárā* in (2) is an example.

(2) maːtár -aː   =pitár -aː
    mother -DUAL =father -DUAL

'mother and father' (both semantically singular)

A case of non-vacuous repetition from Bole is given in (3) (Gimba 2000). The same pronominal suffix *mu* 'we' is repeated in two places in the clitic group, but this is not a case of multiple exponence, as the two *mu*s arguably have different uses: The first indicates the subject, while the second modifies 'body,' serving as an "intransitive copy pronoun" (see §10.3). (Incidentally, the PL-1PL sequence in (3) *is* a case of multiple exponence, but not one involving affix repetition of the type that is the focus of this paper.)[1]

(3) 'yòr -áː -mú   =jìː -mú
    stand -PL -1PL =body -1PL

'(let's) stand!'

Finally, because the Bole verbs analyzed below involve vacuous repetition of the same morpheme, they are unlike cases of multiple exponence involving redundant specification of a feature using distinct morphemes. Examples of this type from Choguita Rarámuri are provided in (4) (Caballero 2008).

(4) a. pá   -s   -ki   -ma
       throw -APPL -APPL -FUT.SG

'he/she/it will throw for someone'

---

[1] I employ the following abbreviations: 1, 2, 3 (first, second, and third person), ADD 'additive,' APPL 'applicative,' CAUS 'causative,' F 'feminine,' FUT 'future,' FV 'final vowel,' ICP 'intransitive copy pronoun,' INF 'infinitive,' M 'masculine,' NULLO 'null object,' O 'object,' PL 'plural,' PROG 'progressive,' R 'root,' REC 'reciprocal,' S 'subject,' SG 'singular,' TOT 'totality,' and VENT 'ventive.' In some cases in Bole, the same object suffix varies in its interpretation as direct or indirect depending on extraneous factors; these are glossed appropriately, but without comment.

b. sú -n -ki -ma
sew -APPL -APPL -FUT.SG
'he/she/it will sew for someone'

Three bona fide cases of affix repetition qua multiple exponence (all three treated by Caballero and Inkelas 2013) are now reviewed before turning to the Bole data. First, in Jita, the causative suffix *y* is realized two (or more) times in certain verbs, such as (5) (Downing 2005). Note that (5) is not a double causative semantically.

(5) oku= gus -y -áːn -y -a
INF= buy -CAUS -REC -CAUS -FV
'to sell to each other'

Second, consider the Chichewa verb in (6) (Hyman 2003). The reciprocal is doubled, but, once again, the verb is not semantically a double reciprocal. The rationale for doubling is "morphocentric," as Hyman (2003) puts it (see also Ryan 2010).

(6) a- ku- máŋ -íts -an -ir -aːn -a
3PL- PROG- buy -CAUS -REC -APPL -REC -FV
'to make each other tie for'

Third, Breton plural diminutives require marking the plural both before and after the diminutive, as in (7) (Stump 1991).

(7) bag -où -ig -où
boat -PL -DIM -PL
'(little) boats'

In agreement with Caballero and Inkelas (2013) and others, such cases cannot be analyzed as reduplication or assimilation. For one thing, vacuous repetitions of the same affix almost never surface adjacent to each other cross-linguistically, in contradistinction to reduplication, where adjacency is the norm (though not without exception). This lack of adjacency also makes it difficult if not impossible for a hypothetical reduplication analysis to define the part of the base that gets copied in phonological terms, since the duplicated material is not aligned with one of the edges of the base, and may have varying prosodic profiles depending on its immediate context. In Bole, for instance, the reduplicant, if taken to be the second copy, would have to reach into its base to copy the penultimate as opposed to adjacent VC. Moreover, semantically vacuous affix repetition is unlike reduplication in that RED usually contributes independent semantic content. It is true that some cases of reduplication do not involve a contentful RED (e.g. copy epenthesis, Stanton and Zukoff forthcoming; cf. also Zuraw 2002). But the present cases are not like copy epenthesis, since they are not phonologically motivated. Finally, even if it were possible to analyze doubling as RED, it would not simplify the morphological analysis below, since one would still need to account for the conditions under which the double appears, which do not reduce to phonology.

The remainder of the paper is organized as follows. The contexts in which doubling is found in Bole are characterized in §10.2. These contexts include outside-in conditioning, by which doubling is conditioned not only by the availability of applicable doublers and interveners, but also by the morpheme immediately following the locus of the second copy, as treated further in §10.3. Some comparative notes on West Chadic are then provided in §10.4, suggesting that doubling may have arisen *in situ* in the suffix string in Bole, though this premise is not critical for the analysis that follows. An analysis in terms of bigram morphotactics is developed in §10.5 and §10.6, the latter focusing on morphotactic extension (i.e. analogy in affix ordering). Finally, §10.7 concludes by considering other possible approaches to doubling in Bole and some outstanding questions.

10.2 Contexts for doubling in Bole

BOLE, SPOKEN IN NORTHEASTERN NIGERIA (Yobe and Gombe States), is part of the Bole-Tangale subgroup of West Chadic (Afro-Asiatic). The focus here is the analysis of the rampant multiple exponence found in Bole's verbal system. Aspects of the verbal morphology that are not critical to this discussion are put aside; see Gimba (2000), Gimba and Schuh (2014), and references therein for paradigms and further background.[2] Multiple exponence in Bole involves the semantically gratuitous doubling of a suffix across another single suffix, as with plural subject agreement (PLS, boldface) in (8). In (8a–b), subject agreement /an/ doubles across object agreement /to/. In (8c), /an/ doubles across the totality extension (TOT), which might be glossed 'up' or 'well.' Note that the second copy of the doubled suffix precedes TOT in (8b) but

---

[2]Gimba's (Gimba 2000) paradigms give surface forms, such that the perfective suffix is not made explicit when it is segmentally null. As discussed in §10.3, the perfective conditions doubling even when segmentally null, so this point requires caution.

follows it in (8c).[3]

(8) a. [ŋgòrántáŋgó]
 ŋgor -an -to -an -ko
 tie -PLS -3FSGO -PLS -PERF
 'they tied her'

 b. [ŋgòrántántì]
 ŋgor -an -to -an -ti
 tie -PLS -3FSGO -PLS -TOT
 'they tied her up'

 c. [ŋgòrántùŋgó]
 ŋgor -an -ti -an -ko
 tie -PLS -TOT -PLS -PERF
 'they tied up'

The allomorphy in 8 and elsewhere in this article is phonologically conditioned, reflecting local processes such as assimilation, ablaut, resolution, and tone rules (Schuh 2001). As such, it is not important for the treatment of doubling. In every case, both copies of the doubled morpheme are reflexes of the same underlying form (e.g. /an/ in the case of PLS); there is no suppletion, portmanteaux, etc.[4] Subject agreement is confined to the perfective, but doubling not involving subject agreement is also found in other aspects.[5] The perfective is marked by /ko/ = [ko ~ go ~ wo] (various tones and lengths), though it is not realized segmentally in all perfective forms (§10.3). I usually employ the Class A1 root *ŋgor(u)*- 'tie' in examples here.

I term suffixes that can double DOUBLERS, suffixes that can intervene between doubles INTERVENERS, and suffixes that can immediately follow the second copy FOLLOWERS. All possible doublers, interveners, and followers are enumerated in Table 10.1. The doublers include all subject agreement, which

---

[3] In glossed forms from this point on, I give a surface phonetic form first, with tone, followed by a morphological parse (roughly, underlying form), without tone. This is not to imply that morphemes lack tones underlyingly; but their underlying tones, which are sometimes difficult to establish, are largely irrelevant for present purposes.

[4] The ventive suffix, for its part, comes in three suppletive allomorphs depending on aspect, but it is always the same version that doubles within a word. This concurrence is expected on the present approach. For example, the ventive that subcategorizes for the perfective could hardly be inserted in, say, a subjunctive form, regardless of how many times it is inserted.

[5] Limited subject agreement occurs also in the imperative, but does not furnish a context for doubling.

10.2. Contexts for doubling in Bole

comprises only two suffixes, namely, plural (any person) and feminine singular (2nd or 3rd person). The ventive, also known as *Entfernungserweiterung* ("indicates event initiated at a distance with effect at point of reference," Schuh p.c.), is also a doubler in both of its suppletive variants /in/ and /it/.[6] These variants are synonymous but the former is found in the perfective and the latter in the subjunctive (in Bole, Ngamo, etc.; probably reconstructable as such in Proto-Bole-Tangale).[7] The interveners include all object agreement as well as two extensions, namely, totality (Tot) and additive (Add; "sort of 'pro-adjunct'; can indicate repetition," *id*.). Schuh (p.c.) suggests that Tot and Add are "probably reconstructable" as *ti and *di, respectively, "but there are many shifts." In Bole, they are realized as such word-finally, but as [tu(ː)] and [du(ː)] nonfinally. Tot and Add cannot cooccur within a verb, but either can combine with Vent. Finally, possible followers include Tot and Perf (including its segmentally null realization). As mentioned above, Tot can be both an intervener and a follower.

Table 10.1: Suffixal doublers, interveners, and followers in Bole

Doublers	/ak/	23FsgS	/an/	Pls
	/in/	Vent	/it/	Vent
Interveners	/no/	1sgO	/mu/	1plO
	/ʃi/	2FsgO	/ko/	2MsgO
	/ku/	2plO	/su/	3plO
	/to/	3FsgO	/ni/	3MsgO
	/di/	Add	/ti/	Tot
Followers	/ko/	Perf	/ti/	Tot

A schematic representation of verb forms with doubling is provided in (9). The first copy of the doubler immediately follows either the verbal root or a post-root suffix such as ventive /aːkoː/ or a theme vowel, which do not participate in doubling.

---

[6] Suffixes given as /VC/ here might also be analyzed as /C/. This question is not critical for present purposes.

[7] A third suppletive allomorph of the ventive, namely, /aːkoː/, occurs in the future/progressive and habitual. This version is not involved with doubling.

(9) Schematic representation of verb forms with doubling

		Doubler	Intervener		Follower
Root	(Suffix)	{ Subject Agr. / Ventive }	{ Object Agr. / Additive / Totality }	Copy of Doubler	{ Perfective / Totality }

A verb with doubling is built up progressively in (10). In (10a–b), NullO indicates that the transitive verb is employed without an explicit object. When no subject agreement is explicit, the verb is interpreted as M3SG, as in (10a) and (10c). Plural subject agreement doubles in (10d) (across object agreement), but not in (10b) (across aspect). Note that /to/ is realized with a low vowel nonfinally, as in (10c–d).

(10) a. [ŋgórwòːyí]
ŋgor -ko   -yi
tie   -Perf -NullO

'he tied it'

b. [ŋgòráŋgòːyí]
ŋgor -an -ko   -yi
tie   -Pls -Perf -NullO

'they tied it'

c. [ŋgórtáːwó]
ŋgor -to   -ko
tie   -3FsgO -Perf

'he tied her'

d. [ŋgòrántáŋgó]
ŋgor -an -to   -an -ko
tie   -Pls -3FsgO -Pls -Perf

'they tied her'

An example of doubling in the subjunctive (as opposed to perfective) is given in (11). In this case, in order to set up a context for doubling, all of the examples involve the totality extension, which is always final in (11). The ventive doubles in (11d) (over object agreement), but not in (11b) (over totality). Although Tot can be an intervener, an appropriate follower is not present in (11b) to condition doubling. The subject is glossed X because subjunctives do not exhibit subject agreement. But they do exhibit object agreement, as (11c–d) exemplify. The object must be interpreted as an indirect object in this context, though it is the same /to/ as above (see footnote 1; Gimba 2000: 220).

(11) a. [ŋgòrtí]

ŋgor -ti
tie   -Tot

'that X tie (it) up'

b. [ŋgòrítí]

ŋgor -it   -ti
tie   -Vent -Tot

'that X tie (it) up and bring it'

c. [ŋgòrtáːtì]

ŋgor -to   -ti
tie   -3FsgO -Tot

'that X tie (it) up for her'

d. [ŋgòríttátti]

ŋgor **-it**   -to   **-it**   -ti
tie   -Vent -3FsgO -Vent -Tot

'that X tie (it) up for her and bring (it)'

10.3 Outside-in conditioning

AS MENTIONED IN §10.2, DOUBLING only occurs before an appropriate "follower" suffix, a case of OUTSIDE-IN CONDITIONING. Two followers are possible, namely, the totality extension /ti/ and the perfective aspect /ko/. The latter can be realized in any of its allomorphs, including segmentally null, as discussed in this section. Both followers were illustrated in §10.2. Non-doubling due to the lack of an appropriate follower is now illustrated in (12). In (12a), ventive /it/ cannot double before NULLO, despite the eligible intervener. In (12b–c), it cannot double when no suffix follows, again despite the interveners.

(12) a. [ŋgòríttàːyí]
     ŋgor -it   -to   -yi
     tie   -Vent -3FsgO -NullO
     'that X tie her and bring her'

   b. [ŋgòríttó]
     ŋgor -it   -to
     tie   -Vent -3FsgO
     'that X tie (it) for her and bring (it)'

   c. [ŋgòríttí témʃí]
     ŋgor -it   -ti   temʃi
     tie   -Vent -Tot sheep
     'that X tie up the sheep and bring it'

The lack of doubling in forms like (12) cannot be explained by phonology. In general, Bole words can end with plosives and nasals, as exemplified in (13a–b) (Gimba and Schuh 2014). This is equally true for verbs, as illustrated by (13c–d). (13d) furnishes a near-minimal pair vis-à-vis (12c). In (13d), subject agreement — /ak/, realized as [(a)t] due to assimilation — doubles across totality, yielding word-final [t]. Doubling is conditioned in (13d) by the null perfective, which is absent from (12c), a subjunctive. There is thus a morphological difference between (12c) and (13d), but the point here is that there is nothing wrong phonologically with word-final [t] arising from doubling. The explanation for the lack of doubling in (12c) must be morphological.

(13) a. [dài ʃít]
     'bright red'
   b. [ájàp]
     'amazement'
   c. [ŋgòrát tèmʃí]
     ŋgor -ak   -ko   temʃi
     tie   -23FsgS -Perf sheep
     'she tied the sheep'

   d. [ŋgòráttùt tèmʃí]
     ŋgor **-ak**   -ti   **-ak**   -ko   temʃi
     tie   -23FsgS -Tot -23FsgS -Perf sheep
     'she tied up the sheep'

10.3. Outside-in conditioning

Similarly, consider the "intransitive copy pronoun" (ICP), a subject agreement enclitic (P. Newman 1971, Schuh 1983, Gimba 2000: 150–153). Gimba (2000) suggests that the ICP is the intransitive counterpart of totality, hence my translation '(completely).' Morphologically, the ICP comprises two parts, namely, [jiː] 'body' followed by a normal pronoun (see Table 10.1), as in (14). PLS does not double in (14), as it does not contain an eligible intervener.

(14) [dáːndé 'yòrán jiːsú]

daːnde 'yor -an -ko =ji -su
children stop -PLS -PERF =body -3PLO

'the children (completely) stopped'

Doubling can apply before the ICP, but only when the (null) perfective is there to condition it, as in (15a–b). In other words, the ICP itself is not a follower, and does not condition doubling. This is clear from (15c), which has the ICP but no perfective suffix, and hence no doubling. Once again, as far as the phonology is concerned, doubling would be licit in (15c). As (15b) shows, [jj] (as would occur with doubling) is distinct from [j]. The lack of doubling in (15c) is due to the lack of an eligible follower, not phonology.

(15) a. [dáːndé 'yòrándùn jiːsú]

daːnde 'yor **-an** -di **-an** -ko =ji -su
children stop -PLS -ADD -PLS -PERF =body -3PLO

'the children (completely) stopped again'

  b. [ítá 'yòráddùj jiːtó]

ita 'yor **-ak** -di **-ak** -ko =ji -to
she stop -23FSGS -ADD -23FSGS -PERF =body -3FSGO

'she (completely) stopped again'

  c. ['yòríddí jiːnì]

'yor -it -di =ji -ni
stop -VENT -ADD =body -3MSGO

'that he stop here (completely) again'

At least five considerations favor the underlying presence of perfective /ko/ in forms like (15a–b) even when it is not realized segmentally on the surface. First, deletion occurs in a predictable context, namely, when /ko/ immediately precedes another word. Compare (16a), without deletion, to (16b), which adds 'yesterday' to the same verb, triggering deletion.

(16) a. [ŋgòrántáŋgó]
   ŋgor -an -to   -an -ko
   tie -PLS -3FSGO -PLS -PERF
   'they tied her'

   b. [ŋgòrántán nzònó]
   ŋgor -an -to   -an -ko nzono
   tie -PLS -3FSGO -PLS -PERF yesterday
   'they tied her yesterday'

Second, the perfective suffix has effects on tone even when it is segmentally null. In particular, it blocks an otherwise general process of high tone spreading to a syllable not beginning with a voiced obstruent (Gimba 2000: 140). For example, 'sheep' is /tèmʃí/. After a high-final verb, its low becomes high, as in (17a). But spreading is blocked in perfective forms such as (17b). This blocking makes sense if the perfective leaves a floating low tone even when it is segmentally unrealized. In this sense, the perfective is overtly realized even when segmentally null.

(17) a. [ŋgòrtí témʃí]
   ŋgor -ti   temʃi
   tie -TOT sheep
   'that X tie up the sheep'

   b. [ŋgòrát tèmʃí]
   ŋgor -ak   -ko temʃi
   tie -23FSGS -PERF sheep
   'she tied the sheep'

Third, as seen in passing above, certain suffixes have final and nonfinal allomorphs. Such suffixes appear in their nonfinal forms before segmentally unrealized /ko/, again suggesting that /ko/ is overt. For instance, totality /ti/ is [tu(ː)] nonfinally, as in (18a). In (18b) it remains [tuː] on the surface even though it is ostensibly final in its word, thanks to underlying /ko/.

(18) a. [ŋgórtùwó]
   ŋgor -ti   -ko
   tie -TOT -PERF
   'he tied (it) up'

b. [ŋgórtù: tèmʃí]
   ŋgor -ti   -ko temʃi
   tie -Tot -Perf sheep
   'he tied up the sheep'

Fourth, perfective /ko/ is stably realized on the surface in related languages where it is inferred in Bole (Schuh p.c.). Finally, without a uniform perfective suffix in the perfective (whether realized or not), it is more difficult to explain the distribution of doubling. For instance, doubling applies across Tot in the perfective (13d) but not in the subjunctive (12c). Schuh and I explain this contrast by invoking null /ko/ in the former. Without /ko/, one might imagine stipulating that doubling is constructionally limited to the perfective. But this would not work, since doubling occurs in the subjunctive under other circumstances. Moreover, it would miss that even in the perfective, doubling is limited to certain followers; the generalizations are positional (i.e. morphotactically conditioned), not constructional (i.e. featurally conditioned).

In sum, doubling is crucially conditioned by the suffix following the second copy. Two suffixes, the perfective and totality, trigger doubling as followers. The perfective triggers doubling even if it is segmentally unrealized, in which case other evidence, such as tone, confirms that it is still overt.

10.4 Comparative Bole-Tangale notes

SCHUH (IN HIS HALF OF RYAN AND SCHUH 2010) HIGHLIGHTS four innovations of Bole verbal morphology relative its West Chadic relatives: (1) the 23FsGS subject agreement suffix /ak/, (2) the null object suffix /yi/, (3) the elision of /ko/ (and /yi/) just discussed in §10.3, and (4) the suffix doubling that is the topic of this paper. Some Bole-Tangale cognates are provided in Tables 10.2 and 10.3, which cover Bole, Karekare, and two dialects of Ngamo. I adapt Schuh's transcription slightly for Bole to bring it into line with the rest of this paper (e.g. showing nasal assimilation), but do not do so for the other languages.

These cognate sets suggest that the emergence of multiple exponence in Bole was not due to the univerbation of formerly separate words expressing agreement, such as light verb constructions akin to 'they tied it, they did.' Rather, the whole suffix string was likely already intact when Bole innovated doubling. Compare Yaya Ngamo [ngàr-án-tó:-tì] to Bole [ŋgòr-án-tá-n-tì] 'they tied up for her.' Note that the lengthened [ó:] in Yaya corresponding to Bole [á-n] is presumably driven by open-syllable lengthening/closed-syllable

Table 10.2: Cognates in four Bole-Tangale languages: perfective verbs with a third-person plural subject. Subject agreement doubles in Bole.

	Karekare	Ngamo (Gudi)	Ngamo (Yaya)	Bole
	às-án-kò	ngàr-àn-kô	ngàr-án-kò	ŋgòr-áŋ-gòː-yí
+3FsgO	às-ân-tó	ngàr-àn-tò	ngàr-án-tǒ	ŋgòr-**án**-tá-ŋ-gó
+Tot	às-án-sì-kó	ngàr-án-kò	ngàr-án-tù-kó	ŋgòr-**án**-tù-ŋ-gó
+Tot +3FsgO	às-ân-tá-sì	ngàr-àn-tòː-tî	ngàr-án-tóː-tì	ŋgòr-**án**-tá-**n**-tì
+Vent	às-àː-néː-kò	ngàr-àː-nô	ngàr-à-nô	ŋgòrú-ŋ-gòː-yí
+Vent +3FsgO	às-àː-nê-tó	ngàrì-n-tò	ngàr-á-n-tǒ	ŋgòr-**ín**-tá-ŋ-gó

Table 10.3: Cognates in four Bole-Tangale languages: perfective verbs with a singular subject. The ventive doubles in Bole.

	Karekare	Ngamo (Gudi)	Ngamo (Yaya)	Bole
+Vent +3FsgO	às-nê-tó	ngàrì-n-tò	ngàrí-n-tǒ	ŋgòr-**ín**-tá-ŋ-gó
+Vent +Tot	às-néː-sí-kò	ngàrí-n-kò	ngàr-nó'ò	ŋgòrú-**n**-tù-ŋ-gó
+Vent +Tot +3FsgO	às-nê-tà-sí	ngàrì-n-tòː-tî	ngàrí-n-tóː-tì	ŋgòr-**ín**-tá-**n**-tì

shortening, an otherwise general process in Bole-Ngamo, and need not reflect compensatory lengthening.[8] Moreover, a light verb origin is implausible on the grounds that there were never light verbs to begin with. The perfective and totality markers never require supporting auxiliaries in Bole-Tangale; they are added directly to the root verbal complex. That said, these historical considerations are not critical for the synchronic analysis that follows, and are provided mainly by way of background. They are, however, consistent with my proposal, in that I argue that doubling is motivated by local analogical pressures in the form of bigram morphotactics.

10.5 Morphotactic analysis

Ryan (2010) argues that arbitrary affix ordering restrictions — which cannot be motivated by independent semantic, syntactic, or phonological considerations — are grammatically encoded as adjacency bigram constraints, as in (19), in which X and Y are (classes of) morphemes.

---

[8] Reconstructing the Bole doubling pattern to Proto-Bole-Tangale would be less parsimonious because doubling would then need to be lost independently in multiple branches, including at least Karekare and Ngamo (separately in the latter case, assuming that Bole and Ngamo form a subgroup to the exclusion of Karekare).

10.5. Morphotactic analysis

(19) **X-Y**: Penalize a candidate lacking X-Y.

For instance, such constraints can motivate counterscopal ordering, in which two mutually scoping affixes, such as the causative and reciprocal, are fixed in a certain order regardless of which scopes over the other. X-Y ≫ Y-X ensures that X and Y are realized in that order regardless of scope and other considerations. (Additional constraints penalize deleting or duplicating morphemes.) Ryan (2010) argues that adjacency bigrams are superior to other proposals for arbitrary ordering including precedence bigrams ("X must precede Y"; cf. Paster 2006, Caballero 2008), affix alignment (cf. Trommer 2003), affix movement (cf. Embick and Noyer 2001), and a monolithic template of more than two position classes (cf. Hyman 2003). Adjacency bigrams are argued to better capture nontransitive ordering restrictions, gradient variation in ordering (including predicting possible vs. impossible types of variation), analogical extension in ordering (as discussed presently), learnability (e.g. how are language-specific movement rules or monolithic templates inferred if not from surface adjacency relations?), and context-sensitivity in ordering (e.g. only X-Y is permitted unless Z immediately follows, in which case only Y-X is permitted).

To exemplify two such cases before returning to Bole, first, Chumbivilcas Quechua (Muysken 1988) exhibits nontransitivity in ordering (Ryan 2010). Consider the three verbal suffixes *ri* 'inchoative,' *schi* 'assistive,' and *na* 'reciprocal.' In a doubly derived verb, *ri* can only precede *schi* and *schi* can only precede *na*. If transitivity held, this would entail that *ri* precede *na* when the two cooccur. But in fact *na-ri* is the only acceptable order. This system is captured by adjacency bigrams in (20), which contains three tableaux. They cannot be motivated by a template or position class system.

(20) Adjacency bigrams in Chumbivilcas Quechua

			ri-schi	schi-na	na-ri
a.	☞	-ri-schi-		*	*
b.		-schi-ri-	*!	*	*
a.	☞	-schi-na-	*		*
b.		-na-schi-	*	*!	*
a.	☞	-na-ri-	*	*	
b.		-ri-na-	*	*	*!

Second, consider context-sensitive reorderability. In Tagalog, for instance, the "contemplated aspect" reduplicant RED is free to occur either immediately before or immediately after the prefix *ka* ("telic") when the root ("R") follows: RED-*ka*-R-an ∼ *ka*-RED-R-an (Schachter and Otanes 1972,

Ryan 2010: 766). But in verbs of the form *ka–pag*-R, RED cannot immediately follow *ka*. Schematically, X-Y ~ Y-X, except before Z. This case is akin to outside-in conditioning, in that it cannot be motivated by precedence relations alone.[9] Adjacency conditions must be invoked, as in (21), which is a simplified sketch (and not the only possible bigram analysis of this fragment). See Ryan (2010) for a full analysis of Tagalog and for other cases of context-sensitive reorderability.

(21) Context-sensitive reorderability in Tagolog

			ka-pag
a.	☞	RED-ka-R-an	*
b.	☞	ka-RED-R-an	*
a.	☞	RED-ka-pag-R	
b.		ka-RED-pag-R	*!
c.	☞	ka-pag-RED-R	

Returning to Bole, I employ the representative data set in (22), which abstracts away from allomorphy. These data include doublers both doubling (d, i, k) and failing to double (b, f, g, j), such that all of the conditioning variables discussed in §10.2 are instantiated. They also include cases of totality as both an intervener (k) and a follower (i). R is the root, *ko* PERF, *yi* NULLO, *an* PLS, *to* 3FSGO, *ti* TOT, and *it* VENT. Forms with *ko* are perfective, and those without it are subjunctive. Because allomorphy is not analyzed here, the segmental (but not tonal) elision of suffixes is moot.

(22) Bole doublers
    a. {R, ko, yi}   R-ko-yi
    b. {R, an, ko, yi}   R-an-ko-yi
    c. {R, to, ko}   R-to-ko
    d. {R, an, to, ko}   R-**an**-to-**an**-ko
    e. {R, ti}   R-ti
    f. {R, it, ti}   R-it-ti
    g. {R, it, to}   R-it-to
    h. {R, to, ti}   R-to-ti
    i. {R, it, to, ti}   R-**it**-to-**it**-ti
    j. {R, it, to, yi}   R-it-to-yi
    k. {R, an, ti, ko}   R-**an**-ti-**an**-ko

---

[9] For just the second tableau in (21), one could invoke two precedence constraints to the effect that "RED must precede *ka*" and "RED must follow *pag*," freely ranked with each other to generate the variation. However, (b) in the first tableau is then not generated. There is no system-wide solution with precedence.

10.5. Morphotactic analysis

The grammar is then set up as follows. Every observed bigram is encoded as a constraint. Presumably, the learner posits these constraints as it encounters pairs of affixes, effectively tracking possible transitions in the language. For example, *R-ko* and *ko-yi* are posited as constraints, while *ko-R* and *yi-ko* are not. In some cases, both orders are observed, in which case both are posited as constraints (e.g. *it-to, to-it*). In total, 17 bigrams are observed in (22). Additionally, I posit a constraint against doubling, say, *Feature-Split (henceforth *Split) (Xu and Aronoff 2011), though others (including *Struc) may work equally well here. *Split penalizes each instance of multiple exponence (here, each double). An input for this simulation is taken to be an unordered set of morphemes (with no duplicates, assuming that doubling is not semantically motivated). Inputs in principle encode more information than this, but this is all of the information that is necessary for present purposes. Inputs are given on the left side in (22), in braces. The candidate set for each input includes all ordering permutations and all possible suffix duplication schemes. For example, for {R, ko, yi}, it includes *R-ko-yi, R-yi-ko, yi-ko-R, R-ko-ko-yi, R-ko-yi-ko, ko-R-ko-R-yi*, and so forth. In principle, candidates containing more than two repetitions are available (e.g. *R-ko-ko-ko-yi*), but for the purposes of simulations I cap doubles at two copies. More complex candidates are harmonically bounded in this case, so this simplification is not harmful.

A tableau file was generated automatically and submitted for evaluation to OT-Help2 (Staubs et al. 2010), yielding the grammar in (23). Additionally, I assume that RealizeMorpheme (Kurisu 2001) is undominated, such that a morpheme in the input cannot go unrealized altogether (segmental Max might also work, but it is often violated). Affixes also cannot be inserted if they are not input-licensed; I assume that this follows from Dep, not shown.[10]

(23)
Stratum 1: R-an, R-it, an-ko, an-ti, an-to, it-ti, it-to, ko-yi, ti-an, to-an, to-yi
Stratum 2: R-to, to-ko, to-ti, *Split
Stratum 3: R-ko, R-ti, to-it

Tableau 24 illustrates doubling across object agreement before totality. Only a handful of contenders are shown. The constraints in the top stratum can only be jointly satisfied if *Split is violated, resulting in doubling.

---

[10]Doubling does not violate Dep, as both copies correspond to the input.

(24) Doubling across object agreement before totality

{R, it, to, ti}	R-an	R-it	an-ko	an-ti	an-to	it-ti	it-to	ko-yi	ti-an	to-an	to-yi	R-to	to-ko	to-ti	*Split	R-ko	R-ti	to-it
a. ☞ R-it-to-it-ti	*			*	*	*			*	*	*	*	*	*	*	*	*	
b. R-it-to-ti	*			*	*	*	*!		*	*	*	*	*			*	*	*
c. R-to-it-ti	*	*!	*	*	*	*		*	*	*	*		*	*		*	*	

Tableau 25 illustrates totality as an intervener rather than follower.

(25) Totality as an intervener

{R, an, ti, ko}	R-an	R-it	an-ko	an-ti	an-to	it-ti	it-to	ko-yi	ti-an	to-an	to-yi	R-to	to-ko	to-ti	*Split	R-ko	R-ti	to-it
a. ☞ R-an-ti-an-ko		*			*	*	*	*		*	*	*	*	*	*	*	*	*
b. R-an-ti-ko		*	*!		*	*	*	*	*	*	*	*	*	*		*	*	*
c. R-ti-an-ko	*!	*		*	*	*	*	*		*	*	*	*	*		*		*

This grammar as it stands is purely morphotactic, and one might object that it is brute force. However, bigram morphotactics is not brute force in general; there are plenty of logically possible ordering scenarios that it cannot generate (Ryan 2010, Ryan and Schuh 2010). But to the extent that the present analysis is brute force, it can be considered a baseline or proof of concept. As one adds general principles of affix ordering to the grammar, the morphotactic component can be simplified. But as long as bigram morphotactics are available, a working analysis of Bole morphology is ensured. Moreover, given arbitrary differences between languages, morphotactic constraints cannot be whittled away entirely (*ibid.*). Compare, for instance, Bole and Yaya Ngamo in Table 10.2. The paradigms are close, the main difference being that Bole adds multiple exponence. The theory needs to generate both cases.

10.6 Morphotactic extension

Bigram morphotactics can also motivate the emergence of doubling through a process called morphotactic extension, which essentially amounts to analogy in affix order. Ryan (2010) describes morphotactic extension for Tagalog aspectual red (see above) using the following example. In relatively simple verbs like (26), red usually occupies the second position in the word.

(26) a. ma-red-ka-R
     b. pag-red-pa-R

10.6. Morphotactic extension

However, in more complex cases, such as *ma-ka-pag-pa*-R, it can vary freely between the second position and a position deeper into the prefix string, as depicted by Figure 10.1. In this case, the relative frequencies of the two options are 75% and 25%, respectively. Morphotactic extension explains this optionality as being driven by a tension created by forms such as (26). (26a) supports RED between *ma* and *ka*; (26b) supports it between *pag* and *pa*. In *ma-ka-pag-pa*-R, both options are available, and indeed both are employed. Because *SPLIT is highly ranked in Tagalog, free variation emerges, not doubling.

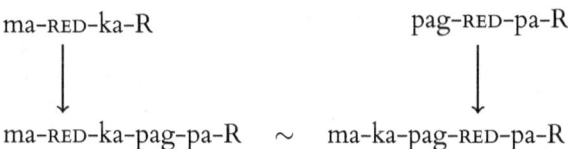

Figure 10.1: Morphotactic extension as a source of variation in Tagalog.

A similar process of analogy can motivate the emergence of doubling in Bole, as schematized in Figure 10.2. However, because Bole ranks *SPLIT low, doubling rather than free variation emerges as the optimal response to the morphotactic tension created by the simpler forms.

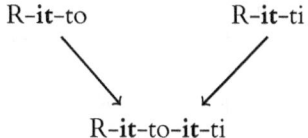

Figure 10.2: Morphotactic extension as a source of doubling in Bole.

To be somewhat more concrete, consider the hypothetical pre-Bole to Bole developments in (27).[11] Pre-Bole in (27) is based on Ngamo.

		Pre-Bole		Bole	Parse
(27)	a.	*R-an-ko	>	R-an-ko	R-PLS-PERF
	b.	*R-ti-ko	>	R-ti-ko	R-TOT-PERF
	c.	*R-an-ti-ko	>	R-**an**-ti-**an**-ko	R-PLS-TOT-(PLS)-PERF

---

[11] For simplicity, I omit the NULLO *yi* from modern Bole in (27a), as it was an independent innovation, irrelevant here.

Imagine that a hypothetical bigram-morphotactic learner is exposed to these three pre-Bole forms with relative frequencies of, say, 10, 2, and 1, respectively. The bigram learner matches its training data here, as it should (since this is essentially the stable situation in Ngamo). But in order to simulate language change, something has to give; learners must occasionally converge on a different grammar. I shall now illustrate that with bigram morphotactics, the pre-Bole learner is particularly conflicted between R-*an-ti-ko* (without doubling) and R-**an**-*ti*-**an**-*ko* (with doubling) above and beyond all other logically possible contenders. One might investigate this question in a few ways. First, one could expose the learner to fewer training data and then wug-test it. Second, one could increase the learner's smoothing factor (i.e. propensity to generalize). Third, in a framework such as maximum entropy Harmonic Grammar (maxent HG) in which candidates are assigned probabilities, one could check which candidate has the second-highest probability, and with what proportion. I pursue this last tack here.

Using maxent HG learning software by Wilson and George (2008) with a relatively strong smoothing factor of $\sigma^2 = 100$, I train the grammar on the data in (27) with the aforementioned relative frequencies. As always, all ordering and doubling permutations are included in the spreadsheet as candidates, and constraints include all observed bigrams as well as *S<small>PLIT</small>. For the key input {R, an, ti, ko}, R-*an-ti-ko* is by far the most probable output (98.9%), as expected. Among innovative mappings, however, R-**an**-*ti*-**an**-*ko* is the most probable by a wide margin (0.6%). The probability of R-**an**-*ti*-**an**-*ko* increases as σ^2 decreases, but under any reasonable σ^2, it is the best unfaithful mapping; that, not the precise values, is the point. To unpack why this particular unfaithful mapping is the silver medalist (and with nonnegligible probability), consider that the learner sees mostly R-*an-ko*, which supports the constraints *R-an* and *an-ko*. Now the learner has to decide what to do with the less common combination {R, an, ti, ko}. It has two options. First, it can maintain a one-to-one mapping, but at a morphotactic cost: *R-an* and *an-ko* cannot be simultaneously satisfied without doubling, assuming that *ti* also has to intervene between R and *ko*. But doubling allows the learner to simultaneously satisfy both morphotactic constraints, as sketched in (28). Admittedly, as an anonymous referee points out, this discussion treats only the actuation of doubling, and not its eventual entrenchment as the only grammatical outcome. I leave intergenerational modeling to future work.

(28)

	Output	Satisfies	At The Expense Of
a.	R-an-ti-ko	R-an, *S<small>PLIT</small>	an-ko
b.	R-**an**-*ti*-**an**-ko	R-an, an-ko	*S<small>PLIT</small>

10.7 Other approaches to vacuous affix repetition

I NOW ADDRESS TWO ALTERNATIVE APPROACHES to semantically gratuitous affix repetition before concluding with some further issues. First, Downing (2005) analyzes Jita causative *y* doubling (as seen in §10.1) using stem alignment (cf. McCarthy and Prince 1993) and Optimal Paradigms (McCarthy 2005). The constraint motivating doubling is ALIGN-y "align CAUS to the end of the the stem" (assuming that the inner copy also surfaces faithfully). For stem alignment to work for Bole, some domain must be specified as the stem, to which the second copy aligns. But outside-in conditioning renders such a stem undefinable. For example, in (29), doubling is absent. Therefore, on the stem analysis, one would have to say that the relevant stem closes before *to* (as discussed in §10.3, the absence of doubling in cases like (29) cannot be motivated phonologically). But in other contexts, doubling (even of the same ventive suffix) is permitted across *to*, resulting in a contradiction. Moreover, TOT can occur both before and after the second copy. If TOT closes the stem when it is final, such that the second copy immediately precedes it, it must do so when it is nonfinal as well, predicting that doubling never crosses TOT.[12]

(29) [ŋgòríttàːyí]

ŋgor -it -to -yi
tie -VENT -3FsGO -NULLO

'that X tie her and bring her'

Second, Caballero and Inkelas (2013) analyze doubling in terms of weakness-driven augmentation. In such cases, the inner morph is insufficiently salient, so it is augmented with an outer morph. For example, consider Choguita Rarámuri *sú-n-ki-ma* 'sew-APPL-APPL-FUT.SG,' as seen in §10.1. Caballero and Inkelas (2013) (see also Caballero 2008, 2010, 2011) observe of this form that "an inner, lexicalized marker (e.g. *-n*) weakly marks Applicative, while

---

[12] An analysis in terms of morpheme-morpheme alignment is viable, since it essentially duplicates bigram morphotactics. However, morpheme-morpheme alignment is more powerful than bigrams, and the extra power is unneeded. For a pair of morphemes X and Y, four alignment constraints are possible (left-left, left-right, right-left, right-right), vs. two bigrams (X-Y, Y-X). Furthermore, alignment introduces an unneeded dimension of gradience, since its violations scale with distance, whereas bigrams are categorical, evaluating only strict adjacency (cf. McCarthy 2003 pro categorical constraints).

a second, regular, outer exponent (-*ki*) brings target meaning to minimum threshold level." They implement this insight using gradient violations of M-Faith (e.g. -*n* contributes only 0.5 to the exponence of the applicative). In general, weaker affixes are characterized by properties such as less productivity, less segmentability, more allomorphy, and smaller size (Hay and Plag 2004). This type of analysis is well motivated for many cases, but not viable for the Bole system treated here. First, note that unlike Choguita Rarámuri, the same morpheme is copied in Bole, so there is no issue of differential salience or productivity. There is also little independent evidence of weakness: All doublers are fully productive and regular, frequently appearing undoubled. For example, plural subject agreement /an/ is extremely common, and usually occurs undoubled, as in most simple verb forms. This approach would also have to contend with outside-in conditioning, in that suffixes like /an/ double only if certain other suffixes follow. But there is no look-ahead in cyclical construction of the type that Caballero and Inkelas (2013) assume.[13] Finally, even if one assumes weakness, one still needs a theory of morphotactics to determine the doubles' placement. The bigram analysis of Bole is parsimonious in that it motivates both the placement of the doubles and the fact of doubling with the same machinery: Doubling is driven by the same morphotactic constraints that control affix order in non-doubling contexts.

In sum, given these issues with the two aforementioned alternative approaches to multiple exponence, I pursue a morphotactic analysis of Bole here, though I do not contest the other approaches in general. The present analysis leaves some issues unresolved. First, it ignores allomorphy, allomorphy that is so extreme in some instances that it eliminates surface traces of the affix altogether, as with the deletion of perfective /ko/. While segmentally deleted /ko/ can leave tonal effects in its wake, in some forms, such tonal evidence is unavailable, meaning that /ko/ is realized wholly abstractly. The morphotactic analysis here takes /ko/ as a given in such cases, assuming that learners posit it even when null, as supported by various evidence in §10.3. But this is a substantial promissory note. Second, I gloss over the issue of whether the morphemes treated here are best analyzed as suffixes or enclitics, assuming them to be the former (as in Ryan and Schuh 2010, but cf. Gimba 2000). At any rate, this question is not critical for the bigram analysis, since bigrams can apply equally to suffixes and enclitics, and the issues are the same either way. Finally, the present analysis appears to miss a generalization: All doublers have the form /VC/ (or possibly just /C/ depending on one's analysis

---

[13] Cyclicity does not rule out that the suffix might be copied and then deleted in a later cycle in a kind of "Duke-of-York gambit." But in that case establishing a phonological motivation for deleting is problematic.

10.7. Other approaches to vacuous affix repetition

of the morphophonology),[14] while all interveners (and followers) have the form /CV/. On the present approach, this is a coincidence, but not a massive one, since only a few suffixes are doublers (viz. the ventive and two subject agreement suffixes), and the generalization may have an unrelated explanation, since doublers and interveners tend to occupy different positions of the suffix string. These questions invite further research.

Acknowledgments

In the spring of 2010, as a graduate student at UCLA, I had the pleasure of working with Russ on his Yobe Languages Research Project, an NSF grant (BCS-0553222, P.I. Russell G. Schuh). On April 22nd, 2010, we co-delivered the annual joint UCLA–USC phonology seminar, entitled "Suffix doubling and suffix deletion in Bole" (Ryan and Schuh 2010). This paper is based on my half of that talk, which draws on empirical data from Russ's half, Gimba (2000), and Gimba and Schuh (2014).

---

[14]For example, Schuh (2001) and Ryan and Schuh (2010) takes PLS to be /an/ (parsing surface [-an-] in some cases), while Gimba (2000) takes the same [a] to be part of the stem, or a theme vowel. Similarly, Schuh (2001) gives the 23FsGS as "/(a)G/" (where G indicates the first part of a geminate), avoiding the issue.

11

CiV lengthening and the weight of CV

Donca Steriade
MIT

11.1 Two problems for CiVL

CIV LENGTHENING (CIVL) TURNS a stressed non-high vowel followed by a string of the form CiV into a long vowel, to be later diphthongized by the rule of Vowel Shift (Chomsky & Halle, 1968).[1]

(1) CiVL alternations
    Cán[ə]da   Can[éɪ]dian   pál[ə]ce   pal[éɪ]tial
    Pánam[ə]   Pànam[éɪ]nian   Ár[ə]b   Ar[éɪ]bian
    Áb[ə]l   Àb[íː]lian   molýbd[ə]num   molỳbd[íː]nian
    Hánd[ə]l   Hand[íː]lian   Béethov[ə]n   Bèethov[íː]nian
    Bóst[ə]n   Bost[óʊ]nian   mél[ə]dy   mel[óʊ]dious
    cól[ə]ny   col[óʊ]niəl   fél[ə]ny   fel[óʊ]nious[2]

---

[1] I deviate from IPA's conventions on marking stress: I place an acute or grave accent on the vowel, sidestepping questions about syllabic division.

11.1. Two problems for CiVL

The pattern described in this note is that reported for American English in the online version of the Oxford English Dictionary, with results checked against Merriam Webster's website and Kenyon and Knott (1953). To assess the productivity of CiVL, a list of Latinate forms containing the strings éCiV, óCiV, áCiV was obtained through regular expression searches in the OED. I retained all the forms which, like (1), are synchronically related to an English base, if that base does not itself contain the corresponding VCiV string. The vowel qualities in the data follow the OED except in the few cases where Kenyon and Knott or Merriam Webster's entries deviate from it. Inspection of this list confirms the unrestricted productivity of CiVL, at least among the editors of the OED[3]. The list is available from the author.

What is the Structural Description of this productive process? Chomsky and Halle (1968: 182, 242) and subsequent writers, most recently Baković (2013: 81), identify it as $V_{[-high]}$CiV. This SD and its OT translations are rejected here as unable to answer two questions.

The first question involves the contribution of the right context _CiV to the lengthening effect. Beyond insuring that the target vowel is in an open syllable, why should it be precisely iV that's needed to open that syllable? Why not any vowel, in any context? CiVL is limited to English, while open syllable lengthening under stress is widespread.[4] This suggests that the complexity of the context in the SD VCiV hides English-specific interactions of simpler constraints.

What could those simpler constraints be? In other phonological systems, including North Germanic, West Germanic, and earlier forms of English (Dresher & Lahiri, 1991), a short vowel lengthens under stress in all open syllables, no matter what follows. The Stress to Weight Principle (SWP; Prince 1991) provides a well-understood incentive for open syllable lengthening and has broad typological support. The proposal here will be to reduce the effect of CiVL to that of SWP, interacting with further aspects of English prosodic structure.

The second question raised by CiVL involves the interpretation of the Derived Environments Effect (DEE; Kiparsky 1973). Although fully productive in forms like (1), CiVL fails morpheme internally: *onion, valiant, cameo, tilapia,*

---

[3] On the productivity of CiVL: apparent exceptions like *Maxw[é]llian* were thought predictable by Chomsky and Halle (1968: 182, fn. 17), who took orthographic geminates to reflect aspects of the underlying form. Alternative explanations follow. There remain, among the better known items, three words: *Itálian, compánion, medállion.* Historically, at least, these are not exceptions: they are borrowings of *Italien, compagnon, médaillon,* which preserve the quantity of their sources, not generated as English derivatives of *Italy, company, medal.*

[4] Cf. Revithiadou (2004) for a survey of open syllable lengthening in trochaic systems.

patio, amianth, manioc, Cheviot, aria, Iscariot[5]. This is part of the DE syndrome, but the application of CiVL is restricted beyond what a standard DE effect demands: the rule is blocked if stress stays on the same vowel in the derivative as in the base, e.g., *Color[á]do* vs. *Color[á]dian*, a fact first noted by Burzio (2005: 68ff).

This is unusual. The original interpretation of DEEs (Kiparsky, 1973) is that the SD of the rule must be new relative to strings contained in the underlying forms, or in the outputs of earlier cycles. That condition is met in *Color[á]d-ian*, if the SD of CiVL is $V_{[-high]}$CiV. Generally, any strings of the form $V_{[-high]}$ + CiV, $V_{[-high]}$ C +iV, $V_{[-high]}$Ci + V (where '+' = affixal boundary) should satisfy a standard DE condition on CiVL, whether stress has changed on the target vowel, or not. As Burzio notes, that is clearly not so: CiVL operates only if the target vowel is newly stressed, as in *Canádian*.

(2) CiVL is blocked if the derivative's main stress is identical to base

Color[á]do	Color[á]dian	Alab[á]ma	Alab[á]mian
Nep[á]l	Nep[á]lian	Balz[á]c	Balz[á]cian[6]
Som[á]li	Som[á]lian	Lapl[á]ce	Lapl[á]cian
Mal[á]wi	Mal[á]wian	Pasc[á]l	Pasc[á]lian
Haw[á]ii	Haw[á]iian	Louisi[ǽ]na	Louisi[ǽ]nian
Rav[έ]l	Rav[έ]lian	Cincinn[ǽ]ti	Cincin[ǽ]tian
D[έ]lhi	D[έ]lhian	Gorbatch[έ]v	Gorbatch[έ]vian
Pantagru[έ]l	Pantagru[έ]lian	Gorbatch[ɔ́]v	Gorbatch[ɔ́]vian

Next to (1), the forms in (2) show the productivity of this DE effect in the dialect of the same speakers for whom CiVL is otherwise unrestricted. Both the basic process and its blockage are fully general. In the list described above I found a small number of exceptions to the pattern in (2). Most of these can be explained in one of two ways: (a) the base of the CiV-derivative is different from the one first assumed (e.g. *Orig[έ]nian* based on *Orig[έ]nic*, with stress identity blocking CiVL, rather than *Órig[ə]n*; (b) the CiV-derivative in A.English contains unexpected lengthening, given (2), because it follows

---

[5]Regarding *aria, Iscariot*: contemporary speakers may neutralize the <eɪr> – <ɛr> contrast. But these words are recorded by Kenyon and Knott (1953) as containing nuclear sequences they transcribe as <ɑr, ɛr, ær> and <ær> respectively, not <ɛr>; <e> is the grapheme used by KK to record the CiVL output transcribed here as [eɪ]. More on the interpretation of <ar>, <er>, <or> in the CiVL context appears in the full version of this note.

[6]Spelled <Balzackian> by William James, with <ck> signaling a short V, i.e. blockage of CiVL: "a real Balzackian figure—a regular porker, coarse, vulgar, vain, cunning, mendacious." (Letters 11 Apr. (1920) I.318, *apud* OED).

a British model, where CiVL is justified (e.g. *polyg[óʊ]nial*, A.English *pólyg[ɔ]n*, British *pólyg[ə]n*.

If a syllable starts out with some stress in the base and merely acquires primary stress in the derivative, the evidence in (3) shows that CiVL is blocked. Apparent exceptions are found in (4). I take blockage to be the invariant rule: the base of one of two apparent exceptions in (4), *Amazon*, has a variant *Ámaz[ə]n* that licenses CiVL in *Amazónian*; the other form, *Cycl[óʊ]pean*, can be derived without CiVL from the plural *Cycl[óʊ]pes*.

(3) CiVL blocked if main stressed V is stressed in base

Trínid[à]d	Trìnid[á]dian	Élg[à]r	Èlg[á]rian
Cónr[æ̀]d	Cònr[ǽ]dian	Yúgosl[à]v	Yùgosl[á]vian
Bórg[ɛ̀]s	Bòrg[ɛ́]sian[7]	Sómers[ɛ̀]t	Sòmers[ɛ́]tian
Hjélmsl[ɛ̀]v	Hjèlmsl[ɛ́]vian	Whíteh[ɛ̀]d	Whìteh[ɛ́]dian
Nímr[ɔ̀]d	Nìmr[ɔ́]dian	Slóv[à]k	Slòv[á]kian

(4) CiVL of base [ɔ̀] licensed in the derivative?
   Ámaz[ɔ̀]n   Àmaz[óʊ]nian | Cýcl[ɔ̀]ps   Cỳcl[óʊ]pean
   cf. variant Ámaz[ə]n | cf. pl. Cỳcl[óʊ]pes

The question raised by the data in (2-3) – why is suffixation insufficient to create a DE for CiVL – arises equally under OT formulations of DEEs: McCarthy's 2003 Comparative Markedness, and alternatives in Burzio (2005), Wolf (2008), and Storme (2017). What I propose to do here is not rethink the DEEs–on that see Storme (2017). Rather the project is, in part, to show that on a better understanding of CiVL no DEE question arises.

11.2 SWP under stress change

BOTH CIVL PUZZLES – the unexplained requirement that CiV follow the vowel to be lengthened, and the unusually stringent DEE – are eliminated if CiVL reduces to the Stress to Weight Principle Prince1991, which bans light stressed syllables, interacting with a new version of Trisyllabic Shortening, TSS. I discuss first the interpretation of SWP needed here.

Several facts obscure SWP's activity in English. The most obvious is that hundreds of monomorphemic words, like *cólor, léper, cámel*, violate it. I explain this by letting SWP itself be subject to DE blockage. For simplicity, I use

---

[7] In the OED, this form is recorded as an alternate to the CiVL'ed *Borg[íː]sian*. I pair this form with the variant *Bórg[ə]s* of the base word, which licenses CiVL.

here McCarthy's (2003) $_N$M constraints in formalizing DEEs. These penalize only marked structures distinct from the underlying form or the derivational base of the candidate. Using this interpretation, a DE-version of SWP, $_N$SWP (BD), prohibits only stressed short vowels that differ, in being stressed, from the corresponding Base vowel. The annotation (BD) indicates that $_N$SWP requires a difference between the surface Base vowel and its output counterpart in the Derivative – as opposed to one between the underlying and surface forms.

(5) $_N$SWP (BD):
assign a * to any stressed light syllable in D's stem that is new relative to B.

It is to this constraint that I attribute the lengthening that was earlier chalked up to CiVL: $_N$SWP (BD) explains the difference between *Canádian* and *Colorádian*: $_N$SWP (BD) is satisfied in *Colorádian* without any change, because the short stressed vowel isn't *new* there.

(6) $_N$SWP (BD) under stress change: *Canadian* vs. *Coloradian*.

B	kǽnədə	$_N$SWP (BD)	I$_D$[±LONG] IO/OO
a.	kənǽdiən	*!	
b. ☞	kənéɪdiən		*
B	kàləɹádoʊ	$_N$SWP (BD)	I$_D$[±LONG] IO/OO
a. ☞	kàləɹádiən		
b.	kàləɹéɪdiən		*!

By letting $_N$SWP (BD) refer to all stressed vowels we explain the fact that a mere change from secondary to main stress can't trigger CiVL:

(7) Main stress shifts, but stress doesn't change

B	nímɹɔ̀d	$_N$SWP (BD)	I$_D$[±LONG] IO/OO
a. ☞	nìmɹódiən		
b.	nìmɹóʊdiən		*!

The analysis must explain why other stress changes, in non-CiV contexts, don't trigger lengthening. There are four cases to consider. The first involves short stressed vowels in a closed syllable, as in *párent, paréntal*. They are explained by assuming that the active version of the SWP, the one stated in (5), is satisfied by a closed syllable, without lengthening.

11.2. SWP under stress change

The second case represents the bulk of apparent counterevidence to $_N$SWP (BD): derivatives like *gener[ǽ]lity*, **gener[éɪ]lity*, with stress shifted from *géneral*. In such cases, the newly stressed vowel is subject to Trisyllabic Shortening (TSS). One component of the revised analysis will be to assume that the Markedness constraint triggering TSS outranks $_N$SWP (BD). The best understood part of this TSS trigger is a bimoraic maximality condition on the English trochee Prince1991, coupled with the independent requirement that at most one syllable at the right edge stay unfooted: this allows parses like [(dʒɛnə)(ɹǽl-ə)ɾi], and excludes *[(dʒɛnə)(ɹéɪl)-əɾi] (too many unparsed syllables), and *[(dʒɛnə)(ɹéɪl-ə)ɾi] (too many moras in the last foot). A foot-free interpretation of TSS, based on the idea of moraic lapse (cf. Kager 1993) is possible, but involves complexities that can't be explored here. A narrower statement of TSS follows in (8), engineered for upcoming developments in this study, along with an illustration:

(8) TSS: Assign a * to a long V followed by a mora in its foot.

B	dʒénəɹəl	TSS	$_N$SWP (BD)	ID[±LONG] IO/OO
a. ☞	(dʒɛnə)(ɹǽl-ə)ɾi		*	
b.	(dʒɛnə)(ɹéɪl-ə)ɾi	*!		*

The third case involves stress advancement in *–ic* forms, whose suffix attracts stress to the penult (*átom, atómic*). These forms also typically shorten an underlying long tonic vowel (*c[óʊ]ne, c[ɔ́]nic, *c[óʊ]nic*), in addition to inhibiting lengthening (*at[ɔ́]mic, *at[óʊ]mic*). This doubly idiosyncratic pattern is attributed by Myers (1987), as interpreted in Prince (1991), to the fact that *–ic* must be parsed in a minimally and maximally bimoraic foot: shortening is a consequence of just this fact. This idea can be incorporated into our analysis: the newly stressed vowel in *atómic* doesn't lengthen because Myers's constraint forces a right-aligned trochee in *a(tómic)*. Under this parse TSS blocks lengthening.

(9) Shortening in right-aligned trochees

B	átom	MYERS-ON-*ic*	TSS	$_N$SWP (BD)
a. ☞	ə(tɔ́mɪk)			*
b.	[ə(tóʊ)mɪk]	*!		
c.	[ə(tóʊmɪk)]		*!	

The fourth source of apparent counterexamples to $_N$SWP (BD) comes from derivatives whose stress shifts backwards, as in *stàtistícian* from *statístic*.[8] What is relevant for ₙSWP (BD) is that the stem-initial vowels that gain stress under this retraction recover full quality, but don't lengthen: it's *st[æ̀]tistícian*, not **st[èɪ]tistícian*. The retracted stress always lands at distance of one syllable from the main stress. I attribute this instance of non-lengthening to TSS as well. (Here too, a foot-free interpretation is possible, based on Kager's ideas about moraic lapse.)

Beyond such cases and beyond CiVL, are there any other stress shifts that license SWP lengthening? Yes. A pattern parallel to, but distinct from CiVL is found with newly stressed vowels in hiatus. Some of the data has been earlier presented under the rubric of PreVocalic Tensing (Chomsky and Halle 1968: 242; Halle and Mohanan 1985: 81; Hammond 1997: 7), but tensing is a misnomer.

First, as Halle and Mohanan (1985: 81) observe, PreVocalic Tensing does not induce Vowel Shift, while PreVocalic Lengthening does. Compare Tensing in *várious*, *mániac* with Lengthening+Vowel Shift in *varí-ety*, *maníac-al*. Second, Tensing operates regardless of stress, while Lengthening requires a newly stressed vowel as its target. The data in (10) shows this: a short unstressed vowel placed in prevocalic position by affixation lengthens and vowel-shifts *when stress lands on it*. The data in (11) shows that, in the same hiatus configuration, when stress does not change between the base and the derivative, the vowel tenses without Vowel Shift, that is without Lengthening. In other words, the instance of Lengthening in (10) is subject to the same DE condition as the Lengthening in *Canádian*: the target vowel must be newly stressed. The contrast between (10-11) lends support to an analysis in terms of ₙSWP (BD), because it is predicted by it.

(10) Lengthening in hiatus under change of stress
    álgebr[ə]   àlgebr[éɪ-ɪ]c   Júd[ə]h   Jud[éɪ-ɪ]c
    fórmul[ə]   fòrmul[éɪ-ɪ]c   délt[ə]   dèlt[éɪ-ɪ]c
    mán[ɪ.æ]c   man[áɪ.ə]c-al   vár[i]   var[áɪ-ə]ty
    simultán[ɪ-əs]   simultan[íː-ə]ti   notór[ɪ-əs]   notor[áɪ-ə]ti

(11) No Lengthening in hiatus without change of stress
    Mac[áʊ]   Mac[á.-ɪ]st   Júd[ə]   Júd[ə-ɪ]st
    Dád[ɑ]   Dád[ɑ.-ɪ]st   Chín[ə]   Chín[ə-ɪ]st
    Niétzsch[ə]   Niétzsch[ə-àɪ]te   Káfk[ə]   Kàfk[ə-é]sque

---

[8] These shifts were seen as word-internal effects of the Rhythm Rule (Hayes, 1982; Kager, 1993; Kiparsky, 1973) or as consequences of PARSE » IDENT STRESS (Pater, 2000). A third proposal is defended in Stanton and Steriade (in progress).

[8] The OED lists also the lengthened form they transcribe as ['dʒudeɪɪst]. I assume this pro-

The present analysis builds on Halle and Mohanan's distinction between Prevocalic Tensing and Lengthening. I differ on two points from those writers: I claim that stress conditions the lengthening in (10), which is triggered by $_N$SWP (BD), and that the process is fully regular, like CiVL. Halle and Mohanan believe, to the contrary, that Prevocalic Lengthening is an idiosyncratic minor rule, so minor in fact that they neither state nor name it. But both its application in (10) and its failure in (11) are predicted by the current analysis. Once we recognize the stress change requirement imposed by $_N$SWP (BD), there appear to be no exceptions to this instance of lengthening. What does have to be explained is not its application, or apparent exceptions to it, but rather the fact that TSS does not *undo* the effects of this lengthening, in items like *variety* or *algebraic*. That failure is predictable too, as we see next.

11.3 The weight of C_0V

WE COME NOW TO A HARDER QUESTION: why doesn't TSS cancel out the CiV-induced lengthening in *Canadian*? Our current analysis says it should:

(12) TSS and CiVL

B		kǽnədə	TSS	$_N$SWP (BD)
a.	☞	kənǽdiən		*
b.	☺	kənéɪdiən	*!	

Similarly, why doesn't TSS block or cancel the effects of PreVocalic Lengthening in *notoriety* and *maniacal*? Why, given Myers' conjecture about trochee-final parses of *–ic* forms, are the effects of PreVocalic Lengthening allowed to surface in *algebraic*? And similarly why does TSS allow underlying long vowels to be preserved in items like *Barbadian* and *Boolean*? In all these cases, an unexpected long vowel surfaces when it is in hiatus itself (in *algebraic, maniacal*) or followed by hiatus (in *Canadian, Boolean*). Clearly it is a fact about hiatus that underlies these exceptions to TSS: what is this fact?

I propose that prevocalic vowels weigh less than their non-prevocalic counterparts. A first version of this idea is spelled out next, in moraic language. The moraic analysis is revisited in the last section. Suppose then that the syllable of prevocalic short [i] is shorter than one mora. That explains why TSS doesn't block CiVL in *Can*[éɪ]*dian*: there is no full mora after [éɪ], in its foot.

---

nunciation contains a tertiary stress on the middle syllable and is based on *Judáic*.

(13) Submoraic C_0i satisfies TSS without shortening

B		kǽnədə	TSS	$_N$SWP (BD)	I_D[±LONG] (BD)
a.		kə(nǽdi)ən	(i/_V < 1μ)	*!	
b.	☞	kə(néɪdi)ən	(i/_V < 1μ)		*

Suppose, *mutatis mutandis*, that the syllables of the prevocalic long vowels, or perhaps of prevocalic Vi dipthongs, are shorter than *two* moras. Then they are less than fully bimoraic and it is natural to suppose that TSS doesn't prevent these items of intermediate quantity from preceding another mora within their foot. That's why *var*[áɪ-ə]*ty* and *algebr*[éɪ-ə]*c* surface with unshortened stressed vowels: their quantity has already been reduced by hiatus.

(14) Sub-bimoraic C_0V:/_V satisfies TSS without shortening

B		vǽɹi	TSS	$_N$SWP (BD)	I_D[±LONG] (BD)
a.	☞	və(ɹáɪ.ə)ri	(aɪ/_V < 2μ)		*
b.		və(ɹí.ə)ri		*!	
B		ǽldʒəbɹə	TSS	$_N$SWP (BD)	I_D[±LONG] (BD)
a.	☞	(ǽldʒə)(bɹéɪ.ək)i	(eɪ/_V < 2μ)		*
b.		(ǽldʒə)(bɹí.ək)		*!	

Stress is also sensitive to the lighter quantity of prevocalic nuclei: stress avoids falling on V_1 in V_1V_2 sequences, especially if V_1 = short [i], as noted by Liberman and Prince (1977: 276), and by Hayes (1982: 247ff). These authors' examples include medial Lapse violations in forms like *mét*[iə]*ròid*, *amél*[iə]*ràte*, where the expected stress for these suffixes should skip just the immediately presuffixal vowel: in fact the entire V.V sequence is invariably skipped. We should add under the same rubric examples of Extended Lapse violations in forms like *meríd*[iə]*nal, septéntr*[iə]*nal, obsíd*[iə]*nal, spírit*[uə]*l*, and the rare *énemious*, all derivative types where antepenult main stress is otherwise the rule[9]; and perhaps Extended Lapse violations like *áx*[iə]*matìze*, *ál*[iə]*nable*, although the source of these latter lapses is harder to untangle.

Stress on $V_1.V_2$ is allowed if V_1 is lengthened, as in the cases like *algebraic* seen earlier in (10). And stress on the V_2 element of $V_1.V_2$ is always

---

[9]For iV sequences, avoidance of stress on V_1 is the rule, while for uV the pre-antepenult stress in *spíritual* is isolated, the normal pattern being that of *habítual, resídual, ambíguous*. Either way these deviations from normal stress patterns involve only hiatus sequences and suggest that at least short [i] in V_1 is always too short to bear stress.

fine, including when V_2 is short, as in b[aɪ.ɔ́]$logy$, av[i.ɔ́]$nics$, $therm$[i.ɔ́]nic, $histr$[i.ɔ́]nic, showing that it is only the weight of V_1 that is reduced in hiatus.

In analyzing this stress data, the first thing to note is that the syllable defined by V_1 in $V_1.V_2$ *is not invisible to stress*: an invisible V_1 would predict **Cánadian*, **cústodial*, **félonious*. This observation weighs against accounts in which [iV] originates as /jV/, with /j/ vocalizing after stress (Hayes, 1982: 267).[10] Our proposal is that submoraic V_1 in $V_1.V_2$ is visible, in the sense that it counts as a syllable for purposes of LAPSE and/or PARSE, but is poorly suited to *carry* stress, because it is too short. Because the syllable of V_1 is visible, stress is forced to advance in forms like *Canádian* from the first syllable of its base *Cánada*, to the second syllable of the suffixed derivative. Because V_1 is too short to carry stress, stress can't advance in *merídional*, from *ri* to prevocalic *di*, and an extended lapse ensues. Similarly, stress can't advance from the initial of *méteor* to the submoraic second syllable in *méteoròid*.

Lengthening V_1 in hiatus does happen, as in *variety*, but this only mitigates rather than solves the stress-to-weight problem posed by these forms: as suggested above, a lengthened vowel in hiatus still falls short of the optimal bimoraic weight for a stressed syllable. For this reason, stressing-cum-lengthening V_1 in $V_1.V_2$ remains a strategy limited to a minority of suffixed derivatives:

(15) a. $_\text{N}$SWP(V_1V_2) (BD): assign a violation to any new prevocalic stressed short V.

  b. $_\text{N}$SWP (BD): assign a violation to

   i any new prevocalic stressed long V: *$V{:}_1V_2$

   ii any new preconsonantal stressed short V: *V_1CV_2

---

[10]Can Hayes' (1982) j→i account be rescued if stress on the antepenult, at the intermediate stage **félon*[j]*ous*, is excluded on the grounds that the closed penultimate *lon* should attract stress? No: first, if the syllabic parse is *felón.*[j]*ous*, then CiVL, which never affects closed syllables, will be incorrectly blocked. Second, the distribution of underlying /j/ must be controlled to prevent preconsonantal [i]s, originating as /j/s, from being skipped by stress in other contexts where [i] surfaces, e.g. in *habitual*. Even if we ignore Richness of the Base issues, the morpheme structure constraint analysis that Hayes advocated in 1982 misses a key point: what English avoids is a *surface stressed [i] in prevocalic position*, regardless of its derivational history. A surface generalization like this can't be guaranteed by a Morpheme Structure Condition.

c. Lapse and no lengthening in *méteoròid*

B	míːtiəɹ	ₙSWP(V₁V₂) (BD)	ₙSWP (BD)	*Lapse
a.	(mìː)(tíə)(ɹòid)	*!		
b.	(mìː)(táɪ.ə)(ɹòid)		*!	
c. ☞	(míːti)ə(ɹòid)			*

d. Antepenult stress and preV lengthening in *variety*.

B	væɹi	ₙSWP(V₁V₂) (BD)	*ExtLapseR_{ITY}	ₙSWP (BD)
a.	və(ɹí.ə)ti	*!		
b.	(vǽɹɪ)əti		*!	
c. ☞	və(ɹáɪ.ə)ti			*

e. Penult stress and preV lengthening in *algebraic*.

B	æld͡ʒəbɹə	ₙSWP(V₁V₂) (BD)	Myers-on-ic	ₙSWP (BD)
a.	(æ̀ld͡ʒə)(bɹǽ.ɪk)	*!		
b.	(æ̀l)(d͡ʒébɹə).ɪk		*!	
c. ☞	(æ̀ld͡ʒə)(bɹéɪ.ɪk)			*

f. No lengthening and extended lapse in *merídional*.

B	məɹídiən	ₙSWP(V₁V₂) (BD)	ₙSWP (BD)	*ExtLapse
a.	(mèɹə)(díə)nəl)	*!		
b.	(mèɹə)(daí.ə)nəl		*!	
c. ☞	mə(ɹídi)ənəl			*

Summarizing: a conjecture about the lighter weight of prevocalic vowels explains apparent exceptions to TSS found in or before hiatus sequences, as well as the stress-avoiding behavior of V₁ in V₁V₂. The conjecture is that the syllable projected by a prevocalic vowel is lighter than that projected by its preconsonantal counterpart. That makes a short prevocalic vowel, and especially *i*, generally unsuited for stress. A lengthened prevocalic vowel is still less suitable than a lengthened preconsonantal one. The same conjecture explains the hiatus exceptions to TSS: the stress foot in *Ca(nádi)an* is followed by less than a full mora, and thus satisfies TSS without any need for shortening, while the main stress feet in *alge(bráic)* and *va(ríe)ty* don't contain the fully long vowel that's penalized by TSS.

11.4 No CuVL

SPE's STATEMENT OF CiVL (Chomsky & Halle, 1968: 182, 242) is justified in singling out prevocalic [i], to the exclusion of its closest counterpart [u] or any other vowel. Alternations like *gr[eɪ]de - gr[æ]dual, tr[aɪ]be - tr[ɪ]bual* (the OED pronunciation of an obscure version of *tribal*) show that TSS effects surface before CuV. Items like *perpetual, innocuous, strenuous, tenuous, annual, manual, casual* display invariably lax vowels in the antepenult, contrasting in this with their counterparts in CiV, like *menial, venial, odious, copious, facial* etc. It seems significant that, even in non-derived contexts, the general rule in the Latinate vocabulary is to have a long nucleus before CiV, but a short one before CuV. We have to recognize then that if prevocalic C_0i can be submoraic, prevocalic C_0u is mostly not.

The two high vowels differ systematically beyond English. The vowel *i* is more likely than *u* to form a post-nuclear glide (Kubozono 2001 on Japanese, Steriade 1984 on Romanian). When it occupies the position of postnuclear glide, [i̯] is more likely to be a light, C-like glide, while [u̯] is invariably heavy (Steriade 1990 on Greek word-final dipthongs in [Vi̯] vs. [Vu̯]). This divergence between the high vowels could stem from a difference in duration or loudness that would explain the *i-u* asymmetry observed in English, but studies available to me do not provide clear evidence to bear on this conjecture.

11.5 The [aɪ] problem

THIS ACCOUNT JUST PROPOSED has a flaw. To identify it, we review how the SPE answers the question about the interaction between CiVL and TSS (Chomsky and Halle 1968: 242; Halle and Mohanan 1985: 78, 83; cf. Baković 2013: 52ff). SPE's proposal is that CiVL follows TSS, counter-feedingly. Then, if TSS shortens an underlying long vowel, as in a case like *Ambr[oʊ]sian*, CiV Lengthening later restores it:

(16) SPE-style derivation of *Ambrosian*, cf. *Ambrose*
Stress   àmbróːz-ian
TSS   àmbróz-ian
CiVL   àmbróːz-ian
Other rules   æ̀mbróʊz-iən

A counterfeeding order also has to hold between TSS and PreVocalic Lengthening so the latter process comes too late in forms like *variety* to have its effects canceled by TSS.

(17) SPE-style derivation of *variety*, cf. *var[ĭ]*
 Stress   varí-iti
 TSS   n/a
 PreVLength varí:-iti
 Other rules vəɹái-əti

Now, SPE's TSS and CiVL rules differ in the height of vowels they target: TSS is unrestricted by height while CiVL operates to lengthen only non-high vowels. This difference describes something that our own account doesn't, as yet. Long high vowels are shortened by TSS and this shortening effect is not undone by later lengthening: it is not undone because CiVL doesn't apply to the high vowels. This part of SPE's analysis describes the shortening found in items like *li:ne, línear*; and the non-alternations in *cívil, civílian*, **civ[áɪ]lian*; *pérfidy, perfídious*, **perf[áɪ]dious*.

(18) SPE-style derivation of *linear*, cf. *line*; *civílian*, cf. *cívil*
 Stress   lí:n-iar   sivílian
 TSS   lín-iar   n/a
 CiVL   n/a   n/a
 Other rules lıniəɹ   sıvílıən

The present account predicts length preservation in *linear*, as *[láıniəɹ], because this long nucleus is followed by a hiatus sequence, as it is in *Bóolean*, where length is indeed preserved. Our account also predicts lengthening in *civílian*, because *[sɪ(váɪli)ən] has a better score than [sɪ(vɪli)ən] on the length-inducing constraint SWP.

(19) a. *línear* fails under the present analysis

B	láın, -iəɹ	TSS	$_N$SWP (BD)	Id[±LONG] (BD)
a. ☞	(láɪ.ni)əɹ	(i/_V < 1μ)		
b.	(lí.ni)əɹ	(i/_V < 1μ)		*!

11.5. The [aɪ] problem

b. *civílian* fails under the present analysis

B	sɪvɪ́l, -iən	TSS	ₙSWP (BD)	Id[±long] (BD)
a. ☞	sɪ(váɪli)ən	(i/_V < 1μ)		*
b.	sɪ(víli)ən	(i/_V < 1μ)	*!	

To get to the root of the problem, we should first understand the source of descriptive success in SPE's analysis. That source is two stipulations. First, that TSS and CiVL stand in counterfeeding order. Second, that CiVL does not target high vowels. I can't offer here a deeper reason for exempting high vowels from lengthening under stress in pre-C position. Short of an explanation, one can still plug the descriptive gap by matching SPE's stipulation with one of our own. We need to prohibit [iː] or its Vowel Shifted transform [aɪ] *in preconsonantal, foot-nonfinal position*. This will allow our analysis to generate *var*[áɪ.ə]*ty*, with lengthening in directly prevocalic position, but *civ*[í]*lian*, without lengthening, and *l*[í]*near* with shortening.

(20) a. *(aɪ CX): a * to any aɪC that's non-final in its foot.
b. *(aɪ CX) blocks CiV Lengthening of high vowels.

B	sɪvɪ́l, -iən	*(aɪ CX)	ₙSWP (BD)	Id[±long] (BD)
a.	sɪ(váɪli)ən	*!		*
b. ☞	sɪ(víli)ən		*	
c.	(sìvɪ)(láɪ)ən		*	*!

c. *(aɪ CX) does not block PreVLength of high vowels

B	vǽɹi, -əti	ₙSWP(V₁V₂) (BD)	*(aɪ CX)	ₙSWP(BD)
a.	və(ɹí.ə)ti	*!		
b. ☞	və(ɹáɪ.ə)ti			*

d. *(aɪ CX) triggers shortening

B	láɪn, -iəɹ	*(aɪ CX)	ₙSWP(BD)	Ident ±long
a.	(láɪni).əɹ	*!		
b. ☞	(líni).əɹ			*

With the addition of *(aɪ CX), the real results of our analysis are maintained. First, *modulo* some account of the Vowel Shift alternations, we now have a transparent analysis: the counterfeeding order between TSS and the two lengthening rules, CiVL and PreVocalic Lengthening, is eliminated. TSS ranks above $_N$SWP(BD), but TSS does not block satisfaction of $_N$SWP(BD) whenever the target vowel is followed by a submoraic syllable (in *Canadian*), or when the target syllable is itself less than bimoraic (in *algebraic*). Second, we understand the conditioning factors of lengthening in pre-CiV and in directly prevocalic position: they jointly amount to the DE version of SWP, $_N$SWP(BD). Finally, we begin to understand the role of hiatus in English lengthening, shortening and in stress. All these effects reduce to one: vowels are shorter – or rather syllables are lighter – in hiatus.

11.6 Intervals and weight in hiatus

I RETURN IN CLOSING TO THE KEY hypothesis about weight that allowed a reanalysis of CiVL as lengthening in a newly stressed open syllable: the idea that when two syllables stand in hiatus, $V_1.V_2$, the first is lighter relative to its weight in pre-consonantal position, i.e. V_1CV_2. Weight-reducing effects of hiatus are not limited to English. Stress on prevocalic [i] is avoided in Norwegian (Lunden, 2010); in Finnish (Karvonen, 2008), with consequences that include lapse and extended lapse; and in Romanian, whose stress pattern for $CiVC_0\#$ words is similar to that of Norwegian. Stress on any prevocalic high vowel is impossible in Iskunun Bunun (Huang, 2005). Tukang Besi avoids secondary stress on any V_1 of any quality in hiatus (Donohue, 1999). In Bhojpuri, primary stress is avoided on any V_1, whether long or short, in $V_1.V_2$; and secondary stress is avoided on short V_1 in $V_1.V_2$ (Shukla, 1981). The lighter quantity of prevocalic long nuclei is observed in the quantitative meter of Greek and Vedic (Devine & Stephens, 1994: 256). This last effect may be the source of *correptio vocalis ante vocalem*, the categorical neutralization of the length contrast between prevocalic long and prevocalic short vowels.

In closing, I note that there is a theory of weight that predicts lighter quantity for the first rhythmic unit in $V_1.V_2$ compared to the first such rhythmic unit in $V_1 CV_2$. This theory operates with units that differ slightly from syllables in that they begin with a nucleus and include the entire consonantal interlude separating it from the next nucleus, or from the end of the prosodic domain. A unit with exactly this organization is used under the name of *vowel-to-vowel interval* in phonetic studies of durational compensation (Farnetani & Kori, 1986; Kato, Tsuzaki, & Sagisaka, 2003; McCrary, 2006). I ar-

11.6. Intervals and weight in hiatus

gue for its phonological uses, under the abbreviated name of *interval* (Steriade n.d.; cf. Sturtevant 1922). To briefly illustrate the composition of intervals, the words *quantity* [kʷɑntəti] and *nuclear* [nukliɚ] are parsed into such units, with boundaries marked by 'l', as kʷlɑntlətlil and nluklliləˑl.

If the duration of each segment in an interval contributes to that interval's weight, then a number of finer weight distinctions are predicted than those available to the theory of weight defined on rimes alone. Thus, VC intervals are predicted to be, all else equal, lighter than VCC: this allows an interval-based computation of weight to distinguish 'light' from 'heavy penults' in words like *cámera* vs. *agénda*, as VC vs. VCC intervals. "Light" CC clusters, like the *br* of *algebra* are predicted to add weight to an interval in proportion to their duration: if they are longer than single consonants, such clusters should attract stress (Hirsch, 2014).

Relevant to present concerns is the fact that the parse into intervals distinguishes the penults of *rádial* and *rádical* (a pair from Baković 2013), and thus contributes to an explanation of CiVL: the penultimate interval in *rádi.al* is a V interval, while that of *rádical* is a VC interval. Likewise, intervals ending in a long vowel or diphthongs (like the antepenult in *variety*) should be lighter than those ending in V:C or diphthong-C (like the antepenult in *Canadian*). This explains why there is no reluctance to stress the antepenult in *Canádian* comparable to the reluctance to stress, even with lengthening, the antepenult in *merídional*: *merid[áɪ]onal* is less acceptable than *Can[éɪ]dian* because their stressed intervals differ in size, VV vs. VVC.

The interval-based computation of weight predicts all the distinctions documented in this note: the unit identified in syllabic terms as a C_0V syllable will be lighter if directly followed by another nucleus than if followed by a 'C-initial syllable'. An interval parse explains this because all postvocalic consonants belong to the interval defined by the preceding vowel and thus add to its weight: the fewer such postnuclear consonants the lighter the interval. The rime-based computation of weight does not predict these asymmetries.

Although this opens a different topic, we should note also that the difference between 'light,' generally unstressable final VC rimes, as in *origin*, and 'heavy,' generally stressed medial VC rimes, as in *agenda*, follows from the division into intervals as well: the former are VC intervals, the latter VCC. A further relevant point is that word-final short vowels (= V intervals) are, with negligible exceptions, unstressable in English and under certain circumstances altogether invisible for stress (e.g. *pársimony* and similar data in Liberman and Prince 1977: 297). It seems significant that the uncounted final [i] in words like *pársimony*, and with the unstressable prevocalic [i] of *merídional*, define the shortest intervals. In this they differ from what, in syllabic terms, we would call, medial 'preconsonantal C_0V' syllables, which *are* stressable: the latter are VC intervals, while final and prevocalic Vs are just V intervals.

The original grounds for developing interval-based computations of weight did not include the effects of hiatus on stress and quantity. The present study, which confirms predictions arrived at independently, suggests that the interval idea is on the right track.

Acknowledgments

The study is dedicated to the memory of Russ Schuh, my valued UCLA colleague and neighbor, and a frequent advisor in all matters phonological. I would like to thank Bruce Hayes, Joan Mascaró, Juliet Stanton and an extremely helpful anonymous reviewer for comments on early drafts. A longer version of this text, in preparation, seeks to address more of their comments.

12

On morphological palatalization in Chadic

H. Ekkehard Wolff
Universität Leipzig

12.1 Introduction

PALATALIZATION, OFTEN DISCUSSED ALONG WITH LABIALIZATION, has intrigued scholars of Chadic languages for quite some time (Gravina, 2014: 71-86). A comprehensive study of its distribution across, and of the domains of palatalization within, all of Chadic remains one of the *lacunae* in comparative typological linguistic research on Chadic: this includes the reconstruction of palatals and palatalization (often referred to as *Y-prosody*) for proto-languages. The present paper focuses on palatalization as the most salient prosody in Chadic, in both synchronic and diachronic perspective. Its starting point are three observations attributed to the eminent Chadicist Russell G. Schuh, to whose memory this paper is dedicated:

- The observation that West Chadic (WC) Miya shows morphological palatalization, which "is unattested elsewhere in West Chadic," but is "quite wide spread in the Biu-Mandara group, particularly Biu-Mandara A" (Schuh, 1998: 33-36).[1]

- The distinction between "morphological palatalization," as opposed to "palatalization as a local phonological process" (cf. Schuh, 2002).

- The assumption that Proto-Chadic determiners are a likely source of morphological prosodies in some present-day Chadic languages (Schuh 1983, expanded by Wolff 2004: 60, Wolff 2006, 2017).

Palatalization in WC Miya comes associated with a minimal inventory of synchronic vowel phonemes, namely two vowel qualities and a single contrast in length: /ə/, /a/, and /aa/. Minimal inventories of this kind, often reduced to /ə/ and /a/, or simply /a/, are characteristic of quite a few CC-A languages and may be linked to a deep level diachronic process of 'vocalogenesis' within (Central) Chadic (cf. Wolff, 2017). The apparently unique appearance of these typological features in WC in view of their wider distribution in CC raises the question of the age and the areal distribution of some notable features pertaining to the phonological systems within Chadic.

The peculiar nature of Chadic phonological systems with regard particularly to palatalization and labialization prosodies has unhappy repercussions on attempts to reconstruct lexical items of the proto-language(s). Proto-Chadic vowels can hardly be reconstructed with any confidence based on the classic comparative method (cf. P. Newman, 1977), if there is any attempt at all to reconstruct vowels (cf. Jungraithmayr and Ibriszimow 1994, who simply don't). As was suggested by Wolff (1983 and elsewhere), phonological and lexical reconstruction need to take into account diachronic processes of 'vocalogenesis' based on the recognition of prosodies, i.e. Y- and W-prosodies most of all. Minimal inventories of phonemic vowels and the presence of palatalized and labialized consonants, plus diachronic (often lexicalized) or synchronically productive Y- and W-prosodies, are typological features that intimately interact, and which together yield rich surface output in terms of vocalic and consonantal phonetic representation. This typological feature affects the reconstruction of both vowels and palatalized (in particular coronal) and/or labialized (in particular velar) consonants for the proto-language. Schuh (2017: 47) lucidly describes the challenge:

---

[1] Nowadays, the term 'Biu-Mandara', originally introduced by P. Newman and Ma (1966), has been widely replaced by 'Central Chadic', as is the case in this paper. Three of the four presently widely accepted branches of Chadic (Central-, East- and West Chadic) have sub-branches, which are conveniently labelled CC-A/B/C, EC-A/B, and WC-A/B/C. The fourth branch is Masa.

12.1. Introduction

> "[I]t is difficult to use correspondence sets to unequivocally demonstrate the reconstruction of palatalized and labialized velars as phonemes distinct from their 'plain' counterparts. However, languages in most major groups arguably have at least a series of labialized velars, and many also have a palatalized series. As I will argue here and elsewhere, *what is often interpreted as a distinction in vowels is actually a distinction in consonants that influences the pronunciation of vowels.*" (Emphasis mine)

In Chadic languages, both consonants and vowels are subject to palatalization and/or labialization by prosodies. Details may be language-specific. Gravina (2014) suggests a typology of Central Chadic phonologies, depending on whether any, and if so what type of, segment is primarily affected by prosodies: *Vowel prosody* languages, *Consonant prosody* languages, *Mixed prosody* languages, *No prosody* languages (restricted to the CC-B Kotoko Group).

The prosodies (Y- and W-prosodies) may have different sources. The source may be segmental material of the lexical root itself: either underlying approximants */y/, */w/ (which, according to the 'vocalogenesis' theory, surface as full vowels [i] and [u] in syllable nucleus position, cf. Wolff (2017), or palatalized and labialized radical consonants */C^y/, */C^w/. This is referred to as localized 'phonological' palatalization and labialization and shall not be dealt with any further in this paper. Focusing on Y-prosody, we may be dealing with 'morphological' palatalization. These would be cases in which the segmental source of the prosody can be associated with a morphological marker that is or was added to a lexical root but may no longer be present synchronically.

The morphophonological processes may be *synchronically productive,* or we are dealing with petrified results of *diachronic* processes whereby such lexicalized markers have become an integral part of synchronic words. The diachronic hypothesis is simple: Non-palatalized forms and the corresponding palatalized forms of a word or class of words differ with regard to the presence of at least one of a set of hitherto unidentified diachronic morphological markers, which carry the prosodic feature [+PALATALIZATION] and may be symbolized as *$\{Y_1\}$, *$\{Y_2\}$ ...*$\{Y_n\}$. In many languages, such markers are semantically bleached and are thus no longer transparent in their original functions; only seldom have they remained synchronically productive (but cf. below). Such petrified markers surface phonetically either in variant forms of the same word without any functional difference, or they account for lexicalized alternative forms associated with given grammatical functions, in both of which cases the markers may show petrified prosodic effects on either vowels, or consonants, or both. These effects are accounted for by morphophonological distant assimilation (umlaut):[2]

(1)   Ø-prosody form   Y-prosody form
       ROOT => # ᵒCVC(V) #   ROOT + *{Y} => # ʸCVC(V) #

Particular attention will be drawn to the behavior of Y-prosody when the word in question carries segmental /i/ in final position, irrespective of whether /i/ is assumed to be part of the lexical root or represents a (synchronic or diachronic) morphological marker.

12.2 Morphological palatalization in WC

MIYA IS THE ONLY WC LANGUAGE that has been described as showing instances of morphological palatalization, both with nouns and verbs, a fact which must be explained diachronically because "there are no lexical or morphological features that will predict which words will be [PALATALIZED] and which will not. There are even minimal pairs distinguished only by this feature" (Schuh, 1998: 35).

Unlike CC-A languages (but cf. Ga'anda below), WC-B Miya nouns distinguish masculine and feminine grammatical gender, but there is no correlation between gender and palatalized and non-palatalized words. Schuh (1998: 35) further observed that non-palatalized far outnumber palatalized words, and that "the non-palatalized words never vary in pronunciation whereas the palatalized words do". Compare the data in (2).[3]

(2)   Ø-prosody form   Y-prosody form
       ᵒlàbadə (M) 'shoulder'   ʸlébedi~ʸlábadi~ʸlébedə (M)
                                     ʸlyábyadadàw (PL) 'basket sp.'
       ᵒátəm (F) 'song'   ʸátim ~ ʸétim (F) 'nose'
       ᵒmər (F) 'sesame'   ʸmìr (M) 'money'

---

[2] According to current transcription conventions for Central Chadic languages, prosodies are indicated by a word-initial raised grapheme, i.e. ʸCVCV for Y-prosody (palatalization), and ʷCVCV for W-prosody (labialization). ᵒCVCV (Ø-prosody) explicitly indicates absence of any prosody. CVCV shall henceforth symbolize any lexical root; CVC would indicate a root that must be considered to be consonant-final; CVCa, CVCə, CVCi would be roots that lexically end in the specific vowel qualities indicated.

[3] The following abbreviations are used: DEF = definite, DET = determiner, F = feminine, FOC = focus, GEN = genitive, INDEF = indefinite, IPF = imperfective, M = masculine, NOM = nominalization, PL = plural, PRF = perfective, SG = singular, v.itr. = intransitive verb, v.tr. = transitive verb.

With one kinship term, presence and absence of Y-prosody would appear to be linked to number:

(3) Ø-prosody form   Y-prosody form
     $^{Ø}dzàfə$ (PL) $^{y}j\hat{\imath}fa$-na (M) 'male, husband'

Schuh (1998: 36) further notes: "For two adjectives, the masculine form is non-[PALATALIZED] but the feminine and plural are [PALATALIZED]. Among other adjectives, some are non-[PALATALIZED] in all forms and others are [PALATALIZED] in all forms." There is a restricted set of lexicalized *deverbal nouns*, which show palatalization accompanying other segmental marking devices, such as, for instance, prefix a-, while others lack palatalization (Schuh, 1998: 116f). Taking explicit analysis further, I assume the forms to reflect presence or absence of an underlying marker (symbolized by *{-^{y}i}) of hitherto unidentified function, which is deleted in the synchronic surface forms.

(4) Verb   Nominalization
     ^{Ø}CVCa   =>   a-^{Ø}CVCə$_{[NOM]}$
     ^{Ø}tsəga 'sit' =>   á-^{Ø}tsəgə 'sitting'

(5) Verb   Nominalization   Y-prosody
                             + suffix *{-^{y}i}   umlaut + suffix
                                                     deletion
     ^{Ø}CVCa   =>   *a-^{Ø}CVCə$_{[NOM]}$-^{y}i => a-^{y}CVCə$_{[NOM]}$-Ø
     ^{Ø}zəza 'flay' =>   *a-^{Ø}zəza-^{y}i   => á-^{y}zhəzhə 'flaying'

12.3 Morphological palatalization in CC-A

FEW STUDIES ON CC LANGUAGES make diachronic *morphological* palatalization responsible, implicitly or explicitly, for (often lexicalized) variants of words in terms of fronted vowels and/or palatalized consonants. Studies that do are Hoskison (1975, 1983) for Gude, R. M. Newman (1977) for Ga'anda, Wolff (1983) for eight languages of the so-called "Wandala-Lamang" group, Barreteau (1983) for Higi, Jarvis (1989) for Podoko, Wolff (2004) for Wandala, and Wolff (2004, 2006, 2015, 2017) for Lamang-Hdi.

In this section, I will re-visit some more or less transparent cases in three CC-A languages, in which morphological palatalization still functions synchronically with sub-classes of word forms, if not with all members of the particular class of forms. The three languages represent the three postulated prosody types in the phonological typology suggested by Gravina (2014), namely: *Vowel prosody* type (Ga'anda), *Consonant prosody* type (Gude), and *Mixed prosody* type (Podoko). In order to facilitate cross-language comparison, occasionally the transcriptions of the original sources have been slightly modified and unified.

12.3.1 Y-prosody in Gude

Hoskison (1975: 40-44) discusses "Rules marking MOTION-TO-SPEAKER" in Gude (Bata Group). This widespread Chadic verb extension is commonly referred to as 'ventive'. All verbs are synchronically marked exclusively by Y-prosody. The original 'ventive' suffix is partially deleted, i.e. losing the segmental vowel */i/ and leaving behind Y-prosody: *$^{\emptyset}$CVCV-$\{^yi\}_{[VENT]}$ => *^{y}CVCV-$\emptyset_{[VENT]}$ > ^{y}CVCV$_{[VENT]}$.

(6)   Ø-prosody   Y-prosody
      $^{\emptyset}$la   'cut'   /^{y}la/ [ʎɛ]   'cut and come'
      $^{\emptyset}$səba   'drive away'   /^{y}səba/ [ʃɨba] 'drive here'

This is comparable to the deverbal noun formation illustrated under (5) for WC Miya.

12.3.2 Y-prosody in Ga'anda

Ga'anda (Tera Group; R. M. Newman 1977) no longer distinguishes grammatical gender. Nevertheless, nouns fall into two classes, which differ by the rules of formation of their so-called 'modified stems'. Newman refers to them as T-class and Y-class, and relates this distinction to the former presence of gender distinctions. We will here restrict the discussion to the Y-class, in which "the difference between simple and modified stems is marked by both vowel alternations and consonant changes. …the modified stem is used before the indefinite -a and the genitive marker -ì" (R. M. Newman, 1977: 122); the consonant changes affect s → sh, most of all.

(7)   Ø-prosody   Y-prosody
      (simple stem)   (modified stem)
      $^{\emptyset}$hlàr-   /^{y}hlàr-/ [hlèr-]   'root'
      $^{\emptyset}$kəlàr-   /^{y}kəlàr-/[kilèr-]   'side'
      $^{\emptyset}$sàʔ-   /^{y}sàʔ-/ [shèʔ-]   'leaf'
      $^{\emptyset}$pə̀rs-   /^{y}pə̀rs-/ [pírsh-]   'horse'

12.3. Morphological palatalization in CC-A

Y-prosody is blocked with vowel-final nouns (which all end in /i/); their modified stems are unique in terms of absence of Y-prosody:

(8)   Ø-prosody   Y-prosody
      (simple stem)   (modified stem)
      ^{Ø}ŋgàmsì- ^{Ø}ŋgàms-   'spider'
      ^{Ø}ndə́rí- ^{Ø}ndə́r-   'moon'

There are two lexicalized exceptions to this blocking rule, which retain Y-prosody and thus confirm to the 'regular' formations above:

(9)   Ø-prosody   Y-prosody
      (simple stem)   (modified stem)
      ^{Ø}kə̀msì-   /^{Y}kə̀ms-/ [kìmsh-]   'youth'
      ^{Ø}fə̀rɗí-   /^{Y}fə̀rɗ-/ [fìrɗ-]   'mosquito'

In addition to inflectional noun formations, "Y-prosody as a morphologically determined process is also found in the inflectional system of Ga'anda verb stems. Here, it is a property of ...a particular set of tenses where the subject is either a second or third person singular pronoun .... In these tenses, when the subject is the second person singular -ən (~ -n) or the third person singular -ə, then Y-prosody must be applied. The verb stem undergoes vowel fronting and s-palatalization in exactly the same way described for Y nouns" (R. M. Newman, 1977: 127). Compare the following verb forms in the 2nd sg *perfective* (all marked by preverbal {ə}) under (10); note that verbs ending in /a/ replace their final vowel by /i/ albeit observing a rule that the monoverb sà- 'drink' must undergo Y-prosody (11), while polyverbs do not (12):

(10)   Ø-prosody   Y-prosody
       (simple stem)   (modified stem)
       ^{Ø}kar-   ə́^{Y}kèr-ə́n   'you refused'
       ^{Ø}fəɗ-   ə́^{Y}fiɗ-ə́n   'you beat (a drum)'

(11)   a-final monoverb
       ^{Ø}sà-   ə́^{Y}sh-ì-ń   'you drank'

(12)   a-final polyverbs
       ^{Ø}mása`-   ə́^{Ø}más-î-n   'you laughed'
       ^{Ø}pə̀dâ-   ə́^{Ø}pə̀ɗ-î-n   'you went'

12.3.3 Y-prosody in Podoko

In Podoko (Mandara Group), morphological palatalization plays an important role in productively forming *imperfective* aspect forms of the verb (cf. Jarvis, 1989). It should be noted that simple verbal nouns, i.e. those without any extension suffix, carry the ending *-i*; they are, as a rule, not marked by Y-prosody. Extended verbs form their verbal nouns by reduplication. The verb 'die' is irregular in two ways: for its simple verbal noun, it allows a reduplicated form, and it shows Y-prosody with the otherwise non-palatalizing ending *-i*.

(13) a. Regular simple verbal noun formation
Ø-prosody
$^{\emptyset}h$- > $^{\emptyset}h$-*i*   'give birth' > 'birth'
$^{\emptyset}dəg'$- > $^{\emptyset}dəg$-*i*   'beat' > 'beating'

     b. Irregular verb 'die'
Ø-prosody   Y-prosody
$^{\emptyset}məts'$- > $^{\emptyset}mətsə$-*mətsə* $^{Y}məts$-*i* [mitʃi] 'die' > 'dying, death'

Y-prosody marks *imperfective* aspect, whether in focus constructions (marked by preverbal *a-*) or not. Exceptions to this rule are intransitive verbs in focus constructions: they do not palatalize but carry a suffix *-i* instead, which makes them look like simple verbal nouns. Note that Podoko has VSO order, which means that pronominal subject person marking also follows the verb:

(14) a. Focus PRF
a-$^{\emptyset}$kəsá   *mətsərə ta*
FOC-catch:PRF thief   3PL

       'they caught a thief$_{[FOC]}$'

     b. Focus IPF, v.tr.: unblocked Y-prosody
a-^{Y}kəsə   *mətsərə ta*
FOC-catch:IPF thief   3PL

       'they are catching a thief$_{[FOC]}$'

     c. Focus IPF, v.itr.: Y-prosody blocked by vowel ending *-i*[4]
a-$^{\emptyset}$par-i   *ta*
FOC-wash-NOM:IPF 3PL

       'they$_{[FOC]}$ are washing (themselves)'

---

[4] "...le verbe imperfectif intransitive n'est pas marqué par la palatalisation. Il a plutôt une forme identique à celle du nom verbal" (Jarvis 1989: 80).

12.4 Discussion

12.4.1 Morphological sources of Y-prosody

Certain cases of palatalization reflect morphophonological processes of considerable time depth in Chadic (Schuh, 1998, 2002; Wolff, 1981, 1983). Wolff (2004, 2006) identified several petrified markers stemming potentially from a defunct Proto-Chadic determiner system, for which Schuh (1983) had already reconstructed three 'gender neutral' markers of 'definiteness', namely *-k, *-ɗ, *-i, in addition to gender-sensitive *n (M) and *t (F). Schuh discusses these, following J. Greenberg (1978), in terms of evolution from definite determiners to "affixes on nouns which mark gender, lexical class, or simply nominality" and markers of genitive constructions. He also views these determiners in a wider Afroasiatic context, pointing out cognates in Berber and Semitic (Schuh, 1983: 197f).

Gravina's (2014) otherwise excellent study does not attempt to identify any morphological function for Y-prosody, which he reconstructs for Proto-CC as a plainly phonological unit. He arguably reconstructs three vowels *a, *ə, and *i, and, in addition to segmental vowels and consonants, "a palatalization prosody for Proto-Central Chadic that has reflexes that cause front vowel harmony in Vowel Prosody languages and palatalize consonants in Consonant Prosody languages" (Gravina, 2014: 4).[5] By disregarding morphological palatalization, and by not being able to relate Y-prosody to his reconstructed */i/, Gravina's reconstruction of Y-prosody remains somewhat inconclusive and serves as a kind of *deus ex machina*. However and as shown in the present paper, it does make sense to distinguish non-palatalizing */i/ from palatalizing */ʸi/, only the latter being a potential source of Y-prosody.

The languages discussed in this paper clearly suggest that morphological Y-prosody has multiple sources in the history of both nominal and verbal grammar in Chadic. It may be fairly safe to assume that *{Y_1} is an ancient marker in the nominal grammar, which is the likely source of Y-prosody with lexicalized or regular noun formations in CC-A Guɗe (plurals), modified stems of Y-nouns in CC-A Ga'anda, and possibly the lexicalized palatalized adjective and noun forms in WC-B Miya. As a so-called stage-II and stage-III article (J. Greenberg, 1978), it shows up lexicalized either segmentally or

---

[5] Gravina's unfortunate use of the term 'vowel harmony' has nothing to do with typologically better known systems of ATR vowel harmony and assimilation/*umlaut* processes across morpheme boundaries between roots/stems and affixes. For this reason, I have long since (Wolff, 1983, 2015) suggested to speak, with regard to the particular prosodic nature of this feature of Chadic (morpho-) phonology, of (mutual) vowel 'harmonization' instead.

as prosody in many CC-A languages. It also operates synchronically, for instance, as previous reference marker in WC Kanakuru and Zaar as well as in EC East Dangaleat (Schuh, 1983: 160).

The source of *{-Y$_2$} in verbal grammar is less transparent. The palatalized deverbal nouns in WC Miya, as well as the irregular verbal noun for 'die' and the *imperfective* aspect stems in CC Podoko, suggest some connection between the nominalization of verbs and the potential use of such nominalized stems for *imperfective* aspect marking, thus possibly and somehow linking *{-Y$_2$} to *{-Y$_1$}.[6]

No links to *{-Y$_1$} or *{-Y$_2$} would be plausible to assume for the 'ventive' verb extension in CC-A Gude, for which I suggest to tentatively postulate diachronic *{-Y$_3$}.

Likewise, palatalization in Ga'anda with regard to 2nd and 3rd sg subject marking in the *aorist*, *perfective*, and *subjunctive* remains diachronically obscure and is here symbolized as *{-Y$_4$}.

12.4.2 Enigmatic relationship: Final vowel i and Y-prosody

Synchronic /i/ in (Central) Chadic languages may have different historical origins. It either represents a vowel phoneme by itself (cf. Gravina 2014 for CC) or an underlying syllabic allophone of */y/, if not a raised and fronted representation of epenthetic schwa (cf. Wolff, 1981, 1983, 2004, 2006, 2017). In final position, a surface vowel *i* can be either root or affix material. In the latter case, it may represent either a synchronically productive or a petrified and lexicalized diachronic suffix, having undergone parallel developments to stage-II and stage-III articles (J. Greenberg, 1978). Regarding the co-occurrence of Y-prosody and the presence of final *i* in the Chadic languages under review, there are two options: (a) co-occurrence of underlying final *i* and Y-prosody, and (b) a blocking effect of underlying final *i* on predictable Y-prosody.

---

[6]The nature and formation of *imperfective* stems in Chadic has been debated since the mid-1970s. Among others, Wolff (1977, 1979, 1982, 1984) pointed out an occasional accidental similarity and relationship in some Chadic languages between nominalized verb stems (as often used in periphrastic aspect formations, in particular 'progressives/continuatives') and *imperfective* formations in others (cf. P. Newman and Schuh 1974 for Hausa).

Co-occurrence: Final vowel i and Y-prosody

In Ga'anda, the modified stem of consonant-final Y-nouns is palatalized before the genitive suffix -ì (R. M. Newman, 1977: 122) and other determiner suffixes, unless in the plural. If the so-called genitive suffix -ì was the source of Y-prosody, then why would the palatalized stem be used with a whole range of suffixed determiners in the singular, synchronically leaving the simple stem to be used, for instance, before the plural suffix -c(ə)-? A plausible diachronic hypothesis would assume two steps (note the important distinction between consonant-final and vowel-final nouns of the Y-class in Ga'anda):

1. Consonant-final Y-class nouns obligatorily attach a palatalizing stage-II article (J. Greenberg (1978), Schuh (1983: 180ff)) $-^y i_{[DET]}$ in the singular, but not in the plural; cf. SG: $*CVC+^y\text{ì} > [^y CVC\text{-}]$.

(15) Simple stem $*CVC_{[y\,class]}$ (+ PL) (+ DET) > $^{\emptyset}CVC\text{-}$
      Modified stem $*CVC_{[y\,class]}\text{-}^y i_{[DET]}$ (+ DET) > $^y CVC\text{-}$

Examples in (16) are from R. M. Newman (1971: 108-111), in which the 1977 so-called genitive suffix -ì is treated as preposition /ì` ~ yì/ preceding the following noun.

(16) a. Ø-prosody (simple stem)
         /ə $^{\emptyset}$kərsə Musa/
         at back   Musa
         'behind Musa'

     b. Y-prosody (modified stem)
         ə ^{y}kirshə i Musa
         at back GEN Musa
         'at Musa's back'

2. The segmental properties of diachronic $*\text{-}^y i_{[DET]}$ before additional synchronic vocalic determiners would be deleted under retention and leftward anticipation of Y-prosody, cf. a tentative reanalysis of 'back' (17) and for 'bone, bones' (18) (R. M. Newman, 1977: 123):

(17)   Ø-prosody   Y-prosody: umlaut+suffix deletion
          $^{\emptyset}$kərsə Musa   ə ^{y}kirshə i Musa < $*$ə ^{y}kərsə-Ø i Musa
                                 < $*$ə $^{\emptyset}$kərsə-^{y}i i Musa
          at back Musa   at back-DET GEN Musa

(18)   Ø-prosody   Y-prosody: umlaut+suffix deletion
     SG   ʸʔél-á < *ʸʔál-Ø-á < *ᵠʔál-ʸi-á
                                                          bone-DET-INDEF
     PL   ᵠʔál-c-á
           bone-PL-INDEF

Podoko provides examples of two 'irregular' verbal noun formations for its verb 'die'. The one relevant to the present discussion allows the final verbal noun marker -i to be suffixed to a palatalized verb stem. The synchronic rule, however, postulates that verbal noun formation with -i should be restricted to stems that are non-palatalized, cf. examples under (13). Since the suffix -i, being the most frequent nominalizer for simple verb stems (Jarvis, 1989: 57), is not regularly associated with Y-prosody, the source of palatalization with ʸməts-i 'dying, death' must be sought elsewhere.

Transitive and intransitive verbs in Podoko behave differently with regard to their final vowels when used in the unmarked *aorist/perfective* ([-IPF]) and marked *imperfective* ([+IPF]). Slightly at variance with the treatment in Jarvis (1989) and in keeping with conventional comparative Chadic linguistics (cf. also P. Newman, 1975), I assume the following system for Podoko:

(19)   [-IPF]   [+IPF]
     v.tr   ᵠCVCa   *ᵠCVCə + Y-prosody   > ʸCVCə
     v.itr   ᵠCVCə/a   *ᵠCVC-i$_{[NOM]}$ + Y-prosody   > ᵠCVCi

Why the *imperfective* stem of intransitive verbs is not palatalized as opposed to the *imperfective* stem of transitive verbs will be discussed in section 4.2.2.

According to synchronic rules, the simple stem of the intransitive verb *ᵠmətsə 'die' would be expected to form a verbal noun **ᵠməts-i$_{[NOM]}$, i.e. not undergoing Y-prosody, which – on the surface of things – would also be used in the *imperfective*. In order to explain the 'irregular' palatalization of the actually occurring form ʸməts-i, I suggest to assume that the verbal noun was further submitted to regular IPF marking by *-ʸi$_{[IPF]}$ to give *ᵠməts-i$_{[NOM]}$-ʸi$_{[IPF]}$. This reanalysis is based on the assumption that the verbal nominalizer *i$_{[NOM]}$ is different from the IPF marker *-ʸi$_{[IPF]}$. Forms like this with two adjacent /i/ belonging to different morphemes would regularly undergo haplology deletion of the second *-ʸi. For some reason and only with this one verb, regular haplology deletion of the *-ʸi$_{[IPF]}$ marker was only partial, i.e. affecting segmental /i/, but not Y-prosody. (All other intransitive verbs would undergo complete haplology deletion, including Y-prosody.) Again, like in WC-B Miya and CC-A Guɗe and Ga'anda, we would deal

12.4. Discussion

with instances of prosodic umlaut and subsequent suffix deletion, cf. $\sqrt{}$/mətsə 'die'.

(20)   Ø-prosody   Y-prosody: umlaut+suffix deletion
        **^{Ø}məts-i$_{[NOM]}$ =>   *^{Ø}məts-i$_{[NOM]}$ -^{y}i$_{[IPF]}$ =>*^{y}məts-i-Ø
        **verbal noun   verbal noun+IPF

The next step would be neutralization of the original verbal noun and the verbal noun marked for *imperfective* aspect (lexicalized for 'die') to the benefit of the palatalized form, i.e.*^{y}məts-i$_{[NOM]}$ <>^{y}məts-i$_{[NOM, IPF]}$. Both would now be phonetically identical sharing Y-prosody. For different reasons and supporting this reanalysis, formal identity – albeit without Y-prosody – is also the regular outcome of the rule for all other v.itr., cf. (14, with footnote).

Blocking effect of final /i/ on Y-prosody

In Ga'anda again, vowel-final nouns of the Y-class all end in /i/ (R. M. Newman, 1971: 126). If we maintain that all Y-class nouns in the SG took the diachronic marker */-^{y}i/$_{[DET]}$, then like with *-^{y}i$_{[IPF]}$ in Podoko above, we have to assume an automatic deletion of */-^{y}i/$_{[DET]}$ after i-final nouns, i.e. lexical final */i/ would trigger the complete haplology deletion of the stage-II marker *-^{y}i$_{[DET]}$ including its inherent palatalization potential:

(21)   Ø-prosody
       SG   *^{Ø}CVCi$_{[y\ class]}$-^{y}i$_{[DET]}$ => *^{Ø}CVCi$_{[y\ class]}$-Ø$_{[DET]}$ => ^{Ø}CVCi
       PL ^{Ø}CVCi$_{[y\ class]}$-cə$_{[PL]}$ => ^{Ø}CVCi-cə

Internally reconstructed examples (22) assume such 'regular' complete haplology deletion of *-^{y}i$_{[DET]}$ before vocalic determiners:

(22)   Ø-prosody
       SG ^{Ø}ŋgàms-á < *^{Ø}ŋgàmsì-Ø-a < *^{Ø}ŋgàmsì-^{y}i$_{[DET]}$-a$_{[DET]}$
              spider-INDEF
       PL ^{Ø}ŋgàmsì-c-á
              spider-PL-INDEF

R. M. Newman (1977) mentions two exceptional nouns, which retain Y-prosody. These exceptions are here explained by 'irregular' partial instead of regular complete haplology deletion of *^{y}i$_{[DET]}$, cf. again the umlaut+suffix deletion situation described for Miya, Guɗe and Podoko above, cf. for 'youth' and 'mosquito':

(23)   Ø-prosody   Y-prosody: umlaut+suffix deletion
    $^{Ø}kəmsì$- $^{Y}kìmsh$-$á$ < $^{Y}kəmsì$-Ø-$á$ < $^{Ø}kəmsì$-$^{Y}i_{[DET]}$-$a_{[DET]}$
    $^{Ø}fərdí$- $^{Y}fird$-$á$ < $^{Y}fərd$-Ø-$á$ < $^{*Ø}fərdí$-$^{Y}i_{[DET]}$-$a_{[DET]}$

The same processes occur in Podoko with *imperfective* stems. Transitive verbs mark IPF by suffixing -$^{Y}i_{IPF}$ to the verb stem, followed by partial deletion of the suffix, i.e. the ^{Ø}CVCə verb stems undergo Y-prosody umlaut and subsequent suffix deletion.

(24)   v.tr.   Y-prosody (umlaut+partial affix deletion)
              ^{Y}CVCə$_{[IPF]}$ < ^{Y}CVCə-Ø$_{[IPF]}$ < ^{*Ø}CVCə-^{Y}i$_{[IPF]}$

Intransitive verbs, on the other hand, use their verbal noun when used in the *imperfective*. Verb nominalization involves a non-palatalizing suffix *-i (cf. 19): ^{*Ø}CVCə/a-i$_{[NOM]}$ => ^{Ø}CVCi$_{[NOM]}$. The verbal noun is then marked for IPF by the palatalizing suffix -^{Y}i$_{[IPF]}$, leading to complete haplology deletion. After complete deletion of *-^{Y}i$_{[IPF]}$, the resulting *imperfective* stem looks formally identical again to the verbal noun (neutralization):

(25)   v.itr.   Nominalization+IPF marking: Complete affix deletion
                ^{Ø}CVCi$_{[NOM,IPF]}$ < ^{*Ø}CVC-i-Ø < ^{*Ø}CVC-i$_{[NOM]}$-^{Y}i$_{[IPF]}$

Cf. verbal nouns of the shape ^{Ø}CVCi$_{[NOM]}$ in (13).

12.5   Summary and outlook

THE ASSUMPTIONS PROPOSED by Schuh (1998, 2002) were well founded, namely that Chadic languages show two types of palatalization: (a) localized *phonological*, and (b) *morphological*, and that morphological palatalization is of great time-depth in the history of Chadic. The present paper describes the morphological nature of palatalization (Y-prosody) and some of the morphophonological rules involved. The paper suggests a systematic distinction between *non-palatalizing* and *palatalizing* grammatical morphemes that share the segmental quality */i/, namely */-i/ vs. */-^{Y}i/, which are suffixed to both nouns and verbs. Based on this distinction, there is a *caveat* against premature identification of *imperfective* verb stems with *verbal nouns* based solely on phonetic identity, as has been postulated in previous studies, not the least by the present author. The review of the situation in Podoko in this paper exemplifies hitherto overlooked complexities of the issue.

12.5. Summary and outlook

West and Central Chadic languages share rules of *prosodic umlaut* and subsequent *deletion* of the suffix that originally carried the source of the palatalization. Central Chadic Ga'anda and Podoko share a shallow morphophonological rule of *haplology deletion* with adjacent */i/ and */ʸi/, sharing it to the detail of allowing for synchronic 'exceptions' to be explained in terms of *partial* rather than *complete* haplology deletion. Partial haplology deletion would account for the presence of Y-prosody, while complete haplology deletion would leave no traces of otherwise expected palatalization.

For suffixes of the internally reconstructed shape */-ʸi/, at least four different morphemes were tentatively identified. *{-Y_1} is an ancient marker in the nominal grammar of Chadic. *{-Y_2} is a synchronically productive marker of *imperfective* aspect stems in Podoko. *{-Y_3} is a synchronically productive local 'ventive' verb extension in Guɗe. *{Y_4} is a marker of unclear local function in Ga'anda, operating in combination with just the 2nd and 3rd sg subject with certain 'tenses' in the inflectional system of verbs.

Morphological palatalization offers a glimpse into hitherto under-researched comparative Chadic grammar. Y-prosody has considerable time depth reaching into a period preceding the split of pre-WC and pre-CC from a common PC stock—unless WC-B and CC-A shared a common node in a historical family tree model of Chadic; this was tentatively suggested in Wolff (2001), based on totally different evidence. Whether and how this affects genealogical sub-classification within Chadic, or whether this is best explained in terms of shared areal features emerging from language contact within Chadic, remains to be answered by further research.

References

Aboh, E. O. (2004). *The Morphosyntax of Complement–Head Sequences: Clause Structure and Word Order Patterns in Kwa*. Oxford: Oxford University Press.

Abraham, R. C. (1959). *Hausa Literature and the Hausa Sound System*. London: University of London Press.

Adamu, M. A., & Potiskum, U. B. G. (2009). *Ngizim-English-Hausa Dictionary* (R. G. Schuh, Ed.). Potiskum: Ajami Press.

Adonae, D. A. (2005). *Aspects of Kaakyi Tonology*. Legon-Accra: University of Ghana.

Aissen, J. (2000). Yi and bi: Proximate and obviative in Navajo. *Papers in Honor of Ken Hale, MIT Working Papers on Endangered and Less Familiar Languages, 1*, 129–150.

Akinlabi, A., & Liberman, M. (2000). Tonal complexes and tonal alignment. *North East Linguistic Society, 31*, 1-20.

Altmann, G. (2005). Phonic word structure. In R. Köhler, G. Altmann, & R. Piotrowsk (Eds.), *Quantitative Linguistik / Quantitative Linguistics: Ein internationales Handbuch* (p. 191-208). Berlin: De Gruyter Mouton.

Anderson, S. (1992). *A-Morphous Morphology*. Cambridge: Cambridge University Press.

Anttila, A. (2002). Morphologically conditioned phonological alternations. *Natural Language and Linguistic Theory, 20*, 1–42.

Aschmann, H. (1973). *Diccionario Totonaco de Papantla, Veracruz*. Mexico: Instituto Lingüístico del Verano.

Austin, J. L. (1962). *How to Do Things with Words: The William James Lectures, Delivered at Harvard Univ. in 1955*. Oxford: Clarendon Press.

Awagana, E. A. (2001). *Grammatik des Buduma: Phonologie, Morphologie, Syntax.* Hamburg: LIT Verlag Münster.

Bach, E., & Harms, R. (1972). How do languages get crazy rules? In R. Stockwell & R. Macaulay (Eds.), *Linguistic Change and Generative Theory* (p. 1-21). Bloomington: Indiana University Press.

Badan, L., & Buell, L. (2012). Exploring expressions of focus in Ewe. *Nordic Journal of African Studies, 21*(3), 141-163.

Baković, E. (2013). *Blocking and Complementarity in Phonological Theory.* London: Equinox Publishing.

Barreteau, D. (1983). Phonémique et prosodie en HIGI. In E. Wolff & H. Meyer-Bahlburg (Eds.), *Studies in Chadic and Afroasiatic Linguistics* (p. 249-276). Hamburg: Buske.

Barth, H. (1857). *Travels and Discoveries in North and Central Africa.* London: John Murray.

Bender, M. (1974). Phoneme frequences in Amharic. *Journal of Ethiopian Studies, 12*, 19-24.

Berkes, R. (1995). *Comparative Indo-European Linguistics: An Introduction.* Amsterdam: John Benjamins.

Bičan, A. (n.d.). *Frequency of the Czech phonemes.* (Online resource available at http://www.ujc.cas.cz/phword/phonemes-lex.html. Accessed August 1, 2017)

Blackings, M. (2000). *Ma'di-English Dictionary.* München: Lincom Europa.

Blanche-Benveniste, C., Bilger, M., Rouget, C., van den Eynde, K., & Mertens, P. (1990). *Le français parlé: Études grammaticales.* Paris: CNRS.

Blench, R. (2005). A survey of Dogon languages in Mali: An overview. *OGMIOS: Newsletter of the Foundation for Endangered Languages, 3*(02), 14-15.

Blust, R. (1973). The origins of Bintulu ɓ, ɗ. *Bulletin of the School of Oriental and African Studies, 36*, 603-620.

Blust, R. (2013). *The Austronesian Languages, Revised Edition.* Canberra: Asia-Pacific Linguistics, School of Culture, History and Language, College of Asia and the Pacific, The Australian National University. (http://pacling.anu.edu.au/materials/Blust2013Austronesian.pdf. Accessed October 10, 2017.)

Blust, R., & Trussel, S. (2010-2016). *Austronesian Comparative Dictionary.* (Web edition: www.trussel2.com/ACD. Accessed August 25, 2017)

Bobaljik, J. (2000). The ins and outs of contextual allomorphy. In K. K. Grohman & C. Struijke (Eds.), *University of Maryland Working Papers in Linguistics* (p. 35-71). University of Maryland.

Booij, G. (2010). *Construction Morphology*. Oxford University Press.

Borg, M., Bugeja, K., Vella, C., Mangion, G., & Gafá, C. (2011). *Preparation of a Free-Running Text Corpus for Maltese Concatenative Speech Synthesis*. (Research & Development Department, Crimsonwing p.l.c., Marsa, Malta)

Bowern, C. (2012). *A Grammar of Bardi*. Berlin: Walter de Gruyter.

Bryan, M. A. (1975). The I- and U-coloration syndrome: An exercise in morphotypology. In S. H. A. Hurreiz & H. Bell (Eds.), *Directions in Sudanese Linguistics and Folklore* (pp. 63–76). Khartoum: Institute of African and Asian Studies, University of Khartoum.

Buell, L. (2011). Zulu ngani "why": Postverbal and yet in CP. *Lingua, 121*, 805–821.

Buell, L. (2012). *A first look at Ewe VP fronting and derivation by phase*. (Unpublished ms., available at http://www.lingBuzz/001486)

Buell, L., & Riedel, K. (2008). *The conjoint/disjoint alternation in Sambaa*. (TiN-Dag conference talk handout)

Bulakarima, U. (2001). *A Study in Kanuri Dialectology: Phonology and Dialectical Distribution in Mowar*. Maiduguri: Awwal.

Burzio, L. (2005). Sources of paradigm uniformity. In L. J. Downing, T. A. Hall, & R. Raffelsiefen (Eds.), *Paradigms in phonological theory* (p. 65-106). Oxford: Oxford University Press.

Bye, P., & Svenonius, P. (2012). Nonconcatenative morphology as epiphenomenon. In J. Trommer (Ed.), *The morphology and phonology of exponence: The State of the Art* (p. 427-495). Oxford University Press.

Caballero, G. (2008). *Choguita Rarámuri (Tarahumara) Phonology and Morphology* (Unpublished doctoral dissertation). University of California, Berkeley.

Caballero, G. (2010). Scope, phonology and templates in an agglutinating language: Choguita Rarámuri (Tarahumara) variable suffix ordering. *Morphology, 20*(1), 165–204.

Caballero, G. (2011). Multiple exponence and the phonology-morphology interface. *Proceedings of the North East Linguistics Society (NELS), 39*, 177–190.

Caballero, G., & Harris, A. (2012). A working typology of multiple exponence. In F. Kiefer, M. Ladányi, & P. Siptár (Eds.), *Current Issues in Morphological Theory: (Ir)regularity, Analogy and Frequency* (pp. 163–188). Amsterdam: John Benjamins.

Caballero, G., & Inkelas, S. (2013). Word construction: Tracing an optimal path through the lexicon. *Morphology, 23*(2), 103–143.

Cahill, M. (2006). Tone dissimilation or tone polarity. *Gur Papers/Cahiers*

Voltaïques, 7, 5-15.
Cahill, M. (2007). More universals of tone. *SIL Electronic Working Papers*.
Carlin, E. (1993). *The So Language*. Köln: Institut für Afrikanistik, Universität zu Köln.
Caron, B. (2005). *Za:r (Dictionary, Grammar, Texts)*. Ibadan (Nigeria): IFRA.
Caron, B. (2014). *Lexique haoussa de l'Ader*. (Unpublished electronic database, LLACAN, Paris)
Caron, B. (2017). *Macrosyntactic corpus annotation. The case of Zaar*. Ms.
Chen, M. (2000). *Tone Sandhi*. Cambridge: Cambridge University Press.
Chomsky, N., & Halle, M. (1968). *The sound pattern of English*. New York: Harper & Row.
Clairis, C. (1985). *El Qawasqar: Lingüística Fueguina, Teoría y Descripción*. Valdivia: Estudios Filológicos.
Clark, M. (1983). On the distribution of contour tones. *West Coast Conference on Formal Linguistics 2*, 44-55.
Clements, G., & Ford, K. (1979). Kikuyu tone shift and its synchronic consequences. *Linguistic Inquiry*, *10*, 179-210.
Conteh, P., Cowper, E., James, D., Rice, K., & Szamosi, M. (1983). A reanalysis of tone in Mende. *Current approaches to African linguistics*, *2*, 127–137.
Corbett, G. (2007). Canonical typology, suppletions, and possible words. *Language*, *83*, 8-42.
Coupez, A. (1954). *Études sur la langue Luba*. Tervuren: Annaeles du Musée Royal du Congo Belge.
Crane, T. (2014). Melodic tone in Totela TAM. *Africana Linguistica*, *20*, 63-79.
Creissels, D. (2008). *Akhvakh Lexicon*. (Ms., Laboratoire Dynamique de Langage, Université Lyon-2, Lyon)
Creissels, D. (2011). *Liste lexical Akhvakh*. (Unpublished wordlist. Laboratoire Dynamique de Langage, Université Lyon-2)
Creissels, D., & Chebanne, A. (2000). *Dictionnaire Français-Setswana, Setswana-Français*. Mogoditshane & Gaborone: Tatsalls Publishing & Books.
Cresti, E., & Moneglia, M. (Eds.). (2005). *C-ORAL-ROM: Integrated Reference Corpora for Spoken Romance Languages*. Amsterdam: John Benjamins.
Cyffer, N. (1998). *A sketch of Kanuri*. Cologne: Rüdiger Köppe.
Cyffer, N. (2010). *GA, RO & Co: Strategies of complementation and subordination in Kanuri* (G. Ziegelmeyer & N. Cyffer, Eds.). Cologne: Rüdiger Köppe.

Davan, M. S. (2010). *Bup Dzanyi Gwaa*. Ibadan (Nigeria): Ifra-Nigéria.
Devine, A., & Stephens, L. (1994). *The Prosody of Greek Speech*. Oxford: Oxford University Press.
Dole, J. A. J., Goge, U. M., & Gashinge, I. A. (2009). *Ngamo-English-Hausa Dictionary* (R. Schuh, Ed.). Potiskum: Ajami Press.
Donohue, M. (1999). *A grammar of Tukang Besi*. Berlin: Mouton de Gruyter.
Downing, L. (1990a). Local and metrical shift in Nguni. *Studies in African Linguistics, 21*, 261-317.
Downing, L. (1990b). *Problems in Jita Tonology* (Unpublished doctoral dissertation). University of Illinois.
Downing, L. (2005). Jita causative doubling provides optimal paradigms. In T. A. Downing Laura. Hall & R. Raffelsiefen (Eds.), *Paradigms in Phonological Theory* (pp. 122–144). Oxford University Press.
Dresher, E., & Lahiri, A. (1991). The Germanic foot: Metrical coherence in Old English. *Linguistic Inquiry, 22*(2), 251-286.
Dundaa, M. (n.d.). *Kaakyi Noun Morphology and Noun Phrase Constituents*. (Kaakyi project, Ghana Institute of Linguisics, Literacy, and Bible Translation. Unpublished ms.)
Dundaa, M. (2007). *Transitional Primer: Can You Read and Write in Kaakyi?* Tamale, Ghana: Ghana Institute of Linguistics, Literacy, and Bible Translation.
Dwyer, D. (1971). Mende tone. *Studies in African Linguistics, 2*(2), 117.
Dwyer, D. (1973). *The Comparative Tonology of Southwestern Mande Nominals* (Unpublished doctoral dissertation). Michigan State University.
Dwyer, D. (1978a). Idiosyncratic, suprasegmental processes in Mende. *Studies in African Linguistics, 9*(3), 333-343.
Dwyer, D. (1978b). What sort of tone language is Mende? *Studies in African Linguistics, 9*(2), 167-208.
Embick, D., & Noyer, R. (2001). Movement operations after syntax. *Linguistic Inquiry, 32*(4), 555–595.
Embick, D., & Noyer, R. (2007). Distributed morphology and the syntax-morphology interface. In *The Oxford Handbook of Linguistic Interfaces* (p. 289-324). Oxford: Oxford University Press.
Emenanjo, N. (1987). *Elements of Modern Igbo Grammar*. Ibadan: University of Ibadan Press.
Esquerra, I., Febrer, A., & Nadeu, C. (1998). *Frequency Analysis of Phonetic Units for Concatenative Synthesis in Catalan*. (http://www.lsi.upc.edu/ nlp/papers/esquerra98.pdf)
Farnetani, E., & Kori, S. (1986). Effects of syllable and word structure on segmental durations in spoken Italian. *Speech Communication, 5*(1), 17-

24.
Faust, N. (1973). *Lecciones para el Aprendisaje del Idioma Shipibo-Conibo*. Lima: Instituto de Verano.
Fedden, S. (2017). Tonal inflection in Mian. In E. L. Palancar & J. L. Léonard (Eds.), *Tone and Inflection: New Facts and New Perspectives* (p. 67-82). De Gruyter Mouton.
Ferry, M. (1991). *Thesaurus Tenda: Dictionnaire Ethnolinguistique de Langues Sénégalo-Guinnéennes (Bassari, Bedik, Konyagi)*. Paris: Société des Etudes Linguistiques et Anthropologiques de France.
Fiedler, I. (2012). Predicate-centered focus in Gbe. In M. Brenzinger & A.-M. Fehn (Eds.), *Proceedings of the 6th World Conference on African Linguistics (WOCAL), Cologne, August 17–21, 2009* (p. 303-405). Köln: Rüdiger Köppe.
Fromkin, V. (Ed.). (1987). *Tone: A Linguistic Survey*. New York: Academic Press.
Gandour, J., & Potisuk, S. (1994). Tonal coarticulation in Thai. *Journal of Phonetics*, *22*, 477–492.
Ghana Institute of Linguistics, Literacy, and Bible Translation. (2011). *The Book of Mark*. (Translation)
Ghatage, A. (1964). *Phonemic and Morphemic Frequencies in Hindi*. Pune: Deccan College.
Gimba, A. M. (2000). *Bole Verb Morphology* (Unpublished doctoral dissertation). University of California, Los Angeles.
Gimba, A. M., Ali, M. B., & Bah, M. (2009). *Bole-English-Hausa Dictionary* (R. G. Schuh, Ed.). Potiskum: Ajami Press.
Gimba, A. M., & Schuh, R. (2014). *Bole-English-Hausa Dictionary and English-Bole Wordlist*. Berkeley: University of California Press.
Givón, T. (1971). Historical syntax and synchronic morphology: An archeologist's field trip. In *Chicago Linguistic Society 7* (p. 394-415).
Goldsmith, J. (1976). *Autosegmental Phonology* (Unpublished doctoral dissertation). Massachusetts Institute of Technology.
Goldsmith, J. (1984). Meeussen's Rule. In M. Aronoff & R. Oehrle (Eds.), *Language Sound Structure* (p. 245-259). Cambridge: MIT Press.
Goldsmith, J. (1987). Tone and accent, and getting the two together. In *Berkeley Linguistics Society 13* (p. 88-104).
Goldwater, S., & Johnson, M. (2003). Learning OT constraint rankings using a maximum entropy model. In J. Spenader, A. Eriksson, & Ö. Dahl (Eds.), *Proceedings of the Stockholm Workshop on Variation within Optimality Theory* (p. 150-159). Stockholm: Stockholm University.
González, A. (2005). *A Grammar of Tapiete (Tupi-Guarani)* (Unpublished

doctoral dissertation). University of Pittsburgh.
Gordon, M. (2001). A typology of contour tone restrictions. *Studies in Language, 25*, 405-444.
Goslin, J., Galuzzi, C., & Romani, C. (2012). *PhonItalia*. (Available at http://www.psy.plymouth.ac.uk/research/jgoslin/phonitalia/)
Gravina, R. (2014). *The Phonology of Proto-Central Chadic*. Utrecht: LOT.
Green, C. R. (2013). Formalizing the prosodic word domain in Bambara tonology. *Journal of West African Languages XL, 1*, 3-20.
Green, C. R. (2017). *Towards a typology of 'tonal compactness' in Mande*. (ACAL 48, Indiana University)
Greenberg, J. (1963). *The Languages of Africa*. Bloomington: Indiana Univeristy.
Greenberg, J. (1966a). *Language Universals, with Special Reference to Feature Hierarchies*. The Hague: Mouton.
Greenberg, J. (1966b). Synchronic and diachronic universals in phonology. *Language, 42*, 508-517.
Greenberg, J. (1978). How do languages acquire gender markers? In J. Greenberg (Ed.), *Universals of Human Language, Vol. 2* (p. 47-82). Stanford: Stanford University Press.
Greenberg, J. H. (1981). Nilo-Saharan moveable-*k* as a stage III article (with a Penutian typological parallel). *Journal of African Languages and Linguistics, 3*(2), 105–112.
Gribanova, V. (2015). Exponence and morphosyntactically triggered phonological processes in the Russian verbal complex. *Journal of Linguistics, 51*, 519-561.
Grubb, D. (1977). *A Practical Writing System and Short Dictionary of Kwakw'ala (Kwakiutl)*. Ottawa: National Museum of Man.
Haas, M. (1964). *Thai-English Student's Dictionary*. Palo Alto: Stanford University Press.
Hale, K. (1973). A note on subject-object inversion in Navajo. In B. B. Kachru, R. B. Lees, Y. Malkiel, A. Pietrangeli, & S. Saporta (Eds.), *Issues in Linguistics: Papers in Honor of Henry and Renée Kahane* (p. 300-309). Urbana: University of Illinois Press.
Hale, K., Jelinek, E., & Willie, M. A. (2003). Topic and focus scope positions in Navajo. In S. Karimi (Ed.), *Word Order and Scrambling* (pp. 1–21). Malden, MA: Blackwell Publishing Ltd.
Halle, M. (1990). An approach to morphology. In *Proceedings of North Eastern Linguistics Society 20* (p. 150–184).
Halle, M., & Marantz, A. (1993). Distributed morphology and the pieces of inflection. In K. Hale & S. J. Keyser (Eds.), *In the View from Building 20*

(p. 111-176). MIT Press, Cambridge.
Halle, M., & Mohanan, K. P. (1985). Segmental phonology of Modern English. *Linguistic Inquiry*, *16*(1), 67-116.
Hammond, M. (1997). Vowel quantity and syllabification in English. *Language*, *73*(1), 1-17.
Harley, H., & Noyer, R. (1999). Distributed morphology. *Glot International*, *4*(4), 3-9.
Harris, A. (2017). *Multiple Exponence*. Oxford University Press.
Harry, O., & Hyman, L. (2014). Phrasal construction tonology: The case of Kalabari. *Studies in Language*, *38*, 649-689.
Hay, J., & Plag, I. (2004). What constrains possible suffix combinations? On the interaction of grammatical and processing restrictions in derivational morphology. *Natural Language and Linguistic Theory*, *22*, 565-596.
Hayes, B. (1982). Extrametricality and English stress. *Linguistic Inquiry*, *13*(2), 227-276.
Heath, J. (2008). *Grammar of Jamsay*. Mouton de Gruyter.
Heath, J. (2016). *A Grammar of Nanga*. (Unpublished Ms.)
Heath, J., & McPherson, L. (2013). Tonosyntax and reference restriction in Dogon NPs. *Language*, *89*(2), 265-296.
Heine, B. (1993). *Ik Dictionary*. Rüdiger Köppe Verlag.
Hellenthal, A. (2010). *A Grammar of Sheko*. Utrecht: LOT—Netherlands Graduate School of Linguistics.
Higgins, J. (1993). *RP phonemes and minimal pairs*. (Available at https://linguistlist.org/issues/4/4-294.html.)
Hiribarren, V. (2017). *A History of Borno: Trans-Saharan African Empire to Failing Nigerian State*. London: Hurst.
Hirsch, A. (2014). What is the domain for weight computation: The syllable or the interval? *Proceedings of the 2013 Annual Meeting on Phonology*, *1*(1), 1-12.
Hooper, J. (1973). *Aspects of Natural Generative Phonology* (Unpublished doctoral dissertation). University of California, Los Angeles.
Hooper, J. (1976). *Aspects of Natural Generative Phonology*. New York: Academic Press.
Hoskison, J. T. (1975). *Notes on the Phonology of Gude* (Unpublished master's thesis). Ohio State University.
Hoskison, J. T. (1983). *A Grammar and Dictionary of the Gude Language* (Unpublished doctoral dissertation). Ohio State University.
Huang, H. (2005). On the status of onglides in Isbukun Bunun. *Concentric Studies in Linguistics*, *31*(1), 1-20.

Huddleston, R., & Pullum, G. K. (2008). *The Cambridge Grammar of the English Language*. Cambridge: Cambridge University Press.

Hyman, L. (1978). Historical tonology. In V. Fromkin (Ed.), *Tone: A Linguistic Survey* (p. 257-269). New York: Academic Press.

Hyman, L. (1979). Tonology of the Babanki noun. *Studies in African Linguistics*, *10*, 159-178.

Hyman, L. (1986). Downstep deletion in Aghem. In D. Odden (Ed.), *Current Approaches to African Linguistics, Vol. 4* (p. 209-222). Dordrecht: Foris Publications.

Hyman, L. (1987). Prosodic domains in Kukuya. *Natural Language & Linguistic Theory*, *5*(3), 311-333.

Hyman, L. (2003). Suffix ordering in Bantu: A morphocentric approach. In G. Booij & J. van Marle (Eds.), *Yearbook of morphology, 2002* (pp. 245-281). Springer.

Hyman, L. (2007). Universals of tone rules: 30 years later. In T. Riad & C. Gussenhoven (Eds.), *Tones and Tunes: Studies in Word and Sentence Prosody* (p. 1-34). Berlin: Mouton de Gruyter.

Hyman, L. (2010). Amazonia and the typology of tone systems. *UC Berkeley Phonology Lab Annual Report*, 376-394.

Hyman, L. (2014). How autosegmental is phonology? *The Linguistic Review*, *31*, 363-400.

Hyman, L. (2017). Morphological tonal assignments in conflict: Who wins? In E. L. Palancar & J. L. Léonard (Eds.), *Tone and Inflection: New Facts and New Perspectives* (p. 15-40). De Gruyter Mouton.

Hyman, L., & Schuh, R. (1974). Universals of tone rules: Evidence from West Africa. *Linguistic Inquiry*, *5*, 81-115.

Hyman, L., & Tadadjeu, M. (1976). Floating tones in Mbam-Nkam. In L. Hyman (Ed.), *Studies in Bantu Tonology* (Vol. 3, p. 58-111). University of Southern California.

Hyman, L., & VanBik, K. (2004). Directional rule application and output problems in Hakha Lai tone. *Language and Linguistics*, *5*, 821-861.

Inkelas, S. (2011). The interaction between morphology and phonology. In *Handbook of Phonological Theory, 2nd ed.* (p. 68-102). Blackwell.

Inkelas, S., & Zoll, C. (2005). *Reduplication: Doubling in morphology*. Cambridge: Cambridge University Press.

Innes, G. (1969). *A Mende-English Dictionary*. Cambridge: Cambridge University Press.

Itô, J., & Mester, A. (1995). The core-periphery structure of the lexicon and constraints on reranking. *Papers in Optimality Theory*, *18*, 181-209.

Jacobson, S. (1984). *Yup'ik Eskimo Dictionary*. Fairbanks: Alaska Native

Language Center.
Jarvis, E. (1989). Esquisse grammaticale du podoko. In D. Barreteau & R. Hedinger (Eds.), *Descriptions de Langues Camerounaises* (p. 39-127). Paris: ORSTOM; ACCT.
Jelinek, E., & Willie, M. (1996). "Psych" verbs in Navajo. In E. Jelinek, S. Midgette, K. Rice, & L. Saxon (Eds.), *Athabaskan Language Studies: Essays in Honor of Robert W. Young* (pp. 15-34). Albuquerque: University of New Mexico Press.
Jungraithmayr, H., & Ibriszimow, D. (1994). *Chadic Lexical Roots*. Berlin: Reimer.
Kager, R. (1993). Alternatives to the iambic-trochaic law. *Natural Language and Linguistic Theory, 11*(3), 381-432.
Kandybowicz, J. (2008). *The Grammar of Repetition: Nupe Grammar at the Syntax–Phonology Interface*. Amsterdam: John Benjamins.
Kandybowicz, J., & Torrence, H. (2011). Krachi wh-in-situ: A question of prosody. In J. Choi, E. A. Hogue, J. Punske, D. Tat, J. Schertz, & A. Trueman (Eds.), *Proceedings of the 29th West Coast Conference on Formal Linguistics* (p. 362-370). Somerville, MA: Cascadilla Proceedings Project.
Karvonen, D. (2008). Explaining nonfinality: Evidence from Finnish. In C. B. Chang & H. J. Haynie (Eds.), *Proceedings of the 26th West Coast Conference on Formal Linguistics* (p. 306-314). Somerville, MA: Cascadilla Proceedings Project.
Kato, H., Tsuzaki, M., & Sagisaka, Y. (2003). Functional differences between vowel onsets and offsets in temporal perception of speech. *Journal of the Acoustical Society of America, 113*(6), 3379-3389.
Kenyon, J. S., & Knott, T. A. (1953). *A Pronouncing Dictionary of American English*. Springfield, MA: G. & C. Merriam Company.
Kingston, J. (2003). Mechanisms of tone reversal. In S. Kaji (Ed.), *Cross-linguistic Studies of Tonal Phenomena* (p. 57-120). Tokyo: ILCAA.
Kiparsky, P. (1973). Abstractness, opacity and global rules. In O. Fujimura (Ed.), *Three dimensions in linguistic theory* (p. 57-86). Tokyo: Taishukan Publishing.
Kiparsky, P. (2010). Dvandvas, blocking, and the associative: The bumpy ride from phrase to word. *Language, 86*(2), 302–331.
Kirchner, M. (1989). *Phonologie des Kasachischen: Untersuchungen anhand von Sprachaufnahmen aus der kasachischen Exilgruppe in Istanbul*. Wiesbaden: Otto Harrassowitz Verlag.
Konoshenko, M. (2008). Tonal systems in three dialects of the Kpelle language. *Mandenkan, 44*, 21–42.

Korboe, A. J. (2002). *The Study of the Nominal Phrase in Kaakyi* (Masters thesis). University of Ghana, Legon-Accra.

Korsah, S. (2017). *Issues in Kwa syntax: Pronouns and Clausal Determiners* (Unpublished doctoral dissertation). Leipzig University.

Kotapish, C., & Kotapish, S. (1975). *A Darai-English, English-Darai Glossary*. Kathmandu: SIL, and Institute of Nepal and Asian Studies.

Kropp Dakubu, M. E. (1992). Contrast in context: Topic, focus and definiteness in Gã. *Journal of West African Languages*, 22(2), 3-16.

Kubozono, H. (2001). On the markedness of diphthongs. *Kobe Papers in Linguistics*, 3, 60-74.

Kurisu, K. (2001). *The phonology of morpheme realization* (Unpublished doctoral dissertation). University of California, Santa Cruz.

Lacheret, A., Kahane, S., Beliao, J., Dister, A., Gerdes, K., Goldman, J.-P., ... Tchobanov, A. (2014). *Rhapsodie: a Prosodic-Syntactic Treebank for Spoken French*. (Language Resources and Evaluation Conference, May 2014, Reykjavik, Iceland. http://hal.upmc.fr/hal-00968959/document)

Leben, W. (1971). The morphophonemics of tone in Hausa. In C.-W. Kim & H. Stahlke (Eds.), *Papers in African Linguistics* (p. 201-218). Alberta: Linguistic Research, Inc.

Leben, W. (1973). *Suprasegmental Phonology* (Unpublished doctoral dissertation). Massachusetts Institute of Technology.

Leben, W. (1978). The representation of tone. In V. Fromkin (Ed.), *Tone* (pp. 177–219). New York: Academic Press.

Lefebvre, C. (2015). *Functional Categories in Three Atlanic creoles: Saramaccan, Haitian, and Papiamentu*. Amsterdam: John Benjamins.

Legendre, G., Miyata, Y., & Smolensky, P. (1990). *Harmonic Grammar - A Formal Multi-level Connectionist Theory of Linguistic Well-formedness: Theoretical Foundations* (Tech. Rep.). University of Boulder, CO.

Liberman, M., & Prince, A. (1977). On stress and linguistic rhythm. *Linguistic Inquiry*, 8(2), 249-336.

Loriot, J., Lauriault, E., & Day, D. (1993). *Diccionario Shipibo-Castellano*. Lima: Ministerio de Educación and Instituto Lingüístico de Verano.

Luhana, K. K. (n.d.). *Sindhi Online Dictionary (Based on Luhana Sindhi dictionary of Kirshan Kumar Luhana)*. (Available at http://sindhyat.com/database/SindhiDictionary)

Lunden, A. (2010). *A Phonetically-Motivated Phonological Analysis of Syllable Weight and Stress in the Norwegian Language*. Lewiston, NY: Edwin Mellen Books.

Maclachlan, A. (1989). Morphosyntax of Tagalog verbs: The inflectional system and its interaction with derivational morphology. *McGill Working*

Papers in Linguistics, 6(1), 65–84.

Maddieson, I. (2013). Voicing and gaps in plosive systems. In M. S. Dryer & M. Haspelmath (Eds.), *World Atlas of Language Structures Online*. Leipzig: Max Planck Institute for Evolutionary Anthropology. (Available at http://wals.info/chapter/5)

Maddieson, I., & Flavier, S. (2014-2017). *LAPSyD: Lyon-Albuquerque Phonological Systems Database*. (Available at http://www.lapsyd.ddl.ish-lyon.cnrs.fr/index.php)

Maddieson, I., Flavier, S., Marsico, E., Coupé, C., & Pellegrino, F. (2013). LAPSyD: Lyon-Albuquerque Phonological Systems Database. In *Proceedings of Interspeech 2013, Lyon*.

Maddieson, I., & Precoda, K. (1992). Syllable structure and phonetic models. *Phonology*, 9, 45-60.

Mallik, B., Bhattacharya, N., Kunda, S., & Dawn, M. (1998). *The Phonemic and Morphemic Frequencies of the Bengali Language*. Calcutta: The Asiatic Society.

Manker, J. (2014). The syntax of sluicing in Hän. In *Proceedings of the Dene (Athabaskan) Languages Conference*.

Martin, S. (1987). *The Japanese Language through Time*. New Haven: Yale University Press.

Matthews, P. (1974). *Morphology: An Introduction to the Theory of Word-structure*. Cambridge: Cambridge University Press.

McCarthy, J. (2003). Comparative markedness. *Theoretical Linguistics*, 29(1-2), 1-51.

McCarthy, J. (2003). OT constraints are categorical. *Phonology*, 20, 75–138.

McCarthy, J. (2005). Optimal paradigms. In L. Downing, T. A. Hall, & R. Raffelsiefen (Eds.), *Paradigms in Phonological Theory* (pp. 170–210). Oxford University Press.

McCarthy, J., & Prince, A. (1993). Generalized alignment. In G. Booij & J. van Marle (Eds.), *Yearbook of Morphology* (pp. 79–153). Dordrecht: Kluwer.

McCawley, J. (1978). What is a tone language? In V. Fromkin (Ed.), *Tone* (pp. 113–131). New York: Academic Press.

McCrary, K. (2006). *Reassessing the Role of the Syllable in Italian Phonology*. New York: Routledge.

McPherson, L. (2011). *Tonal Underspecification and Interpolation in Tommo So* (Unpublished master's thesis). UCLA.

McPherson, L. (2013). *A Grammar of Tommo So*. Berlin: De Gruyter Mouton.

McPherson, L. (2014). *Replacive Grammatical Tone in the Dogon Languages*

(Unpublished doctoral dissertation). UCLA.

McPherson, L. (2016). Culminativity and ganging in the tonology of Awa suffixes. *Language: Phonological Analysis*, *92*(1), e38-e66.

McPherson, L., & Hayes, B. (2016). Relating application frequency to morphological distance: the case of Tommo So vowel harmony. *Phonology*, *33*(1), 125-167.

McPherson, L., & Heath, J. (2016). Phrasal grammatical tone in the Dogon languages. *Natural Language and Linguistic Theory*, *34*(2), 593-639.

Meeussen, A. (1951). Tone contraction in Ciluba (Kasayi). *Kongo-Oversee*, *17*, 289-291.

Meira, S. (1999). *A Grammar of Tiriyó* (Unpublished doctoral dissertation). Rice University, Houston.

Mugele, R., & Rodewald, M. (1991). Aspects of Bandi tonology. *Studies in African Linguistics*, *22*(2), 103-134.

Muysken, P. (1988). Affix Order and Interpretation: Quechua. In M. Everaert, A. Evers, R. Huybregts, & M. Trommelen (Eds.), *Morphology and Modularity: In Honour of Henk Schultink* (p. 259-280). Holland: Foris Publications.

Myers, S. (1987). Vowel shortening in English. *Natural Language & Linguistic Theory*, *5*(4), 485-518.

Nash, J. (1994). Underlying low tones in Ruwund. *Studies in African Linguistics*, *23*, 223-278.

Nejad, A., & Qaracholloo, M. (2013). Frequency system of phonemes: contrastive analysis of common standard Persian and English consonants in context-based corpora. *Asian Social Science*, *9*, 76-90.

New, B. (2006). Lexique 3: Une nouvelle base de données lexicales. In *Actes de la Conférence Traitement Automatique des Langues Naturelles (TALN 2006)*. Louvain, Belgium.

Newman, P. (1964). A word list of Tera. *Journal of West African Languages*, *1*, 33-50.

Newman, P. (1971). Transitive and intransitive in Chadic languages. In V. Six, N. Cyffer, E. Wolff, L. Gerhardt, & H. Meyer-Bahlburg (Eds.), *Afrikanische Sprachen und Kulturen, ein Querschnitt (Festschrift J. Lukas)*. Hamburg: Hamburger Beiträge zur Afrika-Kunde.

Newman, P. (1974). *The Kanakuru Language*. Leeds: Institute of Modern English Language Studies.

Newman, P. (1975). Proto-Chadic verb classes. *Folia Orientalia*, *16*, 65-84.

Newman, P. (1977). Chadic classification and reconstructions. *Afroasiatic Linguistics*, *5*, 1-42.

Newman, P. (1995). Hausa tonology: Complexities in an "easy" tone language. In J. Goldsmith (Ed.), *Blackwell Handbook of Phonological Theory* (p. 762-781). Oxford: Blackwell.

Newman, P. (2000). *The Hausa Language: An Encyclopedic Reference Grammar*. New Haven: Yale University Press.

Newman, P., & Jaggar, P. (1989). Low tone raising in Hausa: A critical assessment. *Studies in African Linguistics, 20*, 227-251.

Newman, P., & Ma, R. (1966). Comparative Chadic: Phonology and lexicon. *Journal of African Languages, 5*, 218-251.

Newman, P., & Schuh, R. (1974). The Hausa aspect system. *Afroasiatic Linguistics, 1*(1), 1-39.

Newman, R. M. (1971). *A Case Grammar of Ga'anda* (Unpublished doctoral dissertation). UCLA.

Newman, R. M. (1977). Y-prosody as a morphological process in Ga'anda. In P. Newman & R. M. Newman (Eds.), *Papers in Chadic Linguistics* (p. 212-230). Leiden: AfrikaStudiecentrum.

Noyer, R. (1992). *Features, Positions, and Affixes in Autonomous Morphological Structure* (Unpublished doctoral dissertation). MIT.

Noyer, R. (1997). *Features, positions, and affixes in autonomous morphological structure*. New York & London: Garland.

Odden, D. (1982). Tonal phenomena in KiShambaa. *Studies in African Linguistics, 13*, 177-207.

Odden, D. (1998). Verbal tone in Kikerewe. In I. Maddieson & T. Hinnebusch (Eds.), *Language History and Linguistic Description in Africa* (p. 177-184). Trenton, NJ: Africa World Press.

Ohala, J., & Riordan, C. (1979). Passive vocal tract enlargement during voiced stops. In J. Wolf & D. Klatt (Eds.), *Speech Communication Papers* (p. 89-92). New York: Acoustic Society of America.

Osam, E. K. A. (1994). *Aspects of Akan Grammar: A Functional Perspective* (Unpublished doctoral dissertation). University of Oregon.

O'Leary, M. (2017). The interaction of wh-movement and topicalization in Hän. *2016 Dene Language Conference Proceedings*.

Palancar, E. L. (2017). A typology of tone and inflection: A view from the Oto-Manguean languages of Mexico. In E. L. Palancar & J. L. Léonard (Eds.), *Tone and Inflection: New Facts and New Perspectives* (p. 109-140). Berlin: De Gruyter Mouton.

Palancar, E. L., & Léonard, J. L. (Eds.). (2017). *Tone and Inflection: New Facts and New Perspectives*. Berlin: De Gruyter Mouton.

Palmer, B. (1999). *A Grammar of the Kokota Language, Santa Isabel, Solomon Islands* (Unpublished doctoral dissertation). University of Sydney.

Paster, M. (2006). Pulaar verbal extensions and phonologically driven affix order. In G. Booij & J. van Marle (Eds.), *Yearbook of Morphology 2005* (pp. 155–199). The Netherlands: Springer.

Pater, J. (2000). Non-uniformity in English secondary stress : The role of ranked and lexically specific constraints. *Phonology, 17*(2), 237–274.

Payne, D. L., & Ole-Kotikash, L. (2008). *Maa Dictionary*. (Available at http://pages.uoregon.edu/maasai/Maa%20Lexicon/lexicon/main.htm)

Pennington, R. (2014). *Ma Manda Phonology*. Dallas: SIL International.

Petrollino, S. (2016). Hamar-English selected lexicon. In S. Petrollino (Ed.), *A Grammar of Hamar: A South Omotic Language of Ethiopia* (p. 297-318). Köln: Rüdiger Köppe Verlag.

Philippson, G. (1991). *Ton et accent dans les languages bantu d'Afrique orientale: Étude comparative typologique et diachronique* (Unpublished doctoral dissertation). Université René Descartes, Paris.

Picanço, G. (2005). *Munduruku: Phonetics, phonology, synchrony, diachrony* (Unpublished doctoral dissertation). University of British Columbia.

Platero, P. (1982). Missing noun phrases and grammatical relations in Navajo. *International Journal of American Linguistics, 48*(3), 286–305.

Prince, A. (1991). Quantitative consequences of rhythmic organization. In M. N. K. Deaton & M. Ziolkowski (Eds.), *Papers from the 26th Linguistic Society: Parasession on the syllable in phonetics and phonology* (p. 355-398). Chicago: Chicago Linguistic Society.

Prince, A., & Smolensky, P. (1993). Optimality Theory: Constraint Interaction in Generative Grammar; CU-CS-696-93. *Computer Science Technical Reports*.

Pulleyblank, D. (1986). *Tone in Lexical Phonology*. Dordrecht: Reidel.

Revithiadou, A. (2004). The iambic/trochaic law revisited. *Leiden Papers in Linguistics, 1*, 37-62.

Rice, K., & Saxon, L. (2001). *The y-/b- pronouns in Athapaskan languages: Perspectives on content*. (Talk presented at the Workshop on American Indigenous Languages (WAIL)/Society for the Study of the Indigenous Languages of the Americas (SSILA), University of California, Berkeley, July 2001)

Ridley, R. (1983). *Eagle Han Huch'inn Hòdök*. Alaska Native Language Center. (Illustrated by Sandy Jamieson; introduction by Michael Krauss)

Rizzi, L. (1997). The fine structure of the left periphery. In L. Haegeman (Ed.), *Elements of Grammar* (pp. 281–337). Dordrecht: Kluwer.

Rizzi, L. (1999). *On the position of Int(errogative) in the left periphery of the clause*. (Unpublished manuscript, Universitá di Siena)

Roberts, J. (1987). *Amele*. London: Croom Helm.

Rodewald, M. K. (1989). *A Grammar of Bandi and Mende Tone* (Unpublished

master's thesis). University of Texas at Arlington.
Rohlfs, G. (1868). *Reise durch Nord-Afrika vom Mittelländischen Meere bis zum Busen von Guinea: 1865 bis 1867.* Gotha: Justus Perthes.
Ryan, K. (2006). *The Rig-Vedic fate of the devaí'a dvandva (double dual).* (Manuscript, University of California, Los Angeles)
Ryan, K. (2010). Variable affix order: Grammar and learning. *Language, 86*(4), 758–791.
Ryan, K., & Schuh, R. (2010). Suffix doubling and suffix deletion in Bole. (Talk handouts, Joint UCLA-USC Phonology Seminar, April 22)
Sande, H. (2017). *Distributing Morphologically Conditioned Phonology: Three Case Studies from Guébie* (Unpublished doctoral dissertation). UC Berkeley.
Sandoval, A., Toledano, D., de la Torre, R., Garrote, M., & Guirao, J. (2008). Developing a phonemic and syllabic frequency inventory for spontaneous spoken Castilian Spanish and their comparison to text-based inventories. In *Proc. 6th Int. Conf. on Language Resources and Evaluation* (p. 1097-1100).
Schachter, P., & Otanes, F. (1972). *Tagalog Reference Grammar.* Berkeley: University of California Press.
Schuh, R. (n.d.). *The Yobe Languages Research Project.* (Available at http://aflang.humanities.ucla.edu/language-materials/chadic-languages/yobe/)
Schuh, R. (1972a). *Aspects of Ngizim syntax* (Unpublished doctoral dissertation). University of California, Los Angeles.
Schuh, R. (1972b). Rule inversion in Chadic. *Studies in African Linguistics, 3,* 379-397.
Schuh, R. (1978). Tone rules. In V. Fromkin (Ed.), *Tone: A Linguistic Survey* (p. 221-256). New York: Academic Press.
Schuh, R. (1981). *A Dictionary of Ngizim.* Berkeley: University of California Press.
Schuh, R. (1983). The evolution of determiners in Chadic. In E. Wolff & H. Meyer-Bahlburg (Eds.), *Studies in Chadic and Afroasiatic Linguistics* (p. 157-210). Hamburg: Buske.
Schuh, R. (1989). The reality of Hausa "low tone raising": A response to Newman & Jaggar. *Studies in African Linguistics, 20,* 257-262.
Schuh, R. (1998). *A Grammar of Miya.* Berkeley & Los Angeles: University of California Press.
Schuh, R. (2001). Sources of gemination and gemination as a morpheme in Bole. *32nd Annual Conference on African Linguistics (ACAL 32).*
Schuh, R. (2002). Palatalization in West Chadic. *Studies in African Linguistics,*

31(1/2), 97-128.

Schuh, R. (2005a). *The Great Ngamo Tone Shift.* (Manuscript, University of California, Los Angeles)

Schuh, R. (2005b). Yobe State, Nigeria as a linguistic area. In R. T. Cover & Y. Kim (Eds.), *BLS 31: Special Session on Languages of West Africa* (pp. 77–94).

Schuh, R. (2010). *Miya-English-Hausa Online Dictionary.* (Draft)

Schuh, R. (2017). *A Chadic Cornucopia.* E-scholarship: California Digital Library. (Posthumous, ed. by Paul Newman. Available at http://escholarship.org/uc/item/5zx6z32d)

Schuh, R. (2018). Tone spreading, tone shifting, and tonal restructuring. In E. Buckley, T. Crane, & J. Good (Eds.), *Revealing Structure: Papers in Honor of Larry M. Hyman* (p. 230-244). Stanford: CSLI Publications.

Segerer, G., & Flavier, S. (2011-2017). *RefLex: Reference Lexicon of African Languages.* (http://reflex.cnrs.fr/)

Shibatani, M. (1990). *The Languages of Japan.* Cambridge: Cambridge University Press.

Shih, S. S., & Inkelas, S. (2016). Morphologically-conditioned tonotactics in multilevel Maximum Entropy grammar. In G. Ó. Hansson, A. Farris-Trimble, K. McMullin, & D. Pulleyblank (Eds.), *Proceedings of the 2015 Annual Meetings on Phonology.*

Shlonsky, U., & Soare, G. (2011). Where's 'why'? *Linguistic Inquiry, 42*(4), 651-669.

Shukla, S. (1981). *Bhojpuri Grammar.* Georgetown: Georgetown University Press.

Sibanda, G. (2004). *Verbal Phonology and Morphology of Ndebele* (Unpublished doctoral dissertation). University of California, Berkeley.

Siddiqi, D. (2009). *Syntax within the Word: Economy, Allomorphy, and Argument Selection in Distributed Morphology.* Amsterdam: John Benjamins.

Silber-Varod, V., Latin, M., & Moyal, A. (2017). Frequency of Hebrew phonemes and phoneme clusters in a data-driven approach. *Literacy and Language, 5*, 22-36.

Smith, A. (1971). The early states of the Central Sudan. In A. Ajayi & M. Crowder (Eds.), *History of West Africa, Vol. 1* (pp. 158–201). London: Longman.

Snider, K. (1988). The noun class system of Proto-Guang and its implications for internal classification. *Journal of West African Linguistics, 10*, 137-164.

Snider, K. (1990). Tonal upstep in Krachi: Evidence for register tier. *Language, 66*, 453-474.

Snider, K. (1998). *North Guang comparative word list, Chuburun, Krachi, Nawuri, Gichode, Gonja*. Legon, Ghana: Institute of African Studies.
Solnit, D. (2003). Eastern Kayah Li. In G. Thurgood & R. LaPolla (Eds.), *The Sino-Tibetan Languages* (p. 623-631). London & New York: Routledge.
Spears, R. A. (1967a). *Basic Course in Mende*. Northwestern University.
Spears, R. A. (1967b). Tone in Mende. *Journal of African Languages*, 6, 231–244.
Speas, M. (1990). *Phrase Structure in Natural Language*. Dordrecht: Kluwer.
Stanton, J., & Zukoff, S. (2018). Prosodic identity in copy epenthesis: Evidence for a correspondence-based approach. *Natural Language & Linguistic Theory*, 36, 637–684.
Staubs, R., Becker, M., Potts, C., Pratt, P., McCarthy, J. J., & Pater, J. (2010). *OT-Help 2.0. Software package*. (Amherst, MA: University of Massachusetts, Amherst)
Steriade, D. (n.d.). *Intervals*. (Unpublished Ms.)
Steriade, D. (1984). Glides and vowels in Romanian. In C. Brugman & M. Macaulay (Eds.), *Proceedings of the tenth annual meeting of the berkeley linguistics society meeting* (p. 47-64). University of California, Berkeley.
Steriade, D. (1990). Moras and other slots. In D. Meyer, S. Tomioka, & L. Zidani-Eroğlu (Eds.), *Proceedings of the First Meeting of the Formal Linguistics Society of Midamerica* (p. 254-280). University of Wisconsin-Madison.
Stevens, K. (1988). *Acoustic Phonetics*. Cambridge: MIT Press.
Stokhof, W. (1979). *Woisika II: Phonemics*. Canberra: Australian National University.
Storme, B. (2017). *Perceptual Sources for Closed-Syllable Vowel Laxing and Derived Environment Effects* (Unpublished doctoral dissertation). MIT.
Stump, G. (1991). A paradigm-based theory of morphosemantic mismatches. *Language*, 67, 675–725.
Stump, G. (2001). *Inflectional Morphology: A Theory of Paradigm Structure*. Cambridge: Cambridge University Press.
Sturtevant, E. (1922). Syllabification and syllabic quantity in Greek and Latin. *Transactions and Proceedings of the American Philological Association*, 53(1), 35-51.
Tamaoka, K., & Makioka, S. (2004). Frequency of occurrence for units of phonemes, morae, and syllables appearing in a lexical corpus of a Japanese newspaper. *Behavior Research Methods, Instruments, & Computers*, 36, 531-547.
Tang, K. (2008). *The Phonology and Phonetics of Consonant-Tone Interac-*

tion (Unpublished doctoral dissertation). University of California, Los Angeles.

Tarbutu, M. M. (2004). *Bade-English-Hausa Dictionary (Gashua Dialect)* (R. G. Schuh, Ed.). Potiskum: Ajami Press.

Theil, R. (2007). Kafa phonology. *Journal of African Languages and Linguistics, 28*, 193-216.

Thomas, E. (1974). Engenni. In J. Bendor-Samuel (Ed.), *Ten Nigerian Tone Systems* (p. 13-26). Dallas and Arlington: Summer Institute of Linguistics and University of Texas.

Thompson, C. (1989). *Voice and Obviation in Athabaskan and Other Languages* (Unpublished doctoral dissertation). University of Oregon.

Thompson, C. (1996). The history and function of the yi-/bi-alternation in Athabaskan. In E. Jelinek, S. Midgette, K. Rice, & L. Saxon (Eds.), *Athabaskan Language Studies: Essays in Honor of Robert Young* (pp. 81–100). Albuquerque: University of New Mexico Press.

Tikau, A. I., & Yusuf, I. (2009). *Karekare-English-Hausa Dictionary* (R. G. Schuh, Ed.). Potiskum: Ajami Press.

Torrence, H., & Kandybowicz, J. (2015). Wh-question formation in Krachi. *Journal of African Languages and Linguisics, 36*, 253-286.

Tourneux, H., & Daïrou, Y. (1998). *Dictionnaire peul de l'agriculture et de la nature (Cameroun)*. Paris: Editions Karthala.

Trommer, J. (2003). The interaction of morphology and syntax in affix order. In G. Booij & J. van Marle (Eds.), *Yearbook of Morphology 2002* (pp. 283–324). Dordrecht: Kluwer.

Tsoi, W. (2005). *The Effects of Occurrence Frequency of Phonemes on Second Language Acquisition: A Quantitative Comparison of Cantonese, Mandarin, Italian, German and American English.* (Manuscript, Chinese University of Hong Kong.)

Uyechi, L. (1996). The Navajo third person alternation and the pronoun incorporation analysis. In E. Jelinek, S. Midgette, K. Rice, & L. Saxon (Eds.), *Athabaskan Language Studies: Essays in Honor of Robert Young* (pp. 123–135). Albuquerque: University of New Mexico Press.

Vainio, M. (1996). Phoneme frequencies in Finnish text and speech. *Studies in Logopedics and Phonetics, 5*, 181-194.

Vallejos, R., & Amías, R. (2015). *Diccionario Kukama-Kukamiria * Castellano*. Iquitos, Perú: Programa de Formación de Maestros Bilingües de la Amazonía Peruana – FORMABIAP. (Available at https://www.academia.edu/15582960/Diccionario_kukama-kukamiria_castellano)

Veenker, W. (1982). Zur phonologischen Statistik der syrjänischen Sprache.

Études Finno-Ougriennes, 15, 435-445.
Vennemann, T. (1972). Rule inversion. Lingua, 29, 209-242.
Voorhoeve, J. (1971). Tonology of the Bamileke noun. Journal of African Languages, 10, 44-53.
Vorbichler, A. (1971). Die Sprache der Mamvu. Glückstadt: J.J. Augustin.
Vydrin, V. (2004). Areal and genetic features in West Mande and South Mande phonology: In what sense did Mande languages evolve? Journal of West African Languages, 30(2), 113-126.
Vydrin, V. (2008). Dictionnaire Dan-Français (dan de l'Est). St Petersbourg: Nestor-Istoria.
Weber, A., & Smits, R. (2003). Consonant and vowel confusion patterns by American English listeners. In M. J. Solé, D. Recasens, & J. Romero (Eds.), *15th International Congress of the Phonetic Sciences* (pp. 1437–1440). Causal Productions Pty Ltd.
Westermann, D., & Bryan, M. A. (1952). *The Languages of West Africa*. London: Oxford University Press.
Williams, E. S. ([1971] 1976). Underlying tone in Margi and Igbo. Linguistic Inquiry, 7, 463-484.
Williamson, K. (1972). *Igbo Dictionary*. Ibadan: Ethiope Publishing Company.
Williamson, K. (1986). The Igbo associative and specific constructions. In K. Bogers, H. van der Hulst, & M. Mous (Eds.), *The Phonological Representation of Suprasegmentals* (p. 195-206). Dordrecht: Foris Publications.
Willie, M. (1991). *Pronouns and Obviation in Navajo* (Unpublished doctoral dissertation). University of Arizona.
Willie, M. (2000). The inverse voice and possessive yi-/bi-in Navajo. International Journal of American Linguistics, 66(3), 360-382.
Willie, M. A., & Jelinek, E. (2014). Navajo as a discourse configurational language. In A. Carnie & H. Harley (Eds.), *Pronouns, Presuppositions, and Hierarchies: The Work of Eloise Jelinek in Context* (pp. 112-142). New York: Taylor & Francis.
Wilson, C., & George, B. (2008). *MaxEnt Grammar Tool.* (Software package. University of California, Los Angeles)
Wistrand-Robinson, L., & Armagost, J. (1990). *Comanche Dictionary and Grammar*. Summer Institute of Linguistics and the University of Texas at Arlington.
Wolf, M. (2008). *Optimal Interleaving: Serial Phonology-Morphology Interaction in a Constraint-Based Model* (Unpublished doctoral dissertation). University of Massachusetts Amherst.

Wolff, H. E. (1977). Patterns in Chadic (and Afroasiatic?) verb base formations. In P. Newman & R. M. Newman (Eds.), *Papers in Chadic Linguistics: Papers from the Leiden Colloquium on the Chadic Language Family* (p. 199-233). Leiden: Afrika-Studiecentrum.

Wolff, H. E. (1979). Grammatical categories of verb stems and the marking of mood, aktionsart, and aspect in Chadic. *Afroasiatic Linguistics*, 6(5), 161-208.

Wolff, H. E. (1981). Vocalisation patterns, prosodies, and Chadic reconstructions. In W. R. Leben (Ed.), *Précis from the Twelfth Conference on African Linguistics* (p. 144-148). Los Angeles: Department of Linguistics, UCLA.

Wolff, H. E. (1982). 'Aspect' and aspect-related categories in Chadic. In H. Jungraithmayr (Ed.), *The Chad Languages in the Hamitosemitic-Nigritic Border Area* (p. 183-191). Berlin: Reimer.

Wolff, H. E. (1983). Reconstructing vowels in Central Chadic. In E. Wolff & H. Meyer-Bahlburg (Eds.), *Studies in Chadic and Afroasiatic Linguistics* (p. 211-232). Hamburg: Buske.

Wolff, H. E. (1984). New proposals concerning the nature and development of the Proto-Chadic tense/aspect system. In J. Bynon (Ed.), *Current Progress in Afro-Asiatic Linguistics: Papers of the Third International Hamito-Semitic Congress* (p. 225-239). Amsterdam: Benjamins.

Wolff, H. E. (2001). Verbal plurality in Chadic: Typology and grammaticalization chains. In A. Simpson (Ed.), *Proceedings of the Twenty-Seventh Annual Meeting of the Berkeley Linguistics Society: Special Session on Afroasiatic Languages* (p. 123-167). Berkeley, CA: Berkeley Linguistics Society.

Wolff, H. E. (2004). Segments and prosodies in Chadic: On descriptive and explanatory adequacy, historical reconstructions, and the status of Lamang-Hdi. In A. Akinlabi & O. Adesola (Eds.), *Proceedings of the 4th World Congress of African Linguistics (New Brunswick 2003)* (p. 43-65). Cologne: Rüdiger Köppe.

Wolff, H. E. (2006). Suffix petrification and prosodies in Central Chadic (Lamang-Hdi). In D. Ibriszimow (Ed.), *Topics in Chadic Linguistics II: Papers from the 2nd Biennial International Colloquium on the Chadic Languages* (p. 141-154). Cologne: Rüdiger Köppe.

Wolff, H. E. (2015). *The Lamang Language and Dictionary* (Vol. 1-2). Cologne: Rüdiger Köppe.

Wolff, H. E. (2017). 'Vocalogenesis' in (Central) Chadic languages. In S. G. Obeng & C. R. Green (Eds.), *African Linguistics in the 21st Century: Essays in Honor of Paul Newman* (p. 13-31). Cologne: Rüdiger Köppe.

Xu, Z. (2011). Optimality Theory and morphology. *Language and Linguistics Compass, 5*(7), 466–484.

Xu, Z., & Aronoff, M. (2011). A Realization Optimality-Theoretic approach to blocking and extended exponence. *Journal of Linguistics, 47*(3), 673–707.

Yan, Q., Zhizhi, Z., Yong, L., Ming, Q., Wenjun, T., & Kaizheng, T. (1981). *Pug Lai Cix Ding Yiie Si Ndong Lai Vax Mai Lai Hox*. Kunming: Yunnan Minzu Chubanshe.

Yip, M. (2002). *Tone*. Cambridge: Cambridge University Press.

Young, R. W., & Morgan, W. (1980). *The Navajo Language: A Grammar and Colloquial Dictionary*. Albuquerque: University of New Mexico Press.

Zhang, J. (2000). The phonetic basis for tonal melody mapping. In R. Billerey & B. D. Lillehaugen (Eds.), *WCCFL 19: Proceedings of the 19th West Coast Conference on Formal Linguistics* (pp. 603–616). Somerville, MA: Cascadilla Press.

Zhang, J. (2001). *The Effects of Duration and Sonority on Contour Tone Distributions—Typological Survey and Formal Analysis* (Unpublished doctoral dissertation). University of California, Los Angeles.

Zhang, J. (2003). Contour tone distribution is not an artifact of tonal melody mapping. *Studies in the Linguistic Sciences, 33*(1), 73–132.

Zuidema, W. (2009). *A syllable frequency list for Dutch*. (Available at https://eprints.illc.uva.nl/379/1/PP-2009-50.text.pdf)

Zuraw, K. (2002). Aggressive reduplication. *Phonology, 19*(3), 395–439.

www.ingramcontent.com/pod-product-compliance
Lightning Source LLC
LaVergne TN
LVHW051517070426
835507LV00023B/3160